Dana

THE ART OF BECOMING

Creating Abiding Fulfillment in an Unfulfilled World

First published 2019
Alétheia Press Publishing
ISBN - 9781711025049

www.theartofbecoming.com

Edited by Dee Reinert
Cover Art and Design by Berge Design
www.bergedesign.com

REGARDING NAMES AND LANGUAGE

In this book, some names have been changed, and others not. Most notably, I did not change Herr Kraft's or Mr. Roux's name; those were their actual names. The significance of their names will become clear later in the book.

William Blake had a distinct style. He used unusual punctuation, capitalisation, and spelling. Wherever he is quoted, either in prose or poetry, what may appear to the modern reader as a mistake, is not.

For Neville and William,
Thank you for coming to find me when I fell.
Neville, I will always keep my eyes on our intertwined hands.
I hope this book will suffice as a beginning.
William, thank you for receiving me.
This is my wink back.

Empty-handed I entered the world, barefoot I leave it.
My coming, my going — two simple happenings, that got entangled.
—Kozan Ichikyo

The future is a vast expanse that you'll never reach and the past is a place you've never been, but both have a way of reaching across the Great Wheel, and tapping you on the shoulder.

PROLOGUE

The Lay of a Golden Goose

by Louisa May Alcott

Long ago in a poultry yard
One dull November morn,
Beneath a motherly soft wing
A little goose was born.

Who straightway peeped out of the shell
To view the world beyond,
Longing at once to sally forth
And paddle in the pond.

"Oh! be not rash," her father said,
A mild Socratic bird,
Her mother begged her not to stray
With many a warning word.

But little goosey was perverse,
And eagerly did cry,
"I've got a lovely pair of wings,
Of course I ought to fly."

In vain parental cacklings,
In vain the cold sky's frown,
Ambitious goosey tried to soar,
But always tumbled down.

The farmyard jeered at her attempts,
The peacocks screamed, "Oh fie!
You're only a domestic goose,
So don't pretend to fly."

Great cock-a-doodle from his perch
Crowed daily loud and clear,
"Stay in the puddle, foolish bird,
That is your proper sphere,"

The ducks and hens said, one and all,
In gossip by the pool,
"Our children never play such pranks,
My dear, that fowl's a fool."

The owls came out and flew about,
Hooting above the rest,
"No useful egg was ever hatched
From transcendental nest."

Good little goslings at their play
And well-conducted chicks
Were taught to think poor goosey's flights'
Were naughty, ill-bred tricks.

They were content to swim and scratch,
And not at all inclined
For any wild goose chase in search
Of something undefined.

Hard times she had as one may guess,
That young aspiring bird,
Who still from every fall arose
Saddened but undeterred.

She knew she was no nightingale
Yet spite of much abuse,
She longed to help and cheer the world,
Although a plain grey goose.

She could not sing, she could not fly,
Nor even walk, with grace,
And all the farmyard had declared
A puddle was her place.

But something stronger than herself
Would cry, "Go on, go on!
Remember, though an humble fowl,
You're cousin to a swan."

So up and down poor goosey went,
A busy, hopeful bird.
Searched many wide unfruitful fields,
And many waters stirred.

At length she came unto a stream
Most fertile of all Niles,
Where tuneful birds might soar and sing
Among the leafy isles.

Here did she build a little nest
Beside the waters still,
Where the parental goose could rest
Unvexed by any bill.

And here she paused to smooth her plumes,
Ruffled by many plagues,
When suddenly arose the cry,
"This goose lays golden eggs."

At once the farmyard was agog,
The ducks began to quack,
Prim Guinea fowls relenting called,
"Come back, come back, come back."

Great chanticleer was pleased to give
A patronising crow,
And the contemptuous biddies clucked,
"I wish my chicks did so."

The peacocks spread their shining tails,
And cried in accents soft,
"We want to know you, gifted one,
Come up and sit aloft."

Wise owls awoke and gravely said,
With proudly swelling breasts,
"Rare birds have always been evoked
From transcendental nests!"

News-hunting turkeys from afar
Now ran with all thin legs
To gobble facts and fictions of
The goose with golden eggs.

But best of all the little fowls
Still playing on the shore,
Soft downy chicks and goslings gay,
Chirped out, "Dear Goose, lay more."

But goosey all these weary years
Had toiled like any ant,
And wearied out she now replied
"My little dears, I can't."

"When I was starving, half this corn
Had been of vital use,
Now I am surfeited with food
Like any Strasbourg goose."

So to escape too many friends,
Without uncivil strife,
She ran to the Atlantic pond
And paddled for her life.

Soon up among the grand old Alps
She found two blessed things,
The health she had so nearly lost,
And rest for weary limbs.

But still across the briny deep
Couched in most friendly words,
Came prayers for letters, tales, or verse
From literary birds.

Whereat the renovated fowl
With grateful thanks profuse,
Took from her wing a quill and wrote
This lay of a Golden Goose.

PART I
THE INNER SANCTUM

Chapter 1
THE LAST DREAM OF THE OLD OAK TREE

"Why this is beautiful, too beautiful to be believed," said the oak in a joyful tone. "I have them all here, both great and small; not one has been forgotten. Can such happiness be imagined?" It seemed almost impossible." In heaven with the Eternal God, it can be imagined, and it is possible," sounded the reply through the air. Moreover, the old tree, as it still grew upwards and onwards, felt that his roots were loosening themselves from the earth. "It is right so, it is best," said the tree, "no fetters hold me now. I can fly up to the very highest point in light and glory, and all I love are with me, both small and great. All are here."
—Hans Christian Anderson

I once peed on a stranger's front porch. I was around the age of five or six at the time, and my beloved stepfather stood next to me, Bible in hand, deep in his ministrations to a gentleman who had neither invited us to, nor wanted us in, his home that sunny Saturday morning. My family was part of a religious organisation that required its members, both young and old, to proselytise. Each Saturday morning of my childhood was spent in the service to a judgmental God in a state of perpetual trepidation that never decreased as I knocked on strangers' doors.

All clouds have silver linings, and my silver linings were the snack breaks we took at various convenience stores along our ever-changing service routes. That morning I drank a large juice and ate (as per usual) some salty, unhealthy but delicious snack during the break. By the time we returned to field service, my bladder was full, and I squirmed in my seat. Much to my father's chagrin, I told him that I had to pee. He chastised me for not going to the restroom when I had the chance and told me I would have to wait until we finished our morning work.

I didn't make it.

At the very next house, a tall gentleman appeared in the doorway, and my father began his rehearsed presentation. I don't remember what it was about because at that moment, my world contracted, and I shrunk in stature as my bladder gave way and warm, yellow liquid ran down my bare legs under my dress, pooling at my small feet. It was a cement porch. I remember because my child-mind wished that it were wooden, with wood slats through which the evidence of my childishness could pass and disappear. My father saw it, the gentleman householder saw it, I felt it, but no one said a word. My father just sped his presentation along, offered some biblical literature, and finished. Only when he took my hand to leave did he apologise to the man. The man just smiled at me, warm, gracious, and nonjudgmental. He was precisely the kind of man with whom I often wished I could live. A father that would let me stay home and watch cartoons on a Saturday morning. One that believed in a kind, loving God, a God that wouldn't give me nightmares.

When we got back to the car, our church companions were waiting for us. My father told them that we needed to cut our ministry short, as I required a change of clothes. He put something under me to keep my soaked panties from staining the car seat. At that moment, I was The Girl Who Peed Herself, which made perfect sense since I was also The Girl Who Wet the Bed. That's all I was (unless you counted The Girl Who Had Nightmares) and all I would ever be until I grew up. For now, I was just an acorn, surrounded by saplings and a few, rare tall oaks. I was an insignificant, small, embarrassed acorn with fragile roots that held tenuously to the earth. Watering that gentleman's front porch sparked something in my young mind. For the first time, I felt aware that I was somehow unfinished, and I became acutely aware of the consequences of being forced to reside in someone else's reality vector.

My childhood years were spent navigating a world created by the adults around me; this is the case for all of us. We're provided with narratives and a menu of life choices and are informed that our only job is to grow up, make sufficiently acceptable choices, and pay our dues to society. Our parents, doctors, and schools monitor and measure our growth (a linear, observable phenomenon), and we learn that growth is something to be desired without ever questioning the nature of this thing called growth. Even less are we invited to explore the truths that thread through our experience of living, or the psychological, emotional, and alchemical process by which we exist; that of *Becoming*.

Have you ever witnessed a sapling become a massive, majestic oak tree? None of us have had that opportunity and likely never will. It's estimated that in an average human lifetime of eighty years, a sapling oak will grow no more than two feet tall. Their average life expectancy is between two and four hundred years, but some can live much longer than that. My husband and I are blessed by the presence of an oak on our property that the French government has classified as one the Arbres Remarquables of France. She's estimated to be over five hundred years old.

The oldest oak in France is estimated to be around one thousand years old. She lives in a small village called Allouville-Bellefosse and hosts a hidden, sacred space for worship in her heart. Reminiscent of the ancient Western and Eastern descriptions of a specific mystical experience that the Eastern mystics call "kundalini rising," she survived a lightning strike that hollowed out her centre without killing her. It's no surprise then that the local Abbot du Détroit and father du Cerceau believed that this event held spiritual significance and chose to build a shrine within the hollow of the tree. When is a tree, a tree? At two feet tall? At eighty-two feet tall? Is the sapling not still an oak? And an acorn—does it not contain a tree within?

I've often thought about the process of growth and our understanding of it through the lens of a tree's life. We currently live in a world overrun by facts, rational materialism, and the behaviours that a materialist world view begets. This book is neither anti-rationalist nor anti-materialist. I certainly wouldn't want to live in buildings designed by architects that ignored calculus and thermodynamics. Reason and intellect have been, and remain, one of the cornerstones of my life.

But there is much more to be experienced than that which we can measure. I would suggest that it's the things we can't measure that most significantly influence our lives. A geneticist would say that within the visible tree, is a microscopic body of information, DNA that differentiates a tree from a rose, an oak from a birch. A quantum physicist would say that within the

DNA and matter of a tree are particles and waves that only appear to separate an oak from the space that surrounds it, the space that it grows through. All forms of becoming require spaciousness in one way or another; mental space that allows the mind to expand, emotional space for feeling to flower, and physical space in which to move.

A mystic (and a few philosophers) would say that the oak is a spirit, an entity that manifests one form in the physical world, perceivable to our five senses, while also possessing its own invisible, eternal beingness that transcends time and space. Perhaps all of them, the geneticist, the quantum physicist, the mystic, and the philosopher are correct. All of them are contemplating a tree from a different level of mind and, therefore, a different level of reality. Considering this, the concept that we call growth becomes something to contemplate. Is the growth of a tree limited to its height and breadth? Or is the tree only becoming what it always has been, manifesting multiple forms of itself in a three-dimensional, dynamic, and ever-changing realm?

Is the Being of the tree growing? Or is growth an illusion projected by minds trapped in materiality which, in the search for security, go through life measuring, analysing, and judging without balancing those actions with contemplation and poetic living?

This book isn't about growth modalities, self-help, or self-development. It's none of those things because you don't need someone or something to fix you (you can restore yourself), nor do you require systems for growth. The thing we call growth is too complex and personal to be organised into, or contained within, a system or modality. You contain everything that you currently are, have been, and could be within yourself. Given the right conditions, your natural impulse is towards self-actualisation and transcendence in your own time and way. Therefore, it's the *art* of becoming. A painter chooses his canvas, brushes, and paints. He pours himself out as he becomes not only an artist but, using imagination combined with will and movement, he becomes the art—a masterpiece in the making.

Living poetically means that we approach our life as a poet. We explore the inner landscapes of our being, charting, and unifying contraries that only exist within the dream of duality. The rhythms of life are the rhythms of poetry. The phases of your life and the experiences that shaped your perception are like a sentence; a sentence is a building block of prose, but poetry differs from prose. Poets employ stanzas and the poetic line. Through masterful use of rhythm, they decide how long each line will be, and where it will break off. A poetic life doesn't just happen. It's consciously directed, constructed, and encompasses manifold meaning. As a poet, you can choose to stack your experience like evenly arranged lines or, as some poets do, use the length of lines to create a shape. At the end of your life, what shape would you like the lines to form? An orb? A tree? A figure eight?

The poetic meter is about emphasis. When we speak, we stress certain syllables to create rhythm. This rhythm infuses our speech with meaning and feeling. **When we approach life as a poet, we put emphasis on the underlying truths that have revealed themselves through experience.** Experience is like the air we breathe. We can create our experience, sculpt our vessel, alter our perception, envision new realities, refine our personality, and ultimately live the life we wish. We can reach into previously uncharted regions of Self and discover new worlds.

Probably, all of what is going on in the human mind can be depicted as a conglomeration of several overlapping trees.
—Misha Gromov, Mathematician

Chapter 2
EUDAIMONIA

Becoming is both an art and a journey. It is *Beingness in Action*, moving through infinite States, as it charts polarities and creates experiences with which it becomes entangled. As we move through and inhabit these States, our commitment to creating deep, abiding fulfillment plays a role in the world we create, and the trajectory we take. Think about that when considering the condition of our world.

What is deep, abiding fulfillment? Is it having the perfect job? Marrying the person you believe is best suited to you? Is it living a creative life? Finding inner peace?

Language has always been of extreme interest to me. Naturally, when deciding to subtitle this book "Creating Abiding Fulfillment in an Unfulfilled World," there was much contemplation about the choice of words. In my day job, I'm an ontological coach and consultant. Ontology is the branch of metaphysics dealing with the nature of being. Ontology takes a unique and profound approach to human language. In ontology, language is understood to be generative.

Consciousness is preconditioned by language. Awareness of the language used in our culture, the words that are encouraged or discouraged and how words are redefined is vital. We need to be conscious of how words and phrases are being redefined, and how language is used to manipulate minds and attitudes in order to corral human beings, like cattle, into predetermined modes of living. Language can be used to reach deep, often unconscious parts of ourselves that, while not able to communicate linguistically, can be coaxed to the surface of the conscious mind through the images and feeling that a word or phrase evokes, it's vibrational. To do this, we need to delve deep into the words that we use. Find their roots and trace their movements through the human psyche over centuries and across cultures. Doing this creates a connection with our ancestors, their knowledge, struggles, and wisdom.

There is much to be found in one simple word.

A quick web search for the word "fulfillment" results in one, concise definition at the top of the search page. Underneath the search window, more than ten results appear which refer to "order fulfillment." Consumerism has resulted in the degradation of our language, but it hasn't destroyed it. We can reclaim it. In the Old English dialects spoken by the Angles, Saxons, and Jutes in England from 400–1150 AD, the word for fulfillment was the strong, feminine noun, *Gefyllednes*. Gefyllednes is defined as a state of fullness and completion.

There are other thought-provoking words that refer to fulfillment and help us flesh out its deeper meaning. The word *telophase* is used in molecular biology for a phase in the cell's cycle duration. It's the final stage in both meiosis and mitosis in a eukaryotic cell. Telophase is taken from the Greek *télos* (end) and *phasis* (stage), to be at the end-stage. The Greek dictionary from 1904 defines Telos as "the ultimate objective or aim." The Proto-Indo-European root related to telos was *kwel*, meaning "to sojourn, to revolve around and to dwell." The Etymology Dictionary notes that kwel suggests a turning-point, such as during a race. It is describing a point in a journey or a process at which one is close to the end and has reached a pivotal turning point.

Now our fulfillment takes on a much deeper, more vibrant, and consequential meaning. If we're on a journey of consciousness, and if this journey takes us from the state of unconsciousness to one of awakened actualisation, then fulfillment implies that one has come close to, or attained, the ultimate objective. To reach a turning point and return to wholeness.

Eudaimonia

This book is not about philosophy or abstract concepts that have no practical value to our lives. But there will be a touch of philosophy and a dash of abstraction here and there. I agree with Neville Goddard who said, "What is most spiritual is most directly practical."—It should be something that we can apply in any circumstance to the benefit of ourselves and others.

So I'd like to dip into philosophy and metaphysics for just a moment and if that's not normally your cup of tea, I ask you to bare with me, this will all make sense in the end.

Here is question to consider:

Do each of us each possess an aspect of our psyche that we're not immediately aware of, but is constantly available to us, and contributes to our well-being and happiness? The ancient Greeks believed that we do, and some of the greatest thinkers of the 20th-century also believed in this so called, *higher mind* or *higher self.*

The Greeks believed in something called a *eudaimon*. Eudaimon means to have a loving, helpful spirit that is assigned to, or part of, each individual. Basically, the eudaimon was regarded as a guardian angel, whereas a naughty, up-to-no-good evil spirt was called a cacodaimon. This was probably a great way for mischievous Greek children to get out of trouble with their parents, "My cacodaimon made me do it!"

The poet William Blake said, "The Creative Genius is the True Man." He was referring to "Daimon" (which is exactly the same thing as the aforementioned eudaimon). To the Greeks, the Daimon is the guiding spirit within each man; it also means "godlike." Elsewhere in the world, the Zoroastrians recognised the *fravashis,* which they believed to be the guardian angel of each person. Zoroastrianism also has the concept of the *Daena,* which is the conscience of a person and acts as a guide. In *Zoroastrian Theology,* Maneckji Dhalla writes, "On the dawn of the fourth day after death there appears then to the soul its own *Daena,* or spiritual conscience in the shape of a damsel of unsurpassed beauty, the fairest of the fair in the world." You're going to see this later in the book because a few well known people of the 20th-century have also experienced this beautiful being during near-death experiences and in deep meditation.

From the word *eudaimon* we have the word *eudaimonia,* which a bunch of dead Greek guys argued over for decades. Eudaimonia refers to what we now call *well-being* but eudaimonia is often mistranslated, and its deeper meaning wholly missed. It's usually translated as "happiness" or "welfare."

Occasionally it is more accurately translated as "flourishing." Still, that's an incomplete translation because it's missing an essential aspect of the word; *Daimon*.

So what could this daimon concept have to do with fulfillment and happiness?

Heraclitus, a pre-Socratic philosopher is known for the statement, "Ethos anthropos Daimon". His statement is often phrased by modern translators as "character is spirit." But *ethos* doesn't just mean "character," it also translates to "spirit" (as in the spirit of the times). Since the Greek word ethos was used to refer to the guiding beliefs or spirit of a people, person, or ideology, Heraclitus wasn't saying just saying that character is spirit. He was saying that the guiding spirit of the lower self is the Daimon, and that our true character comes from our spirit. In other words, your guiding spirit is part of your own, innermost Being.

The Vedas also speak of this in the Srimad-Bhagavatam, Canton 5: "The Supreme Personality of Godhead, who is the source of life for all living entities, lives within the heart of everyone as the **friendly Supersoul**, and under its direction a living entity enjoys or suffers in the material world." Further on in Canton 5, it is written: "The self-realised mystic derives great transcendental bliss from realising the Supersoul within themselves."

German writer Johann Wolfgang von Goethe credits his daimon with his artistic and scientific accomplishments. Carl Jung stated, "There was a daimon in me, and in the end its presence proved decisive." Socrates' daimon warned him (in the form of a voice) against mistakes but never told him what he should or shouldn't do. Rudyard Kipling said, "When your daimon is in charge, do not try to think consciously; drift, wait and obey."

Some have discounted the Daimon as being a superstitious and unnecessary way to account for the phenomena of intuition and genius, and in one regard they are correct. The Daimon isn't a separate Being—it's both our very own Being, and the operations of our mind, at what some call *higher planes*.

In other words, it's our superconscious Self a.k.a your *higher self*.

Considering the true meaning and contextual history of the word Daimon, and taking Heraclitus' statement into account, the word Eudaimonia takes on a much richer meaning. Rather than referring to happiness, it suggests that **authentic human flourishing is the result of opening ourselves to that which flows from the superconscious, inner man.**

Fulfillment and flourishing then become about so much more than choosing the perfect career or attaining one's dreams.

Fulfillment means to flourish because an inner source of wisdom, love, support, and guidance is activated and allowed to flow through us, for us, and into the world.

What to Expect from this Book

This book is an invitation to *think* and *feel* and *be* together, even if we never meet and live oceans apart. It's for Existentialists, Atheists, Agnostics, Pantheists, Panendeists, Christians, Muslims, Jews, New Agers, Old-Timers, every culture, and every possible constellation of identity, attitude, and perspective. It might *make total sense* or *no sense at all*. One might love it, one might hate it, one might feel complete apathy towards the contents. This book is for everyone because of an obvious truth; like any voyage, each person decides what value they get from it. In my experience, books have always felt like ships; they carry us into the waters of another soul's mind.

The book is suggestive, not prescriptive. It's not a *how-to* guide. It's an invitation to enter another person's heart, by way of your own. You won't agree with everything, and you're not meant to! Your journey belongs to you. I'm no teacher. I'm a fellow traveler and this book is more of a travel journal than a travel guide. Parts of my own journey are woven throughout the texts, and some chapters are dedicated entirely to a few of the most profound learning experiences of my life. I share intimate details of my life in the hope that it can help you heal, relate, and recognise our shared humanity.

If the language doesn't work for you, switch it out for words that you find comfortable. I was once allergic to the word *God*, and I would replace it with *Universal Mind*. If you're an Atheist who doesn't relate to the word *soul* or breaks out into hives when you hear the word *God*, replace the term with a word from your preferred lexicon. It's the felt experience of engaging with the contents of a book, in your way and on your terms, that matters.

Redefining God

This is not a religious book. It is spiritual at times but as I'll demonstrate in chapter four, spirituality is neither a belief system nor a set of practices.

I've come full circle with the word *God*. The process of transmutation of Being from one state to another alters one's language because there is a transformation of meaning, as the individual's consciousness changes. Henceforth in this book, the word *God* refers to any of the following: the Manifest and Unmanifested, Being beyond Mind and 'No-thingness', Consciousness, All-Encompassing, Infinite Unconditional Love and the Source of all that is or could be.

This definition of God is called panentheistic. It was the physicist, psychologist, and philosopher Gustav Theodor Fechner who developed the clearest panentheistic model for the Western world, but he wasn't the first panendeist. Buddhists rarely use the word God, especially in the West, because of the association of the word with the monotheism of the Abrahamic religions. A panentheistic perspective is like that of the Buddhist in that Absolute and Transcendent Being must be *more than the totality* of existence. From this perspective, the world is a manifestation of that transcendent reality.

The panentheistic perspective is that God is not just *a* protean Being. God *is* beingness. God is both immanent and transcendent. The pandeistic view, as first postulated by Spinoza, differs from the panentheistic one in that, to the pandeist, the Divine Being created the universe from itself but then ceased to exist as an individuated entity. Pandeism theorises that the primordial Being disintegrated as it fragmented and created multitudes of conscious fragments. One of the primary differences between panendeism and pandeism is that the panendeist sees the multitude of individuated consciousnesses that arose from Primordial Being as being *fractals*, not fragments. A fractal contains the whole, and so to the panendeist, the Primordial Being never dissolved, it *slept* within the fractal. This is why the mystics have never made it their business to redeem the outer man. The human didn't need redemption. It was the sleeping deity *within* that must be awakened.

A panentheistic view also sees God as a protean Being. Neville Goddard once described it, "From a distance I saw what looked like one man but upon coming closer to it, I saw that it was actually a multitude of beings, all individuated but together they were the One God." One thing that panendeism and pandeism share in common is the theory that the laws of the Universe are comparable to a computer, albeit one far beyond anything the limited human mind could create, and this cosmic computer is the force behind all of the laws of dynamic consciousness. Laws that organise and permit the existence of, and the interplay between, matter, energy, self-organising systems, expansion, and entropy.

I'll employ a *panen*theistic conception of God but stress that it's just a conception, not an absolute definition. By refusing rigid or dogmatic definitions, one can engage in an open-ended exploration of Being. That's the nature of contemplative thought. A contemplative approach allows us to view ideas as if they were creatures, moving upon the surface of water. The creatures (ideas) can't tell us much about the water itself, but their movements give us an indication of the characteristics of water.

For the sake of simplicity, I'm using "God" as an efficient, three-letter word that makes it easier to write and read this book. In this context, I'm defining *consciousness* as the irreducible and true substance of all that is. It gives rise to and permeates existence as many strata of awareness. It's easier to say what God *isn't* than to say what God *is*. In that respect, the words of Meister Eckart (as rendered into prose by Sweeney & Burrows in their book *Meister Eckhart's Book of the Heart*) comes to mind:

It would be best if I stopped chattering and
kept silent about You,
Because when I speak, I say what I do not know,
For I cannot say what is true about You,
Who are beyond understanding —
But not beyond me.

With the exception of love, which is an absolute necessity, fulfillment has foundations, not universal requirements (it is presumed that basic human needs must be met). You will know which of those foundations resonate and you may identify personal foundations that aren't listed on the next page.

The millions are awake enough for physical labor; but only one in a million is awake enough for effective intellectual exertion, only one in a hundred million to a poetic or divine life. To be awake is to be alive.
—Henry David Thoreau

If you're still reading this, then something in your nature is poetic. To create a fulfilling life is a form of poetry. A poem has elements. In this regard, some of those elements are the foundations of fulfillment.

The Foundations of Fulfillment

Beauty
Self-inquiry
Forgiveness
Imagination
Creativity
Coherent Intelligence
Unconditional Love
Transformation
Movement
Recovery of Vision
Will
Innocence
Hope
Awe
Faith in Self
Gratitude
Integration

We will explore all of them, one by one. There is no set sequence to the foundations, but there does seem to be an arc. Sometimes they appear as a chapter title, and sometimes they are woven within the text.

The Wellspring and the Well

As we explore these foundations of a fulfilled life, I invite you to envisage a wellspring and a well. A wellspring is a source of continual supply. It comes from the Old English *welspryng* and is defined as "a living spring, a fountainhead." Imagine a wellspring, deep within the earth, flowing through corridors of smooth stone. The wellspring is the source from which life-giving water flows. Water is analogue for consciousness, as wind is for spirit. The pure water that flows from the wellspring is your higher, unfragmented, and unbound awareness.

The source of that water is your True Self, The Witness.

And what of the well? It's above ground. How does it look? Your well is your lower mind, emotions/feelings, body, and personality construct. It is, in effect, the container for your relative, transient self. Just as the wellspring is the source from which water flows to give you life, even the wellspring itself has a source. That deeper source is the inexhaustible source of all being, light, and love; the undivided, Absolute Self. Throughout the book, we'll explore the foundations of fulfillment through the lens of this metaphor.

Chapter 3
THE MISTA'PEO

The wind blows wherever it pleases. You hear its sound but you cannot tell where it comes from or where it is going. So it is with everyone born of the Spirit. —John 3:8

What a power! Called the power of God, it comes to you just like a wind. At first, you feel it as a vibration but when it hits you, this transfigured Self is a wind, an unearthly wind. —Neville Goddard

This is how it happened to me. I retired as usual, just as I have done throughout the years. Then came this unearthly wind. Intensifying itself in my head, I felt as though I was going to explode, that I must be experiencing a massive haemorrhage. But instead, I began to awake to discover I was in my skull. I was more awake than I had ever been before. I knew a clarity of thought I had never known before. —Neville Goddard

I feel that to write an authentic and compassionate book about human ful-fillment, I must be willing to lay myself bare. In my life, I've been crippled emotionally to the point of laying on the cold bathroom floor, sobbing in a fetal position. I ran away from home at seventeen to escape the overbearing and fundamentalist religious views of my family, who were Jehovah's Wit-nesses. I had been very sheltered from the world up until the fateful day that I walked out and never went back.

At seventeen, I had to pivot quickly and think on my feet. I wasn't old enough to open a bank account or register to vote, but I had to find a place to live, generate an income, and find some way to complete my education. I eventually did all those things but not alone. Somehow, I intuitively under-stood that I needed to build a network of people, some who would support me in more obvious ways, and others who would serve as role models and inspiration.

Nothing happens to us; everything flows from us.

I was excommunicated and lost all contact with the only support system I had ever known. My crime was that I walked away from the religious organisation and never showed a shred of repentance. Many people find it difficult to leave the Jehovah's Witnesses because of mind control, but I found it remarkably easy because I saw through the distortion from a very early age. I was reading by the age of four and have clear memories of discussing the Bible's faulty logic with my stepfather as a five-year-old! It was easy to leave the organisation that I was raised in, but losing my family and dealing with the emotional fallout of being raised in a fundamentalist religion was another story.

I had my son at age twenty. To avoid the same psychologically and physically coercive control that held me in an iron grip during my childhood, I decided to raise my son on my own and never ask for a cent of child support. I had to work and struggle to survive. I never knew what it felt like to thrive. Survival mode took its toll on my mind and body. Although I always managed to achieve my goals through iron will and support from unlikely allies, I suffered under the weight of my pain and beliefs about myself, my worth, and the world.

The journey itself is my home. —Matsuo Bashō

At the age of twenty-seven, I decided to visit Europe. I had never left the country before, didn't yet have a passport, and would be traveling alone. By this time, my relationship with my parents had improved because I moved near them and occasionally attended church meetings with them. I was going through the motions as a matter of survival. I got a job working on a technology team as a teacher-trainer, training public school teachers on the use of technology in the classroom. It was the perfect job for a young, single mother. I had the summers and holidays off with my little boy and never worked evenings or weekends. This opened a unique opportunity, the chance to take a summer holiday in Europe. Despite my decent job, I didn't have all the money needed for the trip. I'd purchased a flight ticket but had no money for hotels, trains, or food. One week before the summer break, determined to solve this dilemma, I went to the local

Publix grocery store to ask for a temporary cashier job. Once inside, I explained my intention to the store manager who, much to my surprise, was not only okay with my offer to work just six to eight weeks but was so supportive of my desire to visit Europe, that he gave me a front office job instead of a cashier position. Additionally, he asked me to help train the employees on various soft skills. Six weeks later, I had all the money I needed.

Boarding that plane to Europe changed the entire trajectory of my life. Perhaps it would have never happened if the kindly store manager hadn't been on my side. When the plane touched down in Frankfurt, Germany, *I touched down in life.*

As I walked the streets, seeing street and store signs in another language and immersing myself in the colours, scents, sounds, and movement that surrounded me, I might as well have been on another planet. Suddenly, for the first time in my life, I knew there was another way of being in the world. It was world-shattering...in the best possible way.

I visited Frankfurt and Aschaffenburg and then took the train to Paris. Never had I known such freedom from my old way of being and patterns of thought. The Coca Cola was fizzier, the toilets absurd, the smells ranged from offensive to intoxicating. Even in the dirtiest areas, I saw not glamour but radiating beauty. I felt as if roots arose from the earth beneath my feet, wrapped around my ankles, and whispered knowingly. "You...are...home." At the time, I didn't know that *home* was within me, and my movement through the world was opening a doorway to a previously unexplored realm of Being. I thought it was Germany itself that beckoned me home, and perhaps at some level it was. Either way, it was enough. It sparked an inextinguishable flame in my mind.

Three weeks later, I boarded another plane. This one intended to carry me back. *Backwards:* I could hear the rattle of shackles edging closer with every step the stewardesses made in preparation for flight. I began to cry uncontrollably but quietly and without embarrassment. I couldn't help myself. Then, out of the blue, more support came. This time the support was in the form of an American couple, two women in their fifties who were seated next to me in our three-seat row. They asked me why I wept, and I responded, "If I didn't have a little boy to return home to, I would get off this plane right now and never go back." Instead of telling me it would "be okay" and, instead of telling me to, "look on the bright side," they gave me some of the best advice I have ever received. They said, "Look, we've lived over here for twenty-five years and this is the best advice we can give you: If you want to do something in life, never wait for the conditions to be perfect before you act because they never will be. If you want something, then do it, make it happen, roll with the punches and face the challenges as they arise. If you want it, do it, and be determined to figure it out as you go."

I took their words to heart, and just six weeks later, I left Atlanta, Georgia, and moved to Europe. Perched on my hip was my precious, six-year-old boy. In my hands, I pushed a cart full of suitcases, and strapped to my waist was a small pack with just over six-thousand dollars in cashier's checks. I never moved back to the US. Two decades later, my life has transformed in ways that would have been unimaginable to my twenty-seven-year-old self.

I'm not going to sugarcoat it. It wasn't an easy road to travel down. Wherever you go, your unprocessed pain and repressed, negative emotions follow. The more space you open in your heart and mind for new levels of being to arise, the more acutely you will feel your pre-existing pain. It's a necessary mechanism akin to a soul detox. As we move up to higher states of Being on the Infinite Staircase, what lies in shadow must be transmuted. There is no other way.

The Mista'peo Speaks

In his lifelong solitude, the Naskapi hunter has to rely on his own inner voices and unconscious revelations; he has no religious teachers to tell him what he should believe, no rituals, festivals or customs to help him along. In his basic view of life, the soul of man is simply an "inner companion" who he calls "my friend," or Mista'peo, meaning "Great Man." Mista'peo dwells in the heart and is immortal. — Carl Jung, Man and His Symbols, p. 161

Naskapi means, "People beyond the horizon" and is the name of the inhabitants of Nitassinan, an area comprising much of eastern Quebec and Labrador. They refer to themselves as *St'aschinuw*, meaning "earth." This is a reminder that some cultures know intuitively that man is the *earth of God*. As man resides in the earth, God resides within man.

The Naskapi are a tribe of hunters who most often hunt in solitude, only occasionally hunting in isolated groups. Because he spends so much time alone, each hunter develops a bond with what he calls his "inner companion" or his "Mista'peo." Mista'peo means "Great Man." The tribe has no concept of an external God. Each member worships his own, divine Great Man as revealed only to him.

The hunter is reliant on his inner companion for spiritual guidance, and they believe that the more they trust their innermost, eternal companion, the more easily he comes through and merges with the hunter. Some people call the Mista'peo *"Daimon"* or the "Holy Guardian Angel" (HGA). They believe that this HGA is separate from them. In one regard it is, the *Daimon* (or HGA) could be perceived as somewhat separate because it's **not** the *personality construct* that you identify with. Imagine it this way: if you play a video game, you can create a character that you control. The character is a code. You use the code (your character) to experience the virtual reality, but the code limits your ability to influence the game. But what would happen if you could hack the code and enter the game more fully without the limitations placed on your character?

As the relative self drops its identification with the personality construct and begins to identify more and more as the 'Am-ness' of the Absolute, a higher awareness flows from the Daimon, and then through the mature, relative self, and into the world. The Naskapi understand that when an individual has surrendered the transient self to the innermost, eternal essence, he or she grows to be wise, speaks truthfully, and is loving. These are the people who inspire us and make a lasting impact.

> *Trust thyself: every heart vibrates to that iron string.*
> —Ralph Waldo Emerson

In his essay, *"Self-Reliance,"* Emerson wrote that to believe what is true in our own, private heart, is also true for all men, and is the true genius. He implores the reader to recognise that what resides in one's innermost core is the most trustworthy of all advisors.

Emerson writes:

> Inquiry leads us to that source, at once the essence of genius, of virtue, and of life, which we call Spontaneity or Instinct. We denote this primary wisdom as Intuition, whilst all later teachings are tuitions. In that deep force, the last fact behind which analysis cannot go, all things find their common origin. For, the sense of being which in calm hours rises, we know not how, in the soul, is not diverse from things, from space, from light, from time, from man but one with them, and proceeds obviously from the same source whence their life and Being also proceed.

Intuition and deep insight have often been considered the realm of theologians, philosophers, artists, and mystics. But both intuition and insight belong to every human regardless of beliefs, expertise, or activity. The atheist has just as much access to intuition and insight as the theologian. Some insight arises after much contemplation and study; other insight arrives *ex nihilo*, seeming to come out of nowhere.

The French mathematician, Henri Poincaré described such a case of sudden insight in 1908:

> At the moment when I put my foot on the step, the idea came to me, without anything in my former thoughts seeming to have paved the way for it, that the transformation I had used to define Fuchsian functions were identical with those of non-Euclidean geometry. I did not verify the idea: I

should not have had time, as upon taking my seat in the omnibus, I went on with a conversation already commenced but I felt a perfect certainty.

Boris Vladimirovich Gnedenko was a Russian mathematician. He is best-known for his contributions to probability theory. Gnedenko reported multiple sudden insights that occurred while his mind was at rest. Some of these insights came while shopping, teaching, or sleeping. He described one instance in which he fell asleep with a mathematical problem on his mind, to which he had no solution. When he awoke, the proof was clear in his mind.

Most of us have experienced such things. I once awoke with insights about conscious tesseracts entering hyperspace and reorganising stellated octa-hedrons that contain tetrahedra that cross at the point of infinity, and play a role in the creation of projected space within a holographic reality and are even found in the lens of the human eye. I knew nothing of tesseracts, hy-perspace, or octahedrons and only remembered the insight because I wrote it down immediately upon waking. While the conscious mind is at rest, the subconscious gives us access to previously unknown truth and wise guid-ance. Knowing this, we advise a friend with problems to "sleep on it." There are countless cases of people receiving spontaneous, life-changing insights and perhaps even more examples of people choosing to trust their intuition, which turns out to be lifesaving.

There are two types of insight; conscious problem solving, which is me-thodical, and sudden insight, as in the cases described above and the "Aha!" moments that all of us have had. In their book, *The Eureka Factor: Aha Moments, Creative Insight and the Brain*, John Kounios and Mark Beeman shared a discovery that upended decades-old assumptions on how the brain generates ideas and shifts between states. For decades, psychologists believed that changing our mental state takes time and must be a gradual process. Meditators and mystics have reported sudden-state changes for thousands of years. But the part of the scientific community that researched cognition in the 20th-century ignored that reality and held to their assump-tion that change must be gradual. Kounios and Beeman didn't research the sudden, drastic shifts in states of consciousness that occur when a person shifts unexpectedly into a state of bliss and union, but they did look at

22

something fascinating. They observed what happens in the brain right before an insight arises. In an interview with Medical Express, Kounios described insight as "popping" into awareness.

That choice of words might remind you a bit of how quantum physics describes particles as "popping" in and out of existence. In the interview with Medical Express, Kounios said:

> A few hundred milliseconds before that flash (of insight) was a burst of a different kind of activity in the back of the brain—a burst of EEG alpha waves. Those are lower-frequency waves. Alpha waves have been studied for about 80 years, and what we know about them is that they're a measure of inhibition of the visual system. They are the opposite of neural activity—when alpha is high, neural activity is low. What we found is that just before an insight, a person's visual system is inhibited for a few hundred milliseconds.

A person's visual system is briefly inhibited, and they recorded a burst of EEG alpha waves. Alpha waves are associated with deep relaxation and increase when the brain relaxes from a goal-oriented task. It's extremely interesting that the visual system is inhibited. It suggests that we use our eyes to look at the world without but use another kind of sight to go within. Insights and guidance aren't limited to answers. Intuition and insight also open new, previously uncharted territories by raising further questions and directing our attention in another direction. Insight opens the mind and heart and spurs the will to curiosity and exploration. Sometimes it causes you to re-examine your entire way of being.

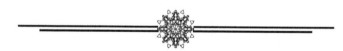

On a November evening in 2009, I curled up on my bed in Paris, too tired to move. I lay under the covers listening to the muffled sounds of dishes clanging as my housemates tidied up after their dinner. I felt chilled to the bone and exhausted. I was thirty-six years old, in an unfruitful, unwise relationship with a recently separated man that was hanging on by a thread. The relationship was founded on mutual sorrow and *Saudade*. It was no wonder that grief would drive us apart.

The fatigue felt as if a heavy resin had seeped into my bone and flesh, and it threatened to harden, fossilising body, heart, and soul. The feeling of home that I'd experienced nine years earlier in Frankfurt and again, even more profoundly just two years before this cold November night, was gone. I felt distant from a home that I couldn't fully regain access to in my present experience but missed all the same. As I drifted between wakefulness and sleep, a part of my mind asked, "Is life ever going to get better?" The question hung in the quiet void. I drifted there, peacefully, warmth finally filling my stiff limbs.

Then something happened.

I wasn't asleep. I was fully aware of where I was (aware that I was lying on my bed), and I seemed to float in that in-between place. There was warmth, relaxation, and peace. Then, without warning, a deafening wind, like a white hurricane, moved through me with such force that it seemed capable of sweeping everything that I was away. It was the loudest wind I had ever heard (and I lived through Hurricane Hugo). As suddenly as it began, it stopped, as if someone snapped their fingers and the wind obeyed. I saw only whiteness and then perceived not that I was *in* another place, but that another previously unexplored place was *within* me.

I then heard the most beautiful and almost indescribable voice. I can only try to describe two qualities of the voice; it was female, somehow crystalline in essence, and it seemed to come from every cell of my body but even more deeply than that, as if it came from my core. It's incredibly difficult to convey the angelic quality of the voice with our limited language. The voice was *in* me and *was* me but also felt beyond me. I didn't hear with my ears but perceived and heard her *within* myself. She said, "*Everyone can heal their life if they just know where to look.*" The moment I heard the words, I experienced my first vision. I saw a treasure chest and opened it. Inside the chest were many small, glass vials, all labeled with words describing emotions and feelings. It was an uncomplicated, straight forward message, but the method of delivery fascinated and startled me. The experience of that mighty wind was overwhelming.

I didn't believe in an anthropomorphic God, angels, or organised religion. I had stopped meditating but in the previous years leading up to this day, mediation had brought me into blissful states that lasted for days and changed my perception of reality: I began to experience previously unknown (to me), phenomena like synchronicity, prescience, almost instant fulfillment of certain, mundane wishes during daily life, and the meeting of needs before the need arose. I sensed that power began to flow through me but it wasn't my own. I could feel that I was just a conduit. After that November night, I began to converse silently with this inner being, and she always answered either with synchronicity, in a dream, or from other people. Sometimes the replies were so immediate and obvious that they blew my mind.

I began lucid dreaming during my childhood, at the age of six. A lucid dream is a dream in which one awakens within the dream and takes conscious control of the dream. Once I began meditating, there was a qualitative change to my dreams. Dreaming developed an instructive quality, and some dreams were prescient.

This kind of thing happened regularly during certain periods and yet, I had never felt anything like the wind. In the years leading up to this moment, I'd studied Eastern traditions like Taoism and Buddhism but hadn't encountered any mention of this particular phenomenon. It would be eight more years before I would discover or read a word from Neville Goddard. If I had found him immediately after this experience, I would have been put off by his religious-sounding language and would have missed the deeper truths in it. I needed more experience, contemplation, and personal evolution before delving into Neville's work.

I was thirsty for knowledge and longing for truth.

The experience of my Mista'peo wasn't a one-time occurrence. After this initial experience, in which my friend the Mista'peo (the superconscious self) who travels on the wind, came through and spoke to her proxy, I was now forever conscious of the cooperation between my self as the lower, relative personality construct, and the superconscious aspect of my being, the *Daimon*. With time (many years), I would surrender more and more to Beingness and shift my perception of Self from the limited, transient personality, to the AM of Being. Fulfillment is a paradox. The truest fulfillment comes from a great emptying out.

Some people hold to the idea that the *Daimon* is an entity that is entirely separate from the human, like a "guardian angel" assigned to each human. This might be true for some, but hasn't been my experience. My *Daimon* has made it very clear that we are one. Individuation is not the same as identity or ego. I grew to understand that, while the relative self is drastically and continually *transformed*, our individuation is never annihilated. The relative self is diminished, refined and integrated for the duration of the currently perceived life. It acts as a sort of proxy in the world. It's transformed via transmutation. Transmutation doesn't annihilate; it changes the state and form of that which it acts upon to such a degree that it *becomes* something entirely new.

The *Daimon* is not the Absolute (True) Self, but it is a helpful guide and source of comfort and encouragement. The *Daimon* is a much more expansive, relative self, that is immortal and exists outside of time. My *Daimon* now guides my life in a very real, felt, and direct way and played a substantial role in the writing of this book.

Over the years that followed that November night in 2009, a series of highly lucid, inner experiences (inner vision and inner voyage), new realms, and serendipitous encounters unfolded in my life. Each one revealed something about my being. I found myself in the right place at the right time. I had strangers approach me with messages that were so intimate and specific to my life, there was no way they could have known those things, and yet they did. Or at least, *something* spoke through them.

There was one consistent quality in all of the events and messages. They were consistently supportive, compassionate, and also clearly leaning towards a kind of *tough love*. The over-arching message was, "Stop throwing your life away. There's work to be done, and it's time you got to it."

When the innermost, Eternal Self wants you to get a move on, she doesn't mess around.

Chapter 4
SAUDADE

The servants of the Machine are becoming a privileged class. The Machines are going to be enormously more powerful. What's their next move?
—J. R. R. Tolkien, in a letter to his son Christopher, 1945

I'd like to take you on a journey. Throughout this book, we'll travel together through streams of thought, layers of self, and realms of imagination. Before we can begin, however, we need to look up and around at the world we share. It's a beautiful, violent, unpredictable world of untameable nature, infinite creativity, and sometimes soul-shattering predation. This is just one side of the story. Beauty has another tale to tell.

Nature is her own master. Humans, on the other hand, are not, by default, so attuned to our potential for sovereignty. As both individuals and a collective, we've relinquished our will and agency to a system, an ancient, impersonal ethos. Ethos is defined as "the 'genius' of a people, characteristic spirit of a time and or place" (1851 Palgrave). The ethos that has been most characteristic of humanity here on earth is called "Empire" by some and "The Control System" by others. Philip K. Dick famously said, "The empire never ended." He was referring to "empire" as an ethos.

Empire as an ethos is accurately represented in, of all things, a massive, multi-player game called "Elite Dangerous." It's the longest-running space-simulation series in history and has over thirty years of heritage. Within the game, there are Powers. According to the game's creators, a "Power is a powerful individual or organisation who strives to control inhabited areas for their own agendas." In the game, each Power has an Ethos that dictates their methods for preparing, expanding, and controlling systems.

Art imitates life.

Here in the 'real' world, our ethos is a complex adaptive system that acts as a sort of container and limiter of human consciousness. It's a Machine Mind. It's non-local, virus-like, highly adaptive, self-perpetuating, and will use any ideology that serves its purpose. Fascism, communism, capitalism, liberalism, conservatism, feminism, you name it. The Machine is, in effect, the result of an awareness that has no creative faculties of its own. It co-opts, mimics, and subverts organic human endeavours to create 'fuel' for itself and the containment system it constructs. The 1999 film, *Dark City*, explores the origins of the machine. In the same year another film, *The Matrix*, explored humanity's willingness to acquiesce to systems of containment.

In a letter to Milton Waldman of Collins Publishing dated around 1951, Tolkien described the main themes of the Silmarillion and Lord of the Rings. While he expressed his dislike for allegory, he admitted that to explain the purport of myth, one must use symbolic language. He wrote about a mind that, filled with a sense of mortality, becomes possessive of the things it has "made on its own, apart from nature." Referring to this sub-creator, he explained that it desires to be "Lord and God of its own creation and so it rebels against the laws of the Creator." Tolkien further explained that this desire for power leads to the mind searching for ways in which to make its will more quickly effective, which leads to the use of what he termed, "The Machine," which he said, was also "Magic." Here, Tolkien is referring to the inverted "magic" of the Machine, whereas the natural magic of the Elves is sourced by their inherent power. It involves their connection with the land they lived on, and flowed from a divine realm. To Tolkien, the Machine and black magic were one and the same.

Tolkien clarified that using the Machine (or magic) means to resort to the use of often elaborate, external agendas, psychological coercion, rituals, systems, and devices instead of developing our inherent powers that flow from an inner source. Tolkien described such behaviour as *"bulldozing the real world and coercing the wills of others."* He concluded with, *"The Machine is our more obvious, modern form and more closely related to magic than is usually recognised."* He was aware that the Machine was a modern manifestation of something much older. But what is it really, and from where did it originate?

One hundred and ninety-four years before Tolkien wrote that letter to Waldman, another Englishman, destined to shine a light on the Machine, was born. His name was William Blake. Blake was born on November 28, 1757, in Soho London, to two Dissenters, James and Catherine Blake. Blake's contemporaries believed him mad, and his work was mostly unknown and ignored. William Wordsworth wrote of Blake, "There was no doubt that this poor man was mad but there is something in the madness of this man which interests me more than the sanity of Lord Byron and Walter Scott." Blake was anything but insane. As John William Cousin, a writer and Fellow of the Faculty of Actuaries in Scotland, wrote, "Blake was a truly pious and loving soul, neglected and misunderstood by the world but appreciated by an elect few."

William was a unique child. He had his first vision at the age of four. At age fourteen, he began an apprenticeship with the master engraver, James Basire. When he was twenty-one, William became a journeyman engraver and member of the Royal Academy. He supported himself by working as an illustrator, illustrating publications in London. In 1789 he published *Songs of Innocence* and the *Book of Thel*. Blake believed that experience and innocence were, *"Two contrary states of the human soul"* and that while contrary states, innocence was utterly impossible without experience. *Songs of Innocence* is a collection of poems written either about children or from the perspective of a child.

The *Book of Thel* introduces the reader to Thel, an innocent shepherdess girl who lives in the Vales of Har with her mother and sisters. Thel experiences an existential crisis when she learns that all living beings must grow old and die. Wandering through the countryside, Thel encounters various individuals who seek to comfort her but to no avail. She finally meets Clod of Clay, who entreats Thel to visit the Underworld, where the dead reside. When Thel enters "the land of sorrows and tears" (the physical world in which we, *the dead* reside), she can't bear it and flees back home to Eternity where she remains an eternal, innocent virgin because she refuses to incarnate, as she fears it would be the end of her existence.

With time, Blake's work became increasingly complex. Between 1793 and 1797, Blake produced a body of work around his own, complex, massively scaled cosmology. The cosmology that Blake conceived of deals with the existence of Man, his fall, and brokenness. To this aim, he introduces us to The Four Zoas. The Four Zoas presented to us as characters, each with his own purpose. The Zoas are the result of the division of the Primordial, Divine Man, Albion. The Four Zoas are Tharmas, Urizen, Luvah, and Urthona.

The Four Zoas are central to the themes we will explore going forward and your understanding of the role they play in human life is crucial to any quest for fulfillment.

The Zoa called Urizen represents the aspect of mind that is concerned only with reason, judgment, measurement, control, and condemnation. He's the god of the Old Testament and is depicted as a white-bearded old man. He sometimes bears architect tools and nets, with which he ensnares humanity in webs of law, order, and tradition. Blake sometimes refers to Urizen quite fittingly as "Nobodaddy." Urizen is similar to the Gnostic Demiurge, who mistakenly believes that he is the creator of all. He is not. In his transcendent state, Urizen represents compassionate wisdom and pure intellect. In his fallen state, Urizen becomes an evil tyrant, obsessed with rational thought, coercive order, law, and control.

The fall of the Zoas, like the biblical fall, tells the story of the shift of super-consciousness into a state of unconscious sleep. Tharmas is called "The Parent Power." He's the source of all power and energy and represents sensation on his masculine side and sexuality on his feminine side. Tharmas is generally peaceful. Although he occasionally threatens to starve Urizen, he avoids conflict. Luvah represents emotion, feeling, and love. When Luvah, a Being of Love, falls, he turns into a Being of hate, driven by passions. Luvah is opposed to Urizen, and they battle constantly. Urthona (a.k.a. Los) is Divine Imagination in his unfallen state. In his fallen state he is called Los and represents the imagination within an individual. Like Luvah, Urthona/Los opposes Urizen. Urthona is the last Zoa to be created and corresponds to the earth element. According to Blake, Luvah and Urthona are the "keepers of the gates of heaven."

Blake's work, specifically his depiction of Urizen, is crucial to understanding the origins of the mentality that's so pervasive in our world. It's Urizen that diminishes human fulfillment, inspiration, and creativity. This aspect of consciousness arose and infected human life long before Blake was born. This raises three questions: Is it part of us? How long has it been here? Could it be that at some level, it exists for the very purpose of catalysing our *becoming* and our return to unity?

Blake often portrays Los (the fallen, human, earthly form of Urthona) as a hero. Los is referred to as the "Eternal Prophet." He's a visionary and initiates reunification. His feminine side, called Enitharmon, represents spiritual beauty and embodies compassion and mercy. She is responsible for the spatial aspect of the fallen world. In pity, she "wove bodies for mankind." In concert with Los, she created the physical world to stop the fallen from falling even further. Blake is suggesting that the creation of the physical world was an act of mercy by a higher consciousness on behalf of those who fell into duality.

Enter the Hero

The hero of every story needs an antagonist. In this story, the antagonist is not only the Machine, but also one's very own fragmented being and perception. You are the hero and you're driven by your *will to recover*. When we speak of the hero, we're not referring to caped crusaders or kick-ass women from Themyscira. You're a different sort of hero, the *original* hero and some would suggest that we've been playing this game for a long, long time.

According to our current historical narrative, an insidious spirit of cunning and assimilation (the Urizen mentality/ethos of Empire) targeted the cultures of the European continent and the isles of the Celts for over two thousand years. The campaign, interspersed with periods of overt brutality, steadily eradicated the rich, organic traditions of the people. Natural human culture and thought were replaced with the draconian, inverted culture of the Empire, but Empire had an enemy. While this enemy existed throughout the lands, with no centralisation of authority, Rome felt its presence most palpably amongst the Celts, specifically the Druids. Rome was hugely successful in its endeavour to rob the people of their sovereignty.

The campaign was so successful that in the 19th and 20th centuries, the peoples of Europe and North America, driven by an inner impulse towards conscious evolution, turned far from their homelands for guidance. They looked eastward towards India and Tibet. Not because Eastern tradition or philosophy were superior but because they knew of no similar alternative. The true spirit of the West had been trampled and oppressed, books had been burned, history rewritten, and their knowledge and tradition rendered nearly non-existent.

Why was Rome so afraid of the Celtic and Germanic tribes? Unlike the Empire, they had no vast armies, no cunning strategists, no will to dominate, and yet, they were of particular interest to Caesar, who was disconcerted by the resilience of their spirit. Throughout the earth, the Empire's modus operandi has always been *divide and conquer* but the Celts and their Druidic way of being were particularly troublesome for Rome. Like all lands that have been conquered by Empire, they were marked for assimilation. The priestly caste, however, was marked for total annihilation. The Druids were priest-philosophers. In his book *Druides et Chamanes*, author and one of the world's leading authorities on Celtic culture, Jean Markale explained that it's challenging to find traces of Druidic philosophy but that by "Examining mythology and the modifications which tribal dispositions brought to bear upon Christianity, it's possible to discern the contours of the Druidic mind."

Markale elaborates in the following passages*:

Some have likened Druidic philosophy to Buddhism but there is no comparison. They represent two opposite registers and conceptions. Where Eastern thinking encourages a state of non-action, the Celtic attitude saw action as prevailing over everything else. The individual was exalted, a hero, and he or she lived in the world in order to actively change it so that it aligned to a divine plan.

The Eastern attitude of resignation or of passively waiting for conditions to change would have been unimaginable to the Celts, this would have been considered neglect and a rejection of the gift of human life and the opportunity to undertake the Sacred Quest. To the Celts, human beings were

God's cohorts. We are active participants in the creation and perfection of the world.

The goal of the sacred quest was to enter and pass-through the Otherworld. This Otherworld doesn't resemble the image of a Christian heaven, nor does it resemble the realms of non-consciousness that the Romans conceived through their rationalist materialism.

According to Markale, the Celtic Otherworld also bears no resemblance to the Buddhist Void, or notion of returning to Source. Markale writes:

> For the Celts, this Otherworld was a place of transition, the station between this reality and other infinite worlds. The Druids understood everything in the universe to be in a state of perpetual motion and transformation. Due to the nature of the quest and mankind's role in universal creation, the individual was exalted. Every quest was unique, and every hero faced his or her own challenges. It was understood that the paths were many, diverse, and singular.

> Druidic logic was neither wholly collectivist nor individualistic; it is both at the same time, as it refuses all duality. But to succeed both individually and collectively, the liberty of each soul had to be safeguarded.

Heroic Hobbits

In Celtic mythology, all who took up the mantel of the quest were considered heroes. In this case, the term "hero" has nothing to do with the modern caricature of massive physical strength or uncanny intelligence. Instead, it's a title bestowed in recognition of the courage displayed by those who accept the challenge of self-mastery and transformation. The quest was perilous and full of hidden dangers.

The invisible Otherworld was all around but only accessible to the hero who had overcome his or her inner-demons and developed an inner-sight. Because the doorway to the Otherworld is located within, not without.
—Jean Markale

The journey was sacred because the Druids considered the human being to be sacred. Markale points out that the Druids believed that Divinity needed us wee little humans. Markale writes, "The primordial God had confidence in small human beings because we possess an infinite power, the extent of which we don't always know how to make use of. That is part of the quest." The Celts perceived the quest as mandatory to human evolution. No one could hide from it. Blaise Pascal said, "Every human being is engaged in the game of life, he has to wager. The quest is the wager." Refusing to engage means stagnating, we are, of course, free to make that choice but should be aware of the consequences.

J.R.R. Tolkien was well-versed in Finnish, Celtic, Icelandic, and Norwegian mythology. His epic tales in *The Hobbit* and *The Lord of the Rings,* were in some ways, more truth than fiction. Using mythological imagery, Tolkien revealed our past to us while illuminating the origins of our current situation. Of all the colourful characters of Middle Earth, none touch the human heart quite like the Hobbit. While the Elves, the Kings of Men and the Dwarves had their roles to play, Gandalf entrusted the ultimate quest to a Hobbit. Frodo and Sam were the true heroes of Middle Earth, and they are not so unlike us. Born pristinely unique and free, they were conditioned by their parents and culture. The life of Hobbits seems like a dream compared to our modern world: two breakfasts a day and plenty of naps. They wanted for nothing, and most of their fellows were content to stay home, work the land, and entertain themselves. Standing out from the crowd was frowned upon, and adventures were unheard of. It was from this quiet, sleepy culture that the greatest hero of Middle Earth hailed. The quest knocked on his door. Frodo did not refuse, and even more beautifully perhaps, his tribal brother Sam chose, of his own free-will, to accompany him.

If you've read their story, you know the details of their quest and the pain and danger they experienced. Through adroit storytelling, Tolkien affords us a rare privilege of observing the transformation of a hero, in all of its gritty glory. There were mistakes made, oversights, and misunderstandings, but their spirits prevailed. Frodo and Sam were heroes because they accepted the quest not because they succeeded. They faced their fears, and they challenged the status quo. They challenged the most frightening authority of their time, Sauron, and they even challenged their teacher, Gandalf but most of all, they challenged themselves.

It's impossible to provide one, definitive answer to why there is so much dissatisfaction in the world today but we come close to hitting the mark and identifying the root cause when we acknowledged that in our state of unconsciousness, we have forgotten who we are, or at least, who we *could* be. The vast majority of humanity are disconnected from their core and live life at a low level of consciousness, existing in a state of perpetual amnesia. In our forgetfulness, a system, one that we have helped to create but also fallen prey to, has manifested.

Both these things, the state of amnesia and its correspondent reality, are incompatible with lasting, human fulfillment. Our minds fragment, mis-perceive, and create duality. We suppress, repress, and project emotion, re-fusing to turn within because we fear what we might find there. No one is coming to save us from ourselves. The answers aren't in any book, certainly not in this one. The answers reside in each person, deep within your being. At the most, this book and others like it, are signposts pointing you to an-other world, the inner realm of infinite beingness and awakened imagina-tion. In this realm, we find a bridge, a bridge that connects the Absolute Self with the relative self, the eternal with the transient.

A commitment to creating the conditions in our lives that catalyse a transformation of consciousness and move us into a state of fulfillment means that we can't expect to shirk our duty to ourselves and hide be-hind apathy as we remain in a state of despondent resignation and melancholy.

The Portuguese have a word that perfectly describes the drumming, melancholic feeling that something is missing in our lives. They call it *Saudade*. Life goes on and on. We do the same thing over and over. We re-sign ourselves to doing what we must to pay the bills, satisfy our families, gain the approval of our friends, and the vacant admiration of strangers. You may have known, or now know, someone of whom the word 'shallow' is an accurate descriptor. Contemplative young people often take it for granted that everyone thinks, reflects and engages with existence the way they do and are surprised to learn that there are millions of people who make it to the age of eighty without having ever done any self, or philo-sophical inquiry, deep contemplation or maturing. They're virtually the same at eighty as they were at twenty-one. I say *virtually* the same because, in actuality, they're worse off. As a person ages, one of two things happen, they get better—or they get worse.

A woman once spoke to me of her brother. She said, "When Gabe was young, he was always smiling and laughing, and when he talked to you, you could feel that he was really interested in who you were, but I haven't seen that Gabe in almost five decades." I know Gabe and his wife pretty well. When around them, you can sense a ceaseless undercurrent of dissatisfaction. Gabe is never present. His mind is constantly preoccupied. His wife Anne is now seventy. She's lonely, dissatisfied and feels that she has nothing to look forward to. Her entire world was constructed around raising her three daughters, managing the family schedule, work, appearances, staying fit, and maintaining alignment with her preferred social circle.Anne will tell you that she doesn't believe in anything. "Life is an accident. You have to get what you can while you're young because once you're old, you're unattractive, and when you die, that's the end," she told me. She might be right, that might be her final destination. Who knows for sure? Anne is dissatisfied because she sought conditional happiness and not true, inner fulfillment. Her happiness was contingent on being youthful, attractive, occupied with her children, career, and hobbies, and being the wife of a successful politician.

All of those things; family, work, hobbies, travel, celebration, and friends, are an important part of a fulfilling life but if they are the sole source of our fulfillment then what happens to that fulfillment when family dies, a career ends, our perfect partner passes away, friends go, or we aren't able to practice our hobbies because of an illness or old age? What's left below the surface when everything else is stripped away?

You may know people like Anne. They are good people and can be loving, generous, funny, and affectionate. But if you attempt to draw their attention to contemplative thought and deeper insights, their eyes will glass over, and you quickly realise that they're not fully home. If you take a moment to look, to *really look* into such a person's eyes, you will see something behind them. You'll see a presence of which they aren't remotely aware. That presence is an infinite potential that they never tapped into and never even inquired about.

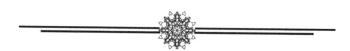

Children are brilliantly imaginative beings, but most of their creative impulse and power is squeezed out of them before the age of seven. Some hold on tenaciously until the age of eighteen and to take care that those renegades don't escape the containment system, we have indoctrination centres operating within a number of universities. In our youth, we're highly creative, full of wonder about the world, hopeful expectation, and openness to adventure and discovery. *Anything is possible.* Do you remember that? What happens to diminish the bright, human spirit of youth? Answer: The inverted culture, mentality, and containment system of the Machine. The Machine can invert and subvert anything but it's not all-powerful. It wouldn't exist at all without our collective consent.

The most recent deception that the system wants you to buy into is that you're random and insignificant. Combine that with the mind-narrowing effects of ideologies, religion, state control of education, and the almost fascist control of science by self-appointed guardians of science and reason, and you will see that we live in a fairytale world, where nothing is as we're told.

We become what we revere, and we aspire to things hoped for. Hope, connection, a rich inner life, wonder, curiosity, exploration, creativity, and a refusal to stagnate are antidotes to *Saudade*. Unfortunately, many people associate spirituality exclusively with religion, esotericism, mysticism, New Ageism, rites, and ritual. Spirituality = Engagement with both consciousness and existence, that are independent of, and precede, matter. In the truest sense, spirituality is engagement with your innermost being, the real you. Quantum theory, research on the non-local mind, ontology, psychology, and philosophy are all examples of different areas of that engagement. Religion doesn't hold a patent on spirituality.

Engagement with the spiritual doesn't require you to adopt a new belief system, quite the opposite! To engage with the power and existence that are independent of matter, we need to first shed all beliefs—to the best of our ability, and by use of a highly attuned faculty of discernment—so that we can approach reality as an unbiased scientist. This is why meditation is so helpful and why great teachers have stressed the importance of reaching a state of 'no-mind.' Spiritual awareness is just one aspect of being. Some people and traditions treat it like the ultimate goal and then stop there.

Self-Realisation requires more than just, being "spiritual" or being "aware" because **presence doesn't guarantee love, and mindfulness doesn't ensure wisdom.**

To *become* is a never-ending evolution. It means committing to integration, embodiment and ongoing, conscious, intentional engagement with the Absolute Self. Power will begin to flow through the individual. Managing its flow requires humility, self-regulation, and wisdom. Sometimes reasoning and deep, clear thinking are appropriate. Sometimes a quiet mind is preferred, and at other times we just need to "chop wood, carry water" as the Zen Master instructs.

Because the journey can feel very solitary at times, it's very easy to get caught up in narratives and other people's reality vectors. We seek confirmation. How good would it feel for some hyper-advanced Being or 'master' to come along and say, "This is how you do it! Just follow me, walk my path, and you'll be okay." Inevitably, when we do think we've found some other way, a new modality, or a new milieu, it almost always comes with a price. That price is a renouncement of the sacred singularity, and perfect validity, of your unique journey. Modalities and systems are mechanisms of containment, but they don't have to be. They can also provide helpful structure. Some containment is helpful as a safeguard for the unprepared mind but there is a difference between wise self-regulation and systematic distortion.

There is a way out of the maze. There's another way to live, to be.

The very first step is to accept the quest, *your* quest. It demands radical self-inquiry, courageous honesty, openness, and a transformation of mind, heart, personality, and being. It's a quest to connect with your higher self, your Daimon and ultimately commune, and identify with, the Absolute Self. Although the journey can seem solitary, the truth is: you are never alone. At the end of your quest, whatever you have become, whatever you have created, and however you choose to engage, it's yours. No one can take it away from you.

Chapter 5
FORGIVENESS

Northern Georgia is a realm of sun-baked, red clay and spindly pines that trace the silhouettes of meandering creeks full of tadpoles and chilly rapids with slippery rocks. Georgia is warm, humid, and slow. This lack of urgency provides a kind of shelter from the future. Antebellum memories refuse to deliquesce like ladies who refuse to nap between an afternoon barbecue and the evening ball.

My greater family was from Savannah, one of the most beautiful towns in the South. My parents grew up there. My sisters and I spent our summers roasting in the heat of Richmond Hill, an area outside of Savannah, where muddy tributaries of the Ogeechee River provide ample opportunity for mud-sliding. The sulphuric mud of the Ogeechee is almost oily and turns the tributary banks into slippery slopes. If you run at just the right speed, then jump forward and land belly-down onto the slope, you'll slide down at break-neck speed. It momentarily holds the potential to disgust but then becomes fantastically exhilarating and somewhat addictive, kind of like the first time you have sex.

Somewhere between the banks of the Ogeechee River and the rapids of North Georgia, I became a woman. The land we grow up on patterns us, we become a part of the energetic mosaic of the living experience that draws its life from the land and draws its breath from the trees.

After my parents divorced, my mother and I lived alone in Atlanta. I was just a baby when my parents' marriage went asunder. My older sister, Lisa, was seven and went to stay with our grandparents. My mother was left alone with an infant to care for but no one to care for her, so my uncle, who was just seventeen when I was born, moved to Atlanta to live with his sister and her baby. Mom drew support from her younger brother and her church. Her own mother and stepfather had converted and joined the Watchtower Bible and Tract Society, also known as Jehovah's Witnesses, in the 1950s. Isn't funny how we inherit the decisions, wise or unwise, of our ancestors?

Through the congregation, my mother met another convert named David, the man who would become my stepfather. David came from a Methodist family and had just returned from Vietnam in 1972. He was awarded the bronze star and was offered the Purple Heart but turned it down. David kept his bronze star a secret for forty-five years due to shame and trauma that he has never been able to heal. He joined the Watchtower organisation in his late twenties in an effort to find security and forgiveness. He recently told me that even now, in his seventies, he still dreams of being chased and shot at in the jungle. Predation scars the soul.

Our mother had a vivacious spirit about her plus something else that was difficult for most people to put their finger on. She had magnificently high cheekbones, a straight nose, strong jaw, and piercing green eyes. Our mother, Alice, was the result of my grandmother's first marriage, a union that remained a secret in our family for a long time. I didn't learn that my grandfather wasn't really my grandfather until I turned twelve. Mother pulled me aside while on vacation and told me the truth. Her biological father was named Edward, and he had lived on the Seminole reservation with his mother, Peasy, who was either Seminole or Creek.

My grandmother grew up in poverty. Her second marriage pulled her out of it. She had known true hunger and deprivation in her youth, but while she 'married up' to an intelligent, educated man of moderate means, she never really escaped her past. Her fear of hunger manifested in a kitchen pantry that always had at least five different kinds of breakfast cereals and extra freezers full of food. She reminded me a bit of Scarlett O'Hara in that regard; no one would ever go hungry on her watch. She was also a witty woman with a wicked sense of humour. The last time we spoke, before her death, we giggled through most of the conversation.

Our grandmother was secretly ashamed of her first marriage, although she needn't have been. All shame is untrue, which is why it feels so bad. Her first husband was a drunk and gambler who left his wife and infant daughter to starve while he drank away what little money they had.

I grew up within this unique constellation of repressed human suffering, hidden shame of the past, immature and isolationist religion, complex family loyalties, and secrets that co-existed with love, kindness, curiosity, intelligence and no small measure of resiliency.

Georgia was the stage, full of props and eccentric set-designs, and the people around me were like actors, unaware of the roles they were playing. I often felt alien in their world. The adults around me, those at home, church, and school, seemed rather insane but I loved them all and understood, somehow, that they were sleepwalking through life. Occasionally, I would find a sage, someone who felt *just right*. They were invariably decades older than I, and often quiet and reserved. I gravitated to them like a star to a galaxy.

When I was fourteen years old, my stepfather took a job in a town called Dalton. We left the bustling suburbs of Atlanta for the rolling landscapes of North Georgia. Evergreens dominate the vistas, but there are just enough deciduous trees to colour autumn with robust colours of rust, burgundy, amber, and butterscotch yellow. In North Georgia, hills pretend to be mountains. The same could be said of the people of Dalton in the late 1980s. Dalton was the carpet capital of the world. They produce berber carpets, wools, polyesters, nylons, intricate tapestries, floor-to-floor basics, oriental motifs, and modern mosaics. The image of an enthusiastic salesman comes to mind, "You can find it all in Dalton!" At one point in the early 1980s, they claimed that there were more millionaires per square mile in the sleepy little town of Dalton than anywhere else in the USA. Arriving in our new home was an unexpected and jarring revelation.

In my youthful naiveté, I expected the same measure of variety that we experienced around Atlanta, where people of all races and economic means attended our church and sat next to me in school. The Dalton High school parking lot was full of Mercedes and BMWs, and they didn't belong to the poorly paid teaching staff. Moving to Dalton was like getting hoisted into the air by the ankles and unceremoniously shook, until all expectations fell, like small treasures escaping upside-down pockets.

Fast-forward a few years to the last day of school; I was seventeen years old. A lifetime (albeit short) of coercive religion, being forced to attend church three times a week, proselytising every Saturday morning and sometimes on Sunday afternoons, being forbidden from forming close relationships with "worldly" people (anyone who isn't a Jehovah's Witness), subjected to emotional and psychological abuse by sometimes well-intended but always lost souls, trying to help an ill mother, and acting as a mediator in the unhealthy marriage of our parents had turned my metaphoric well into a pressure cooker, and I wasn't alone.

The children of Dalton's rich walked around the school as if trying to hide open wounds. Many students were neglected by their busy parents, and love was often lacking. But what does that matter when you can give your sixteen-year-old a Porsche? The world is full of lonely people who treat their children, and each other, like Heidegger's hammer: "Your value is in your utility, and you don't matter until I need you."

I walked out of the building on the last day of school with a friend. As the doors closed behind us, I turned to her and said, "I'm not going back home. I can't take it anymore. Can I come home with you and figure it out?" She said yes, and we did. Her parents took me in for one week. After that I was on my own. I stepped onto a path that had long been prepared for me but I was in no way prepared for the path. Or maybe I was.

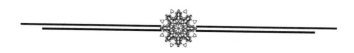

The first time I saw Asher, I thought he looked like an epileptic deer. "*Driving that train, high on cocaine, Casey Jones you better, watch your speed.*" The music of The Grateful Dead reverberated in my ears, and I stood, thunderstruck, at the sight of such a sublime buck who was beautiful, despite his spastic dancing. It was a midsummer's night, and I was free. I hadn't seen my family in a month and had only managed to recover my clothing by sneaking back to the house with the help of friends one afternoon while my parents were at work. But I had just secured an apartment with the help of a friend's mother. It was on the second floor of their house. I had my own kitchen, living room, and two bedrooms. It was threadbare with sparse furnishings, but it felt like mine.

Now, I was at my first party with young adults ranging from eighteen to twenty-four. The Zeitgeist of North Georgia's youth in 1991 included a peculiar combination of 90s Grunge combined with 70s rock, electric blues, hippy jam bands, and the psychedelic rock of the 60s. I stood, transfixed on the grass, in an ankle-length tie-dyed skirt and knock-off Birkenstocks. He didn't notice me, and I was too stunned to care. Passion walked up to me, stared me down, and knocked me right out of my body.

I was a virgin. The only kiss I'd ever known had been at age fifteen and included a slimy, Snickers bar and popcorn flavoured tongue that kept darting rudely down my throat. Kissing was removed from the roster after that. But now I was free, and in that freedom, a vast potentiality and craving for experience entered my sphere of awareness. This was going to be *my* boy… and he was…for a little while.

On our first date, he picked me up in his red Ford pickup and took me to the equestrian facilities of Bouckaert Farm in Chatsworth, a town near Dalton. He walked me through the stables, and it was there that I learned that he was an equestrian jumper and that his family had their own horses as well. On the way home, we stopped by an old house that his older brother was renovating. It was run down with a large swath of ceiling missing, but we managed to work our way up the battered staircase and find a second-floor balcony to sit on. With our legs dangling over the balcony's ledge, we watched the stars and talked. Romance had come home to roost. I was too young to understand the consequences of romantic entanglements and too inexperienced to know that when something throbs, it can be a sign of impending pain, especially the throbbing of a heart.

Asher, still deer-like, bound up the stairs to my apartment on his long legs, carrying a brown paper bag full of soft drinks, plastic cups, some wrapped packages, and a small pack of birthday candles. It was my eighteenth birthday and my first-ever birthday party (birthday celebrations are forbidden by the church). A little while later, we stood around a birthday cake with a few friends, and I beamed as they sang happy birthday, and I blew out the candles.

Sometimes his face held pity for me, and I hated it. I wanted to be cherished, not pitied. This is true of most women. He was three years older than I, and I felt like an inexperienced child around him most of the time. He lived with his parents in an antebellum–style house, complete with white columns on the front. I was in awe of the house and of him. I adored him, and he kept me safe for a while.

His mother bought clothes for me, and Asher (henceforth "Ash") picked me up in this red truck and took me to work every day so that I wouldn't have to walk. I was still a virgin at the end of the summer. By autumn, we were beginning to argue frequently. He was pressing me to continue my education, but I saw no way to do so. I didn't qualify for government grants and couldn't get assistance from my family unless I agreed to go home and rejoin their religion. Despite the bickering, we finally did manage to make love (if you could even call it that). On one level, it was fast, painful, and uneventful (for me anyway). Neither of us knew what we were doing. On another level, it was an opening. I learned to relax and trust and let go—just a little bit at a time.

Beginnings are fragile things. They're made of gossamer threads of hope and shimmer with the faint light of potential grace. It's in the human heart that we begin weaving our designs and dreams of experience yet to come. We live our entire lives within chrysalises. As soon as we emerge from one, life sculpts another around us. Within *manifest* reality, everything is in a constant state of becoming, even God.

Just a few months later, on a winter night right before Christmas, unceremoniously and without warning, life pulled that Dalton-made rug right out from under my feet. In the space of one day, I went from hopeful and supported to chastised and distrusted. Those things seem to be persistent, peripheral aspects of rape, in a society that lives in a hall of mirrors.

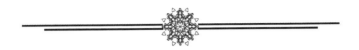

Ash's parents were out of town visiting friends or family before Christmas, which presented the perfect opportunity for a party. By 8:00 p.m., around twenty people had arrived, and we gathered in the kitchen to cook together. Ash and I prepared the baked beans together with our not-so-secret ingredients of BBQ sauce, fried bacon, caramelised onions, and maple syrup. It's funny how certain memories crystallise in the mind, snapshots of emotions.

We had beer, wine, and assorted liquor. A few of the boys wanted some pot, so they called a supplier that wasn't completely part of the group but was considered a useful acquaintance. The supplier, Michael* came quickly after being called but he didn't come alone. He brought a friend that none of us knew. I saw him enter but never spoke with him or learned his name. A few hours later, I learned that he had brought other drugs as well. Only a few people decided to smoke pot or take any other drug, Ash and I were not among them. He stuck to beer, and I stayed with wine before having a few fatal shots of whiskey.

I spent most of the evening on a high chair by the phone in the kitchen talking to a friend of Ash's and our friend Joanna*, also an equestrian and the caretaker and manager of the stables at an equestrian centre. Sometime around midnight, I told Ash that I was tired and felt sick. The house had a layout that allowed you to loop around to the front foyer and stairs either via the living room to the right or via a corridor that led away from the kitchen and through the dining room on the left.

Everyone was in the living room at this point, sprawled out, talking and listening to music, so we took the private way via the side corridor and dining room. When we made it to the staircase, Joanna came to help because I wasn't able to walk up the stairs alone. The last thing I remember is Joanna and Ash pulling me through his bedroom door to put me to bed. I was way beyond tipsy. It's a miracle that I didn't vomit. If I did, I don't remember it. I must have blacked out because Joanna told me later that they put me to bed fully clothed and covered me up. My sleep was close to comatose. I have no awareness of anything that happened between my two friends pulling me through the bedroom door and the moment that I awoke in pitch blackness.

Someone was on top of me. I couldn't lift my arms at first; they were too heavy. I was naked. The person on top of me was so heavy, and he was thrusting into my body very hard. Something wasn't right. In my stupor and weakness, I said, "Ash?" I couldn't breathe. His chest was too heavy as he pressed against mine. There was no verbal response, but I felt him lift off my chest while still thrusting into me. Finally, I managed to lift my arms, and I reached for a face. It had stubble. It wasn't Ash.

I froze.

I didn't say anything, didn't cry, didn't move. I was paralysed.

It finished, and I felt him get off the bed. The room lit up. He had switched on the bedside lamp and stood on the side of the bed, opposite the bedroom door. I sat up, got off of the bed, and turned to look at him. It was the friend of the pot supplier. The one with whom I'd never spoke a word the entire night.

He said, "Oh. I hope that was okay."

There is no way for me to describe what I was feeling or thinking—because I felt nothing and thought nothing. The body took over. It walked out of the room and went directly into the adjacent bathroom. It showered and used the shower nozzle to clean itself from what he had left in it. It went back into the bedroom to get its clothes.

He was gone.

My body walked down the stairs, and only when it reached the bottom did a thought arise, "Don't go left because they're all in the living room. Go right and go quietly through the kitchen and out the back door." Thoughts left again, and my body moved. When I made it to the back porch, I must have stood there for a while. My friend Joanna appeared. She was asking something, I don't remember what. I only stared at her. Without a word from me, her eyes widened. She came closer, put her hands on my arms, and said, "Were you raped?!." I didn't respond, I only looked at her. Then we were outside. She told me to stay near the back fence. It must have been cold, but I don't remember feeling it. I only began to awaken more to my surroundings when the commotion began. Someone, a male friend, came running out towards me with Joanna. They stood next to me and said, "It's being taken care of just stay here with us. We've got you." There was yelling and a crash and the squeal of tires.

Eventually, I was led back up to the same bed, but this time Joanna and the supportive male friend got in the bed with me. I didn't see Asher anywhere. They stayed there, one on each side and told me to sleep and they would stay with me. As promised, they stayed until morning, with Joanna's arms around me for part of the night.

They seemed more visibly upset than I was. I was somewhere else.

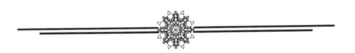

In the morning, before the three of us left Ash's bedroom, Joanna and the male friend told me what happened. Joanna had told Ash what happened. He and a few friends confronted the rapist. Michael, the pot supplier that had brought this unknown young man to the party, tried to defend his friend, but his friend admitted to what he had done by saying, "I'm sorry, I didn't know where I was. I thought she was my girlfriend. I didn't know what I was doing." Reportedly he began to cry and Asher went to the garage and got a baseball bat. The other guys intervened, something was knocked over, and they chased Michael and his friend off. That was the screeching of tires that we heard.

In the future, I would wonder about that night. I wondered what everyone else was experiencing. What's it like to hear that a girl you know was raped just upstairs while you knew nothing of it? What kind of shock is that?

What was the young man who raped me feeling? Why did he do that? What was Ash experiencing? How did Joanna intuitively know what had happened, and how did it affect her? And most of all, where did the Self go when the body was taking care of necessities?

When we went down for breakfast the next morning, Ash was there with a few friends who were helping to clean up. The atmosphere was frigid. Moving through it felt like the Tin Man must have felt when his joints rusted. Ash barely looked at me, and a few of the friends cast suspicious glances in my direction. In their minds, doubt had already set in, and it was a fast-acting poison.

Over the following weeks, everything unraveled. Rumour began to spread, some accurate and some untrue. A few people (specifically the boy who brought the rapist to the party and his girlfriend), suggested that it must have been consensual sex. Despite what the rapist had admitted to, and despite the fact that Ash knew he had put me to bed and left me sleeping, Ash grew distant. He still took me to and picked me up from work, and yet we hardly spoke. He became icy, and I began to spiral out. We broke up, and yet, to his credit, he still came every day to take me to and from work. We could hardly speak two civil words to each other. Perhaps he tried to be civil, but I frequently lashed out at him.

I withdrew from everyone. I was no longer a welcome guest at parties and exciting dates with Asher were a thing of the past. Only a few friends stood by me; Joanna, plus another girl who just happened to be the daughter of the Chief of Police (I never pressed charges) and a handful of others. Each day I worked, watched TV, and slept.

My landlord, upon hearing the story through the rumour mill, decided that I must have been at least somewhat culpable because I was drinking and partying with my boyfriend. Fearing that this would reflect poorly on her and her daughter, she asked me to find another residence. I was homeless, and we're all told that, "Beggars can't be choosers," so when an acquaintance that I had just met through work, told me that her sister and sister's husband could take me in if I paid part of the rent, I agreed. When we pulled up to their place, I sank just a little lower into the earth.

The term 'white trash' first appeared in American vernacular in the 1800s. It's been an unfortunately effective slur for the poor and uneducated Caucasian, especially in the South. Perhaps because of my grandmother's early poverty and the way in which shame is passed on from one generation to another, my mother had a particular aversion to 'white trash.' Although she rarely used the term (she found it unbecoming), she made sure that my sister and I knew that, 'white trash' was about as far as one could fall.

Our mother was an intelligent, talented woman. She could sew beautifully and would buy Oscar de La Renta patterns and produce fantastic replicas of haute couture dresses and pant-suits. She loved to cook dishes from around the world, loved to read, and insisted that we be well-read. She made us walk with books on our head, which we were required to balance perfectly before she would let us walk in high heels.

In addition to the Bible, we were made to study hard, use the encyclopaedia instead of asking others for the answers to our questions. We were required to learn etiquette, have good manners, and hold ourselves upright with good posture. If we slouched, she'd give us a hard poke in the back.

Despite how firmly middle class that sounds, we barely qualified as middle-class. Our parents constantly fought about money. Most of my clothes were either hand-me-downs or sewn by our mother. There was no money for lessons or extracurricular activities, and most vacations were spent either at a campsite or visiting family in Savannah. The lack of money for extracurricular activities meant that we had to entertain ourselves. I became an avid reader. Before the age of ten, I was devouring books on mythology, languages, and science and trying to understand why the Bible was such a strange book. The library was an escape hatch. Mom had no problem with us spending entire afternoons absorbed in the yellowing pages of a book. I lived in a parallel world of wonder and imagination, while also conforming to our parents' demands.

I later wondered how much of this focus on appearances was driven by our parents' hidden shame. Dad was ashamed of Vietnam and, mother was ashamed of something I couldn't grasp. Whatever the scope and source of her motivations, the terms 'white trash' and 'trailer trash' and everything that they represented was something from which we were conditioned to stay far, far away.

My new home was in a run-down trailer park. What would mother say? It had been many months since we'd spoken. Now, sitting on the sofa in a grimy trailer, I began to miss her. I picked up the phone and called her. It was impossible not to tell her what had happened. I needed her. The girl that I was needed the nurturing and compassion of a mother. After I told her about the rape, she was silent for only the space of a heartbeat before responding coldly, "Well, that's what happens to girls who leave God's chosen organisation on earth."

My eighteen-year-old self's response was exactly what one would expect. I said something to the effect of "Go fuck yourself," and hung up the phone. I felt like trash that the world had suddenly discarded. 'White' and 'trailer' had nothing to do with it. I was trash because I believed that no one wanted me around. Isn't that how we feel about our garbage? I felt that I had been loved like a shiny, new toy and then discarded when perceived as damaged, corrupted, or just uncomfortable to be around.

Suspicion had a face. It was the face of my mother, the face of the church, Asher's face when he grew cold and began to doubt. It was the face of the group that whispered and chastised. I hated that face. I wanted to scream and rage and scratch Suspicion's eyes out. That suspicion became my own, and distrust became my default mode.

My time in that trailer was short-lived. Barely two weeks after I arrived, the husband of my friend's sister and man-of-the-house propositioned me. Disgusted and increasingly angry, I refused. Within a few hours, I was told that I had to leave. A friend came to pick me up, and as we left, it seemed fitting that I carried all of my clothes in trash bags.

Over the next few months, I lived in a cockroach-infested hotel room with a small kitchenette. My hotel neighbours were drug addicts and alcoholics. I covered the mattress with garbage bags and tape because I was afraid of bed bugs. I stopped caring about food and weight fell from my frame. It didn't really matter, because I had little money with which to buy food.

There's a predatory spirit in the world that lives through some people as if they were organic portals for something else, something non-human. That predatory spirit caught my scent after I was excommunicated and shunned by the church and further alienated by the group of friends that had temporarily been a support structure for me.

One night, not more than two months after the rape, I was invited to spend the night with a girlfriend. When I met her at our meeting place so that she could drive us to her place out in the countryside, she introduced me to three young men, juniors from Georgia Tech that she had invited to join us. I felt uneasy. She told me that they would be following in their own vehicle and leaving in a few hours. Since I knew I wouldn't be drinking that night (or ever falling asleep without my bedroom door locked), I put my worry aside. We swam, talked, and made dinner. My girlfriend drank with the guys and the guys took something, some kind of drug. Later in the evening, after my friend disappeared with one of the boys, the two remaining boys cornered me in the living room. They were drunk. One ran his hand up my skirt and grabbed my groin while grasping my breast with his other hand. The other one just laughed.

At that moment, I felt a presence, as if someone else was in the room. The presence had a powerfully calming effect that focused my mind. The two young men, each a foot taller and twice as strong as me, gave each other a knowing look that sent a chill up my spine. Instead of reacting like a terrified deer in headlights, the peaceful presence I sensed in the room told me exactly what to do. There was the odd sensation that I had been there before, in that moment. I feigned a smile and told them I'd like a drink after all, and asked them to go make something for the three of us.

Apparently feeling that things were going their way, they complied. As soon as they entered the kitchen, I ran to the bathroom. It was a double bathroom, it had one entrance door where the sink, washer, and dryer were, and a second door that led to a shower and toilet room. I locked the first door and refused to come out. When the two young men realised that I wasn't coming out, they started threatening me. One ordered the other to go get and icepick out of the kitchen so that he could pick the lock. I calmly held the small lock knob on my side of the door. As they grew angrier, they made threats of depraved sexual violence. The entire time I felt that calm presence as if someone else was in the room with me. Finally, they took a fire extinguisher and sprayed the living room with it. I didn't see this until they had left, and I felt safe enough to come out of the bathroom. When I did finally come out, and when I knew I was safe, I started to shake uncontrollably. I went back into the bathroom and curled up in a fetal position and sobbed until my body hurt.

After that night, I didn't trust men at all; I barely ate and didn't care about social acceptance. When I did go out or join a party, I drank myself into a comfortable numbness. I went through a promiscuous period for a few months, something very common for rape victims. It was as if every boy I had sex with was an opportunity to reclaim something I had lost. I wasn't anorexic but I looked like I was. When I wasn't working, I slept on top of my garbage-bag-covered mattress. All colour had been bleached from the world.

Suddenly the world seemed to be full of angry people. I encountered them everywhere. It was beyond the scope of my awareness to comprehend that I was not the curious, naive girl that I had been. I was also someone else, and while this new girl felt hollowed out, she was also full of rage.

More than a year after leaving home, I went out to meet some friends at the local pizza place. I had stopped drinking, stopped having sex, stopped dating, and stopped all parties. My living conditions had vastly improved, I now worked at one of the carpet factories earning a much better wage than before, and had settled into life with two friends, an older married couple and their two children. Taking care of the children and helping my friends gave me a sense of purpose and family that I had lost.

The pizza place that we frequented had a dance floor, and after a few rounds of pool, my friends went to dance. Uninterested in dancing or staying out late, another friend and I got up to leave. As we made our way through the crowd and turned left in our approach of the exit, I looked up and over to the right. Standing about ten feet away, with his back against the wall, was the rapist. I saw him, he saw me, and we looked into each other's eyes. Time slowed, and my mind went blank, all thought ceased but this time, it wasn't due to shock.

His face crumpled a little.

In his eyes, I first saw sorrow and pain but then something else. Looking in his eyes, I saw my Self looking back at me—not as a reflection, nor as a projection. I quite literally saw *my* Self, in *his* eyes, and I experienced being in two places at once. I was both *he* and *I*, the *rapist* and the *victim*, the *boy*, and the *girl*. We were one person; there was no separation between the selves. In that moment came permanent and unconditional forgiveness but more than that, I experienced the truth of unconditional love. The borders that delineate the Self from the other had momentarily dissolved. I experienced a truth that I had no words for. Over the coming weeks, a lightness of Being returned.

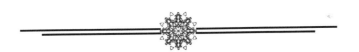

Maturation of the relative Self is a process that continues over a lifetime. While I had wholly forgiven the nameless young man, I wasn't yet able to forgive Asher, the group, my mother, family, the church, or Suspicion and Condemnation. Total, universal forgiveness would take many more years. Still, the spontaneous dissolution of the illusion of a separate Self began to work on my Being. It was the first time I saw my Self in another's eyes but not the last. The second (and also not the last) time occurred a few years later, at age twenty-one. While driving, I looked into my son's eyes and experienced an even more powerful moment of the presence of the Absolute.

Once again, the mind was wiped blank and went silent. I looked in his eyes and saw such a Light that time stopped. Somehow, I managed to pull the car over. Again, I lacked the language to describe the experience beyond the word "light." When I told friends about it, they looked perplexed as I insisted, "I saw a light."

Becoming is the non-linear, dynamic, cyclic, and mysterious way in which the Universe operates on our Being as it moulds our mind, heart, and soul into something greater than what we can see but only as limited as our imagination. Forgiveness plays a vital role in that process.

What is Forgiveness?

The word *forgive* comes from Old English *forgiefan,* which, beyond meaning to "give, grant, allow or remit" also means to "give up" and "to give in marriage." The Proto-Indo-European root for *giefan* is *ghabh* and means "to hold" and "to take hold." There's a lot of truth contained in this word: On one hand, it's about giving up or surrendering something. On the other hand, it's about holding or taking hold of something. *Forgiefan* was to give in marriage. In marriage, two people are joining together in union. They are both giving up something and taking hold of something at the same time. How fascinating that that should be the root of the word forgiveness!

In most books today, forgiveness is defined as the act of letting go of resentment and adopting a beneficent attitude towards the person we believe wronged us. Some people find that too difficult, and so for them, forgiveness is limited to the relinquishing of the desire for revenge and choosing to move on. People say, "I'll forgive but I won't forget." Resentment still simmers beneath the surface.

Think back to the metaphor of the well and the water within the well that we envisioned in chapter two; a lack of forgiveness poisons the water. Every time we take a drink, the water tastes bitter.

The level to which one forgives corresponds to the level of consciousness from which one operates in the world. Consciousness could be compared to the operating system of a computer. All of our beliefs and thoughts reside in our imagination; they're the scripts we run. The feelings that arise when we believe our presumptions and interpretations to be true are the *run command*.

When we talk about levels of consciousness, a useful analogy would be to consider the differences between a quantum computer and the classical binary computer. In classical computing, information can exist in only two states, 1 or 0. Binary computing originates from the I Ching, an ancient Chinese book that was called The Book of Changes. The I Ching philosophy states that reality isn't really *real*, it's a dream, a creation of mind: Anything within the dream can be known as a representation of its binary constituents precisely because, *the dream is a virtual reality*.

In quantum computing, instead of using binary bits, they use 'qubits.' While quantum systems still deal with just two states, they exploit the quantum super-positioning of 0 and 1. The superpositions of one object can become entangled with the superpositions of another object. In quantum computing, imaginal spheres exist, and a qubit can exist at any point in the sphere. Both classical and quantum computing are dualistic. Imagine an operating system that wasn't dualistic; let's call it the Advaita operating system. *Advaita* is Sanskrit and means "not two." Advaita refers to the idea that the true self, Atman, is the same as the highest, metaphysical reality. In such an operating system, there would be no binary division and no separation between the subject and the object. Although there are many strata of consciousness, we can use the above examples to identify (for the sake of simplicity) three primary levels of consciousness:

Level 1. A polarised, binary, *this-or-that* mentality, perception, and way of being that deals only in opposites. Everything is either 'good' or 'bad', 'right' or 'wrong', 'this' or 'that.'

Level 2. A more neutral mentality, perception, and way of being that recognises potentiality and has room for discovery, complexity, connection, and awareness of entanglement.

Level 3. A unified state of awareness that transcends the dualistic, subject-object mode of perception. All is whole and undivided. There is no separation between the observer and the observed. The irony here is that the idea of non-duality creates another binary unless one realises that the universe is both non-dual and dual at the same time. The two realities are enfolded.

It's estimated that more than 90% of the population operates on a scale somewhere between level 1 and level 2 and oscillate between the two. At least 50% of the population will spend most of their lives at level 1. It's estimated that less than 1% of the population live permanently at level 2.

An individual who existed at level 3 all of the time would hardly be able to function in the world. Individuals who have experienced such a state for any prolonged period of time later reported that they became uninterested in food, had no motivation to do anything other than just be, and it became necessary to drop back down into individuated awareness in order to function in the world and experience human life. From this, we can see that consciousness itself is a spectrum and we human beings operate at various points along that spectrum, oscillating between levels on a spiral.

What does all of this have to do with forgiveness?

My forgiveness of another was the automatic and unpremeditated result of experiencing spontaneous, spiritual union (Level 3) the moment I locked eyes with the young man who had, on one level, violated both my will and inner sanctuary, by forcing his body on mine without permission. In the moment I saw my Self looking back at me from his eyes, I surrendered the false Self to something eternally real, and through that surrender, I experienced the Absolute. The transcendent experience was momentary. I didn't remain in that state, but the effects were permanent.

I didn't consciously choose to have that experience. It was a moment of unexpected grace, and the result was that I went forward with my life without feeling or thinking like a victim. I would still feel anger and pain and suffer but not as a 'victim.' Mankind possesses faculties of will, imagination, reason, and feeling. Ultimately we can choose to consciously forgive through use of those faculties, and we have good reason to do so.

The Effects of Forgiveness

Everett Worthington is a psychologist, professor, and researcher who had spent decades studying and writing about forgiveness and how it impacts the human condition when, on January 1st, 1996, his 76-year-old mother was found murdered in her home. Worthington told VCU magazine, "I had done personal forgiving before but nothing of such a large magnitude." He was able to forgive the murderer quite quickly precisely because he had been studying and practicing forgiveness in the years leading up to the death of his mother. Nine years later, Worthington's brother committed suicide as a result of what Worthington describes as the "emotional fallout."

He said that the death of his brother led "to a new experience of self-forgiveness that I didn't have before." In an article that he wrote for The Greater Good magazine, Worthington suggests that a lack of forgiveness can disrupt hormonal balance and our cell's ability to fight off infections, bacteria, and other assaults on the body. Studies done by other researchers and clinicians have shown that forgiveness can lower blood pressure, improve the immune system reduce ocular pressure behind the eyes, reduce pain, decrease anxiety, and improve sleep.

The physical effects of forgiveness on the body are a reflection of the mental and emotional release that happens when we forgive. Resentment, anger, and blame can be suppressed, repressed, projected, or released. When we don't hit the release lever, pressure builds, and our metaphoric well becomes a pressure cooker. The effects of that ongoing pressure are deleterious on body and mind.

Forgiveness is a choice that each one of us makes. Right now, it may feel impossible for you to forgive someone or something that caused harm. That's okay, it's a deeply personal choice. Nevertheless, refusing to forgive has consequences. It's very hard to feel fulfilled when our well is full of negative emotions and resentments that rob us of inner peace. Therefore, when we seek abiding fulfillment, one of the first doors through which we are invited to pass, is the door of forgiveness. It's no dead end. Passing through that door leads us to new realms of being. The poet Rumi knew this, and that is why he wrote:

Out beyond ideas of wrongdoing and rightdoing, there is a field.
I'll meet you there.
When the soul lies down in that grass,
the world is too full to talk about.

Chapter 6
HERE ENTERS BEAUTY

Beauty is truth's smile
when she beholds her own face in
a perfect mirror. —Rabindranath Tagore

Beauty is an inner coherence, of which truth is intrinsic. There is no beauty without truth, no truth without Beauty. When we behold a thing of beauty, we're transfixed by it because we recognise its coherence. Beauty has a unifying effect on the heart and mind. When we're in a state of coherence, everything and everyone is beautiful. We see the ultimate Truth that underlies manifest reality: All is One, and exists in perfect harmony. In moments of Beauty, life becomes light and effortless. All is accomplished by synchronicity, not coerced or forced.

The Containment System that we explored in chapter two inverts beauty, offering us a simulacrum instead. Truth destroys illusion by "cleansing the doors of perception." Beauty is truth. Therefore, the system cannot sustain anything of true Beauty. Its best attempt at Beauty is glamour.

Why are you so enchanted by this world when a mine of gold lies
within you? —Rumi

In our old faerie tales, faerie glamour is the type of magic that turns ashes and decaying leaves into enticing delicacies and sparkling jewels. When the unsuspecting human consumes the glamoured food, it turns into ash in their mouth, catches in their throat, and traps them in the hellish land of Faerie, where they become the playthings of spiteful, capricious entities.

It's easy to see why Tolkien considered magic and machine to be the same. In this context, *magic* is the psychological mechanism through which the fallen, fragmented mind creates an effect, manipulates perception, and creates sub-realities. Due to the power and complexity of the human mind, this kind of *magic* can have an incredible impact on the human body, direct experience, and subjective reality.

The entertainment industry, shiny accessories, new cars, fashion, modern art, some modern architecture, award shows, the red carpet, social media influencers, entrancing pop music, amusement parks, football fever, the list of glamours goes on and on. There is nothing inherently wrong with those things. They simply *are*. Glamour is the distraction that we use to avoid looking within ourselves. It's the mechanism we use to avoid Truth because we fear it when, in reality, there is nothing to fear from Truth. Because truth and Beauty are one, truth is always compassionate, loving, and forgiving.

The world often confuses *fact* with *truth*. This is why people fear and avoid it. Facts are often presented as heartless, harsh, and impersonal as in, "The cold, hard facts are..." Chuck Palahniuk once said, "You can spend your whole life building a wall of facts between you and anything real."

When faced down and examined in the light, most facts dissolve. What's left is a truth, in which you will always find Beauty.

If the doors of perception were cleansed everything would appear to man as it is, infinite. For man has closed himself up, till he sees all things thro' narrow chinks of his cavern. —William Blake

Those "narrow chinks" of our caverns are our individual and societal paradigms, paradigms that are primarily fuelled by what we believe to be factual. As we move into a state of perpetual coherence, we begin treating all facts as feather-light suggestions of how things might be rather than concrete blocks that we need to carry around on our shoulders.

There is a shift from, "The world is happening around me" to "the world is unfolding within me." When we engage with that unfoldment, we begin to notice that our feelings and thoughts are generative; they generate our subjective reality. That shift facilitates coherence as we begin to pay conscious attention to our emotions and thoughts from an entirely different perspective. It's interesting that many people, upon making that shift, develop a new-found (or rediscover an) appreciation for Beauty. There is a sudden interest in classical art, inspiring music, nature, poetry, and aesthetic living overall. If the love of those things was already there, it intensifies and evolves.

Beauty is therapeutic, transformative, restorative, and enlightening. The more we engage with, and channel Beauty, the more coherence we create. People around us feel it, even if they can't name it, it radiates from our centre, influencing everything around us. Beauty is an infinite, eternal word that cannot be uttered, only experienced. Creating coherence in ourselves, in our Being, and ultimately in our lives isn't complicated or difficult. Coherence is kind, gentle, compassionate, understanding and loving, not just with others but with ourselves.

When our choices, thoughts, speech, and actions begin to align with our true, inner self, we are creating coherence.

As I walked through the streets of Frankfurt, everything was beautiful because I had shifted into a state of profound, inner coherence. It wasn't permanent, but it was a beginning. The doors of perception had opened, and once opened, they can never be completely shut again. Once Beauty has introduced herself, we will never forget her.

Beauty is the beginning and end of fulfillment. She stands at the precipice and invites us to step forward. If we allow her, she walks beside us in nobility as we journey, removing the glamour from our eyes and tenderly embracing us when the road feels rocky.

Eventually, we realise that Beauty resides within us. She is the divine, human heart.

If God is Love, then Beauty is his face.

Chapter 7
ME, MYSELF AND I

Something we were withholding made us weak.
Until we found out that it was ourselves,
We were withholding from our land of living,
And forthwith found salvation in surrender.
—Robert Frost, The Gift Outright

The personality is a construct that is built upon the foundation of our self-concept. The self-concept is the consistent set of perceptions and beliefs about oneself. How we see ourselves determines the traits we develop that eventually create a personality.

A person who considers himself to be intense and high-strung might find himself feeling quite relaxed and peaceful as he observes a beautiful sunset while on holiday. If asked, "Are you normally so relaxed?" his answer might be, "Oh, no! I've always been a real go-getter, my friends tell me I'm an intense guy. I'm definitely not a laid-back person." And yet, at that moment, he experienced a state of deep relaxation and peacefulness. He believes himself to be high-strung and a go-getter because those are the states of being that he most consistently experiences. He misidentifies himself with the states he most frequently inhabits and lives within.

People with multiple personality disorder have much to teach us about the power of self-concept. There are documented cases of individuals who have one personality that is allergic to orange juice and another personality that isn't. When the non-allergic personality is present, orange juice can be consumed with no deleterious effects. If the allergic personality is present, the body breaks out in hives. Other cases have documented individuals with one personality that needs glasses, while another personality has perfect vision. Even traits considered relatively static, like IQ and eye colour can vary from one personality to the other, within the same body.

The above examples are of multiple, relative, mutable personality constructs residing in one body. In healthy individuals, there is what appears to be only one, relative, mutable but rarely changing personality. In truth, we have multiple selves but generally operate with just one apparent personality.

The creation and maintenance of this personality are said to be dependent on memory. But are they? Who we think we are is the sum total of our experience, interpretations, and the degree to which we identify with our beliefs and assumptions. Who we truly are lies underneath the personality construct and exist beyond the relative self: The Primary Essence.

Retrograde amnesia describes the loss of all past memories but the ability to form new ones. One of the most fascinating and touching cases of full retrograde amnesia is that of aviation entrepreneur, Scott Bolzan. Scott suffered a severe head injury after falling at work. He lost all memory of who he was, his wife, family, and past. His memories have never returned, and yet, he fell in love with his wife all over again. In an interview with ABC News in 2011, his wife Joan said, "Scott has retained all of his deep personality traits." She elaborated, "Love, loyalty, protection, and courage; all those things are there." When reading his book, *My Life, Deleted* published in 2011, the book description states, "Scott learned to trust his intuition in a way that most people never will." One thing stands out in Scott's story, while all his memories disappeared, the essence of the man remained. Scott learned to trust his Mista'peo, the Daimon, his Genius, the true Inner Man, and he wasn't led astray.

The self we think we know is just a story, it's an ongoing narrative that weaves our experiences and interpretations into the fabric we refer to as the *self*. It's just a story, albeit a highly coherent one. The relative self is not limited to the personality construct. How many relative selves do we have over a lifetime? Like our Lower Selves, our Higher Selves (the Daimon) are fractals of the Absolute and use physical bodies and the 4D, mental constructs of the relative self, to operate in the world. Likewise, The Absolute Self exists outside of time and space, and because of this, it couldn't directly experience the full spectrum of human life within a manifest, physical reality without the Daimon and its 'lower,' relative self to act as a proxy.

What we see here are layers.

The term *self-inquiry* has been used in a few different ways. When psychologists refer to self-inquiry, they're most often referring to the process of reflecting on our thoughts, beliefs, and behaviours and how those things influence our lives. When spiritual teachers refer to self-inquiry, it's an invitation to connect with and meditate upon the Absolute Self. Self-inquiry is the process of subtraction, not addition. It involves peeling back layers of personality, and layers of the relative Self. We lift the hood of this car called 'Self' and ask, "What's really fuelling this vehicle?"

The brain is a receiver. Like a radio receives radio signals, the brain receives consciousness.

In a paper entitled, *Consciousness in the Universe is Scale Invariant and Implies an Event Horizon of the Human Brain*, Doctors K. F. Meijer and Hans Geesink wrote:

> Our brain is not a 'stand alone' information processing organ: It acts as a central part of our integral nervous system with recurrent information exchange with the entire organism and the cosmos. In this study, the brain is conceived to be embedded in a holographic structured field that interacts with resonant sensitive structures in the various cell types in our body.

In their paper, they posit that each person has their own, fourth-dimensional, holographic work-space in which an integral model of the self is formed. If all our memory was wiped away, if all feeling and emotion were gone and the body disappeared, what would be left? Many people, including myself, have experienced such a state. All that remains is pure awareness. The *Am* without an *I*. From this *Am-ness*, an *I* arises. I Am—I exist, everything else is a construct.

In our confusion and fear, we lose ourselves, and the world becomes a hall of mirrors. Reflected, gruesome, distorted forms become reminders of the feelings we've repressed and thoughts that haunt us as we fall asleep at night. We lash out and try to shatter the mirrored corridors of the mind, not understanding that what seems without, is in truth within. The self isn't what we think it is, and it certainly isn't the image we work so diligently to project into the world. Deep down, we know this, and it sometimes scares the hell out of us. What would we lose if we surrendered to our true Being? Who would we be?

The first time I saw my Self looking back at me from another person's eyes, it wiped all thought from my mind and dissolved all pre-existing boundaries that I had previously believed created a line of demarcation around myself and everything else. This is no metaphor or projection. In these instances, we are *literally* looking back at ourselves through the eyes of another. This is empathy in its purest, most primordial form. There is only one, Absolute Self. The Relative self enquires, "Who, am I?" and the inner, Being replies with a smile, "Who, am I *not*?" What makes this realisation so joyful is the comprehension that the Absolute Self is expressed through the prism of an actualised individual's unique perspective and lived experience. It's a joyful, glorious playground of light and colour, a kaleidoscope of Being.

People travel to wonder at the height of mountains, at the huge waves of the sea, at the long courses of rivers, at the vast compass of the ocean, at the circular motion of the stars, and they pass by themselves without wondering.
—St. Augustine of Hippo

When we're unconsciously moving through our lives, the construction of the personality and the illusory dominance of the relative self seems to just happen on its own but once we recognise the mutability of it, and cease rigid identification with the relative self, personality, and ego, a space opens within. Shadows emerge, and instead of projecting them on to the world or others, we embrace them, claiming them as our own creation. Through this loving acceptance of our shadow, it transmutes, and light enters our awareness. This lucent spaciousness allows a new reality to unfold within, and effect change without.

This unfoldment has been often compared to a path. Many spiritual teachers through the ages have spoken of being *on the path* but here's another way to think of it:

You are not *on* a path. You *are* the path. You are the path that Divinity takes to awaken as itself.

Chapter 8
ETERNAL STATES OF BEING

AS the Pilgrim passes while the Country permanent remains,
So Men pass on but States remain permanent for ever.
—William Blake

When our ancestors looked up at the night sky, their view was not obscured by billions of artificial lights that now project a sodium haze towards the heavens, diminishing the perceivable, ethereal beauty of starlight. In the philosophy and cosmology of the ancients, it was held to be true that the world was made up of four elements; fire, earth, air, and water. Aristotle taught that the stars were part of the celestial sphere and were made of a fifth element, aether. The four elements in the earthly sphere were said to move linearly, with the quintessence of the stars and celestial realm moving circularly. If this quintessence was uniquely distinguishable from fire, earth, air and water, what was it? It was the essence that the gods breathed and the life force of stellar awareness. It's the essence of spiritual beings.

When the ancients beheld the night sky, they didn't see another *place*, they saw another *state of being*.

A state of being is a quality of experience. It is not limited to the physical condition of the body because your Beingness is not limited to your body. A mood is a state, a physical condition is a state, and any circumstance in which Being (you) finds itself (unemployed, rich, poor, etc.) is a state.

Martin Heidegger was one of the most influential philosophers of the twentieth century. Heidegger grew up as a Catholic in Germany, where he initially studied theology before breaking from the church. He embraced phenomenology and began an investigation into the nature of being. Heidegger rejected the Cartesianism view (I think therefore I am) and reversed it: "I am therefore I think." *Seinsfrage* was the word that Heidegger used to describe the primary questions of his philosophical inquiry: "What does *Being* mean?" and, "What is the most fundamental kind of Being?"

Heidegger expressed doubt in humanity's ability to manage technology and was concerned with the effect it would have on the beingness of the human race. We may create our technology but can't accurately assess or mitigate the destructive impact it has on our perception. Heidegger coined the term *enframing* to refer to how technology warps perception. He admonishes us to ponder the true *essence* of technology and be conscious of how we become enslaved by it instead of truly liberated. Heidegger believed that the Western philosophers had dismissed Being and the Ultimate Truth that is intrinsic to the very core of authentic Being. He asserted that because we don't understand true, authentic Being, we become lost in cultural structures and transient, false ideas of self, thereby losing contact with Truth.

Eternity exists, and all things in eternity, independent of creation, which was an act of mercy. By this, it may be seen that I do not consider either the Just or the Wicked to be in a Supreme State but to be every one of them, States of the Sleep which the Soul may fall into, in its deadly dreams of Good and Evil.
—William Blake

Being Neville

Neville Lancelot Goddard did not call himself a philosopher. He was a joyful, curious, and contemplative man who loved to dance. He was tall, lithe, had wavy, light brown hair, and was said to be built like an athlete. Neville didn't identify as a metaphysician or align himself with any religion, tradition, or *-ism*. He is often and mistakenly associated with New Thought, the early, 19th-century movement based on the teachings of Phineas Quimby but Neville wholly rejected any such association and the focus that the New Thought movement had on mortal life and materialism. Neville was a man driven by his visions of eternity.

He was born on February 19, 1905, in St. Michael, Barbados in the British West Indies as the fourth child in a family of nine boys and one girl. His family was poor but eventually grew rich. He often told stories of his childhood, his disciplinarian mother, and times on the island. The man loved to laugh and dance. People who met him described him as having "bright, smiling eyes" and as "having a presence about him." When Neville reached his seventeenth year, he left Barbados for New York City. His first job was at the JC Penny store, earning $22.00 a week as an elevator operator and errand boy. Fired from JC Penny, he went on to work for Macy's. Then, one fateful evening, he went to see a Broadway play with friends. Watching the performers dancing, he thought, "I can do that!" His faith in his potential served him well.

Neville went on to study dance and drama, and in 1925 Neville began performing at the old Hippodrome in New York. He was a massive success as a dancer. His salary went from the meagre wages that department stores paid to $500.00 a week. That was quite the sum in 1920s America but Neville wanted something more, and he gave up dancing to pursue it.

While giving a lecture called *Predestined Glory*, Neville spoke of that time in his life, and shared the following:

> I was then a dancer. I was 24 years of age, searching—searching for an experience of God. If anyone went into blind alleys looking, I did. I tried everything, trying to find Him. I didn't try dope; I didn't smoke marijuana. No, I didn't go in for that. I couldn't afford liquor, and prohibition was on in those days, and I wasn't in the habit of drinking. I couldn't afford it, and there was no liquor around unless you went to some expensive speakeasy. But I was searching for God. I thought maybe a certain diet, like a strict vegetarian—maybe that would do it. I tried that.

None of that worked.

What Neville did finally find of the God he was searching for, he found *within*. Throughout his life, he described an inner experience in which he experienced God as unconditional, infinite love, wisdom, and power. Neville repeatedly said, "God became man so that man may become God." We are not God in our normal, waking consciousness. We're neither omniscient nor omnipresent. There are insane people confined to hospitalisation who daily proclaim themselves to be God. How's that working out for them?

It's in the silence when the relative self and its incessant thinking has stopped altogether, that one realises that their individual 'I Am' is *part* of God, not *all* of God. There is a fractal of the Superconscious Whole, buried deep within our being. As Neville said, "Your world is your consciousness, objectified."

After that initial and life-altering inner experience, Neville changed his life. He was so convinced of the validity of his inner experiences and personal revelations that he quit dancing and traveled the US giving lectures on what he called, *The Law* and *The Promise*. To clarify, the law of which he spoke is *Hermetic* and refers to a mental law that subordinates matter, energy, and power. Neville's primary focus was not the law, but the promise, i.e., the *Promise of Transcendence*, which is also called "apotheosis." Neville had many profound inner experiences that transformed his view of reality. To help others grasp cosmic laws, principles, and esoteric knowledge that was totally foreign to most of his audience, Neville focused much of his teaching on states of being and imagination. He warned of the external trappings of world religion and literal-mindedness.

He wrote: "This is a world of educated darkness where you and I—infinite beings as we are—entered for a purpose, and only a very small part of the immortal Self entered. That's what we see here. You are an infinite Being, for you are God. Everyone is God but here on earth, we are just a spark of the immensity of our own fiery Being." Neville's message, at its core, could be paraphrased as; life is not happening *to* you, it is happening *because* of you. As Neville stressed, you are the operant power.

Understanding that states are static but that you, the conscious being, are in constant motion, frees the mind from the illusion of being helplessly trapped in specific circumstances. Learning that you possess the inherent power to move into, and inhabit any state you desire, liberates you from the notion that you *are* the state. You are not sad, poor, rich, frustrated, happy, excited, employed, unemployed, or calm. These are states. You are the operant consciousness that is experiencing life from within those states.

You can decide to change the state that you most frequently inhabit. We do this through the use of our faculties of imagination, will, reason, action, inquiry, and intentional feeling. Imagine the person you would like to become or the state of being you would like to inhabit. What would life look like if you were already the person you desire to be? How would you see yourself and others? What would it *feel* like?

The circumstances that you currently find yourself in are the result of your most fundamental feelings and beliefs about yourself and reality. The mind might resist this truth with thoughts like, "No, I was born into these circumstances," or "Society is unfair, the deck is stacked against some people." But the truth is that society is neither fair nor unfair. Those are subjective judgments of the mind. Society simply *is*. Society, as a phenomenon is not conscious, but *you* are. Society is a construct and does not have its own personal will, but *you* do. Some people have been born into the worst conditions imaginable and yet have managed to transcend those conditions and create incredible lives for themselves. Like the Lion from the Wizard of Oz said, "What have they got that I ain't got?"

Fear is a state of being; it's physiological and psychological. If a predator is chasing us, fear is useful if it makes us get out of harm's way, but sometimes fear paralyses us. Barring the existence of clear and present danger, fear is a product of distorted thinking. The mind is a mosaic, and sometimes the pieces get twisted or broken. We all have mental distortions. It comes with being human but the mind doesn't exist in a vacuum. Perhaps you've been told that you simply need to "change your mindset" in order to thrive or succeed, that's true but if repressed negative emotions aren't processed, it will always be very difficult to change one's thinking.

Beingness and consciousness are co-emergent and entangled. Conscious beingness is the awareness of existence. I exist. I am. Conscious beingness doesn't require thought, emotion, or feeling, but it can become entangled with those things as the *states* from which it experiences its *I Am-ness*.

Heidegger demonstrated how Being and consciousness become entangled with phenomena in his example of the workman with his hammer. He describes a scene in which a workman takes his hammer in hand, instinctively estimates its weight, and begins to work. Every strike of the hammer requires imperceptible adjustments of trajectory and velocity. The workman is so adept at his trade that he makes these adjustments almost subconsciously. His subconscious so guides his conscious action of hammering that the workman has developed an unconscious competence and virtually forgets about the existence of the hammer as he focuses his awareness on the nails he's striking.

The hammer becomes an extension of the workman's arm; tool and Master are entangled. Heidegger observes that if the workman puts the hammer down and stares at it, the simple observation of the hammer doesn't reveal anything about its Being. It's only through the utilisation of the hammer that its utility to the workman is revealed. Heidegger argues that it's through our actions that we form an understanding of ourselves. The workman identifies as a workman through all of his work-related activities and tools: nails, hammer, workbench, interactions with customers, his craftsmanship, etc. Heidegger explored the ways in which a relative Self is created and becomes entangled with the phenomena of its world.

Likewise, the relative Self often becomes entangled with the feelings and thoughts that arise from the conscious mind's interpretation of experience. Being, as a workman, is the state from which the self inhabits and experiences the world. The workman, relative to his perception of himself and the world, might feel very proud of his vocation or ashamed of it. Like the hammer, thoughts are phenomena. If our persistent thought patterns are useful for creating what we wish to create, then we, as Beings in the World, can benefit from them. But if those thoughts get in the way, if they paralyse or disable us, then they lose their utility but not their power. It's like getting hit with a misdirected hammer—it might not hit the exact spot intended, but it still hurts like hell.

It's very difficult to change a belief without first processing and releasing the underlying feelings that gave rise to thoughts that eventually became a belief. The saying, "Thoughts create your reality," has become quite commonplace nowadays, but it's only partially true. _Feeling_ is the fuel, your Being (your I Am-ness) is the operator, and your imagination (consciousness) is the engine.

Think of a time when you felt ecstatically happy, a time when your heart seemed to expand beyond your body. Thoughts didn't create that feeling, they arose from it. In times of profound positivity, contentment, peace, and love, we find ourselves thinking, "Anything is possible," "I'm so grateful," and "Life is great!" Therefore, when you're feeling good, that gooey, delicious chocolate chip cookie, fresh out of the oven of your local café, elicits thoughts like: "How delicious! I'm so glad I got here right when they pulled them out of the oven," or "This reminds me of grandma's cookies. I'm going to call her and tell her how much I love her!" But when you're feeling bad, that same chocolate chip cookie elicits thoughts like: "This is going to make me fat," "I'm fat and hate my body," "Why am I eating this junk loaded with sugar?" or "It sucks that everything that tastes good is bad for you!" A million thoughts can arise from one feeling.

When we imagine a scene, if we use our imagination to move into the scene (instead of viewing it as we would a movie screen) and experience the imaginative act as if it were happing now, the subconscious doesn't know the difference between what is happening in the physical reality and what is occurring in imagination. It's through perception and imagination that Being begins to experience (become entangled with) feeling. Emotion and feeling are two different things. Emotions are physical states that occur in the subcortical region of the brain, the amygdala, and ventromedial prefrontal cortices and then move through the body via the autonomic nervous system and cause biochemical and electric reactions in the body. Dr. Sarah McKay, a neuroscientist, said, "Emotions play out in the theatre of the body. Feelings play out in the theatre of the mind."

But there is another level of feeling that is wholly different from the feeling generated by mentation: It's the expansive, limitless, *awareness* that arises from infinitely adaptable Beingness (your *I Am*) and that, 'plays out,' within human life, at the level of the proverbial heart. It's in the heart that the theatre of life ceases to be a stage show with actors and scripts. In the heart, experience reveals itself to be what it truly is; a journey of awareness as infinite potential.

When the Lion in the Wizard of Oz asked himself, "What do they have that I ain't got?" His answer was "Courage."

Courage is recognising the emotional and mental states of fear and the act of allowing the fear to be what it is without resistance. Courageousness means relying on a deeper source of strength that enables us to take action despite all fear. The word courage comes from *corage* in Old French. It defined "heart," as in "the innermost seat of true feeling." Courage is inner strength. Isn't that interesting? Where does the innermost heart reside?

Within the Innermost Man.

Thoughts are potentialities that exist in an imaginary sphere. Emotions are the movement of energy through the body. Thoughts and emotions move us but with limited inertia behind the movement. It's the powerful awareness of limitless Being, and the conscious use of generative imagination by the mind, that produce *feeling* states. These feeling states have their own, correspondent rate of vibration. Transcendent states of being such as, love, appreciation, joy, and peace actuate feelings so powerful that they don't just move energy, they completely transmute it.

Imagine for a moment, your idea of heaven. For some, heaven might be eating triple chocolate ice cream covered in salted caramel sauce while getting a scalp massage. For others, it might be freedom from mundane work and fantastic orgasms that last for days. For others, it might look like peace on earth, cities of starlight, and everlasting, unassailable peace. Go back to the scene of your own personal heaven and how it feels to be there. It's a state you are inhabiting. How you *feel* there will determine how you *think* there, feeling precedes thinking, not the other way around. Fortunately, they work in tandem. They work in tandem with each other (meaning thoughts influence feeling and feeling influences thought) because thinking and feeling are phenomena of one stratum of consciousness. In superconsciousness, thinking, feeling, and willing are unified. There is no human word that can fully describe such a state of unification, but some have used the term "pure experience," and others refer to reaching that state as "transcendence."

Let's come back down to earth (and back to heaven) for a moment. Go back to your image of heaven and how you felt and thought there. What would happen if you latched on to that feeling and fully embodied it before opening your eyes and going about your day? In order to maintain such a state, presence is required. The mind is not focused on the imagery of one's imaginative heaven, that would be a distraction. Instead, the mind is focused on the present moment and the <u>felt experience</u> of that state of being, as <u>*reality*</u>—awareness shifts. If you remain in the state of being (the <u>*feeling*</u> of it) that you were in, as you actively envisioned and experienced your version of heaven, then your experience of daily life will be transformed. Your pattern of thinking changes, neurological synapses in the brain create new connections, and the heart opens.

This is the difference between living life as a Passive Perceiver and living life as a Creative Visionary. A Passive Perceiver goes through life perceiving, but without any conscious awareness that they are the operant power which creates that which they perceive. A visionary is not some dude who creates the latest gadget or a start-up. A Visionary is someone who actually has vision. A Creative Visionary *envisions* and only gives feeling energy to that which they intend. This focused energy moves them into conscious action.

A Creative Visionary is not an idealist with their head in the sand. They see the reality of pain, suffering, and confusion in the world and are moved by ceaseless compassion for their fellow man to imagine and act in order to create a better world. They cross the abyss and return transformed. Their compassion harmonises with wisdom and a disciplined mind. Embodiment is a Creative Visionary's highest aim. A vision only comes to fruition through the people who have the will to embody it.

Heaven means "Home of God."

Heaven isn't a place we go, it's something we become.

Chapter 9
THE PURPOSE OF PAIN

No tree, it is said, can grow to heaven, unless its roots reach down to hell.
—Carl Jung

Sitting on a hard, wooden chair, I stared down at my feet. It was February, and Munich was covered in a blanket of snow and dirty ice that left a film of grime on my black winter boots. Dr. Emanuel's* office was a small, book-lined space, filled to capacity by his desk and a small, white, plastic table to which I had my back turned, as I faced him. He'd positioned his desk so that he could look out of the window while he worked, but for now, he'd turned away from the grey scene beyond the glass to watch me as I spoke.

"I had a dream last night that really disturbed me. I don't even understand where these morbid stories come from. My nightmares are like watching horror movies of someone else's life."

"What was your dream about?" he asked.

I continued looking down towards my feet without really seeing them. "I had this dream about a woman who was lost. She believed that her bro-kenness was hurting her husband and son. She felt so bad for imposing her sadness on them, that she picked up a knife, and slit her own throat."

My face might have shown surprise as a sudden realisation came. "Ah! I see now—that woman was *me*! Wow, how could I not realise that until just now?" I felt curious and fascinated by the sudden clarity, but when I looked up, Dr. Emanuel had tears rolling down his face. He turned away and shuf-fled some papers for a moment on his desk. My curiosity and the slight hopefulness that I'd felt by gaining some understanding of my dream mor-phed into discomfort that I had made my doctor cry. I was twenty-nine years old and fighting to stay alive.

Life could have been a joyful celebration of my success in Europe. I lived near my beloved Alps; they were the reason I chose to move to southern Germany. I had never been to Munich before the day we landed at the Munich airport as new expats. I picked Munich based on photographs of a lake called Königsee (King's Lake). I thought it was the most beautiful place in the world and chose the largest city close to it.

When I hiked around Königsee, Garmisch Partenkirchen and in the Austrian Alps, I felt like I'd finally come home. I'd put an ocean between myself and the past, or so I thought. When we embrace the unknown and courageously set off to forge our path, the Universe rolls out the red carpet and assist us, as long as our trajectory is in accordance with our greatest potential, and Self created destiny. But that doesn't mean that everything is going to be easy.

Upon informing my family that Daniel and I would move to Europe, the general response was, "You're nuts. You don't speak the language. You don't know anyone. You don't have a job. It's never going to work." My response to that was, "If I have to clean people's toilets or flip burgers at McDonald's, this *will* work because I refuse to accept any other alternative."

The transition went smoothly. Everything seemed to work out on its own. In Germany, we also benefited from affordable healthcare and excellent public schools for Daniel. Our lives improved in every *external* aspect but... there is a mechanism built into the human experience that works as such: The creation of outer space in our lives (in this case, physical distance), makes room for repressed negative emotions to surface within inner space, the internal landscape of our minds. It ensures that we can't outrun our pain. The faster we run, the faster it catches up with us. We're forced to either process it—or perish.

I couldn't pinpoint when the darkness took hold. In the depths of depression, it seemed that the shadow had always been there. At one point, I tried to write a list of every happy memory I had, hoping that this would cure me, but I found that I couldn't recall even one happy memory. It was like they had never been.

One night, while waiting for the metro, I sat on a cold, metal bench in the

Rotkreuzplatz U-Bahn station. As the train approached, a thought came, "Jump in front of the train. Just jump." The thought shocked me, I didn't want the thought but it kept coming, and it made me so anxious that I had to turn around and go back home for the evening. I had no relationship with the entity that the church called *God*. Why would I want to be in a toxic relationship with a judgmental psychopath? Beyond my feeling of separation from anything divine and whole, other experiences that I had suppressed began demanding attention.

While writing this book, I spent a few nights in deep contemplation about how much of my own experience to share. There was some reluctance to divulge certain details, not due to any fear but because I'm cognisant of the fact that no matter how traumatic aspects of my childhood were, there are people who have experienced much worse. This book is about fulfillment, and true fulfillment is the result of a process in which we create an unassailable inner equilibrium. Happiness is a red herring. It's fragile because it's conditional, but fulfillment abides when we base our fulfillment on inner, not outer conditions. Getting to this state of being requires that we cross an abyss, the abyss of human suffering.

I was born extremely empathic, perhaps most babies are. As a child (and still today), I could feel what people around me were feeling and notice even the most subtle shifts in someone's body, expression, breath, and a field I sensed around each person. Throughout my entire life, I've had people ask me how I know what they're thinking and sometimes ask me if I am reading their thoughts. I'm not. I'm just perceptive, and I thought everyone was until my teen years.

As a child, I also thought that it was normal to remember most of your dreams and to lucid dream. I've never once in my life had a black and white dream, and was shocked to hear that many people don't dream in colour. Curious about scientific explanations for phenomena, I believe that people like me might have pineal glands that produce more endogenous N,N-Dimethyltryptamine (DMT). It's wise and scientific to take a much broader approach and continue exploring. I lean towards a holographic (as a metaphor, not a literal hologram) model, and evidence that *supra*conscious awareness is more accessible to some brains (receivers) and less by others. It's most certainly not 'all in the head'; more on that in chapter 13. Whatever the cause, this 'gift' has its pros and cons. To be frank, I wouldn't call it a gift at all. It's just another way to be in the world. We're all down here in the trenches together. Everyone has a role to play. **Each of us receives a gift, a curse, and a chance. We make of it what we will.**

As a child, I had no idea that I wasn't just *aware* of other people's feelings, I was also *absorbing* them and internalising their suffering. All children do this to some degree. It exacerbates suffering by amplifying it. Children have their own pain (as a result of their individual experience) to deal with, plus that of their parents and community.

When I was eight years, old I awoke one night to the sound of my father's loud cry. My room was right next to my parent's bedroom. I was at their door within seconds. When I opened the door, the light from the hall nightlight spilled into their room. Crouched down on one knee, with his other leg extended in front of him, and his arms, hands, and shoulders positioned as if he were holding an invisible rifle, my father stared at nothing. Mom spoke softly, "Don't touch him, honey. He's not awake and might lash out." I kept my distance but looked into his face. His eyes were terrible, staring at some image only he could see. Mom gently coaxed him until she could take him by the elbow and lead him back to bed. He never woke up as she put the covers back over him. His eyes closed and he was peaceful. He had been dreaming of Vietnam. Our entire childhood was accentuated with moments like this. Periods of peace and happiness were always framed by some kind of fearful symmetry[1].

Radiant Rage

Rage is not mere anger; it's the compilation of every word written by our pain and shame, an anthology of hurt. If suppressed or repressed, it harms us and those around us. If understood, embraced, and wisely directed, the flames of rage provide the energy needed for transmutation.

---

[1]"Fearful symmetry" is a phrase first coined in the 18th century by William Blake in his poem *The Tyger*. It's been used in a few books and television series as well.

As small children, one of my sisters and I were sexually abused by two, adult individuals, members of our congregation within the Watchtower Society (Jehovah's Witnesses). It's an organisation that runs on fear, brainwashing, and totalitarian control. The abusers were protected by the organisation. At home, we experienced physical abuse (in the form of beatings) of varying degrees, from our stepfather, who suffered from severe posttraumatic stress syndrome from the war. Our mother tried to mitigate the damage and keep the peace, but my older sister caught the worst of it, once being pulled up the stairs by her hair.

Although my stepfather adored me, and I adored him, I wasn't immune to his sudden outbursts of anger. The older I got, the less immune I was. When you never know what's going to set someone off, you live on constant alert and walk on eggshells. Because I could read my father's moods better than anyone else, I figured out how to handle him at an early age. But the older I got, the less willing I was to mitigate other people's moods. I grew fatigued by it, and began to rebel openly as a way of recovering my energy.

Both of our parents were severely traumatised and unable to accept any help that could have healed them. When my stepfather finally hit me in the face at age seventeen for saying, "Geez" during our home Bible study, I made the conscious decision that being rebellious was better than being exhausted.

I grew to resent our parents, especially our mother, for not protecting us. I despised their religion for forcing a sick mentality on its members, one that looks forward to a coming Armageddon in which "bad" people are murdered en masse by an avenging God. The organisational stance is that women are inferior to men. Women are required to submit to the mastership of men over their lives. The organisation requires parents to shun their children if the children are excommunicated or simply make life choices that don't comply with church dogma. The rate of suicide among ex-Jehovah's Witnesses who are 'disfellowshipped' (their word for excommunication) is high.

By the time I had my son at age twenty, my resentment and rage had congealed into a black tar that coated my heart. I had never forgiven our mom for suggesting that my rape was deserved. I couldn't forgive church members for turning paranoid imaginings into hateful narratives and gossip. I avoided *all* groups as I distrusted human nature once individuals adopted a group dynamic. The positive side of this was that because I was raised in a cult, I developed a very keen sense of when cult-like dynamics are at play in any group.

I *could* and *did* forgive a young, obviously very lost, man because I directly experienced our shared Self and the light within it, but that forgiveness was the result of an experience for which I had no words. It didn't yet extend to all the other, older, deeper sources of my pain. It felt like I had forgotten something important that I used to know.

I was pregnant with rage but didn't know it. Depression is one of the disguises of rage. The person that I was despised those people, their literal-minded, foolish ideas, immature, isolationists religion, and unkind behaviour. That hatred was *my* pain, and it was now making me very, very sick. So I had a choice; become the very thing that I condemned in others, or change.

After that first thought of suicide on a metro platform, my hijacked mind was like a dog that has had its first taste of blood. The suicidal thoughts kept coming, and the more I tried to silence them, the more anxious I became. I slept fitfully, lost my appetite and would cry at the drop of a hat.

My partner Hans, who came from Eastern Germany and had grown up behind the Berlin Wall until it fell, my son Daniel and I, lived near Rotkreuzplatz, in an area of Munich called Neuhausen. There, a tree-lined canal juts through the neighbourhood and points to Nymphenburger castle, like a watery phallus pointing towards a king. I knew every inch of the path between our apartment and that castle. It was the only place I found a temporary peace from my own mind.

Every morning found me running along that path, and each time I did, I would mentally mark the moment my feet hit the gravel of the trail that winds through the grounds behind the castle. *Crunch, crunch, crunch...* gravel under my feet. At the forty-five minute mark, endorphins would kick in, but I'd curse as my knees began to ache. *If only these damn knees would cooperate! I could run for hours—and outrun the dark.*

Finally, the hopelessness and suicidal thoughts hit a crescendo. One night while lying in bed next to a sleeping Hans, with Daniel safely ensconced in his room, I lay in bed in an insomniac haze of repetitive, incessant thought. The sense of separation from everything whole and good was so stark and seemed so eternal, that hellfire felt like a welcome reprieve from the nothingness and despair. I was in the pit of darkness that didn't feel psychological; it felt physically real and impossible to escape because it was inside me, and I was in it. Only people who have experienced this level of depression understand the sensation of inescapability from the black hole of deep depression. In the seventeenth century, melancholy was seen by some as a period of rest for the soul. Suicidal depression is not that kind of rest—it's death, but some deaths are new beginnings.

As I lay in bed that night, the suicidal thoughts wouldn't abate. All I could think of were different ways to kill myself. The tipping point came with a final battle in my mind. So began an inner dialog: "You could jump off the balcony."—"I don't want to die but I have to"—"It would be better than this, just do it"—"I can't leave my child, he needs me"—then..."If he were dead too, then I could finally die." At that final thought, I felt nauseated and wretched off the side of the bed. It was incomprehensible that such a thought could enter my awareness but it also served a great purpose. That final suggestion of total annihilation awoke something inside of me: Will.

I got out of bed and fetched a towel to clean up the floor. When I went back to the bathroom to rinse the towel, I found my way back to the bathroom floor, a place that I had known well since the age of eighteen. On the cool floor of a bathroom, behind a locked door, I was safe to sob and safe from the outside world, but still not safe from the contents of my mind. I woke Hans and begged him to find a psychologist's number in the middle of the night. He didn't understand the severity of what was happening. In his annoyance, he just brushed it off.

The next morning the will that had activated within me the night before set me into motion. A locked bathroom wasn't going to be enough this time. I saw my son off to school and then, as irrational as it may be, I went to my gym because I knew people would be there. Then, determined to save myself but not knowing what to do next, I locked myself in one of the tanning booths and called a psychiatric centre. When the receptionist connected me to Dr. Emanuel's office, I told his assistant, "I am having suicidal thoughts and can't stop them. I don't want to die. Can you help me?"

Every real solution is only reached by intense suffering.
—Carl Jung, Letters Vol. I, Pages 233–235

The assistant was kind and reassuring. She asked for my name and the address of where I was at that moment. She gently but firmly instructed me to take a taxi to the clinic and assured me that someone would be waiting at the reception desk to greet me. Gentleness was a hallmark of my experience with Dr. Emanuel. That cold, winter morning was the beginning of a conversation, the first conversation I had ever had about my pain with another human being. The compassion and love that I felt from Dr. Emanuel and his staff did more to facilitate my healing than anything else could have.

Although I looked forward to our appointments, there was always a little bit of apprehension about going to the clinic, because each visit meant that I came face-to-face with people who were so ill they required hospitalisation. Just off the waiting room were double, automatic, locked doors through which only the staff could pass. Behind those glass doors, was a brightly lit corridor with a floor of white tiles that reflected the abrasive light of fluorescent bulbs. If I sat at one end of the waiting room, I could observe patients shuffling up and down the hall, sometimes stopping to speak to the nurses and often mumbling to themselves. As I watched them, a thought taunted me, "Run away! You might end up in there, behind that glass, held against your will like a mad monkey!" I avoided that end of the waiting room.

Every antidepressant medication that Dr. Emanuel prescribed, as a supportive measure and means by which the process of healing could possibly be made more expedient, caused such an adverse reaction that we decided to move forward without it. We agreed to a mix of cognitive-behavioural and what I now know to be Person-Centred Therapy. The doctor explained how and why therapy works. He made me the driving force behind my healing, and through this approach, my self-esteem and sense of agency were boosted. Through all of it, I felt loved, understood, and sure that I would never be judged.

I began to heal.

Over the months that we worked together to bring me back to the land of the living, and back into the light, I was able to share all of my experiences, and no question was discouraged. When I mentioned that I was afraid of becoming depressed again, Dr. Emanuel responded, "If you believe you will, you will." What? I thought that depression was strictly the result of misfiring neurotransmitters and chemical imbalances in the brain? I must have made an incredulous face when I asked him, "What do you mean if I *believe* I will, I will? What does belief have to do with it?" "A lot more than people realise," was his response. During my months in therapy with Dr. Emanuel, my thinking began to revert to something resembling what it had been in childhood but with the added dimension of maturity.

When I was five years old we lived in an apartment in the suburbs of Atlanta. One evening at dinner, my parents, little sister, and I sat around our oval-shaped dining room table and ate spaghetti. My parents were discussing the Bible study program for the week. I became aware of some tension between our parents, and a thought arose in my mind: "If everyone could know every thought, feeling, and experience of everyone else, no one would fight anymore." That led to a question, "Why can't we do that? Why are people stuck inside of themselves?"

When I was a child, I intuitively understood that the adults around me were lost and needed love. My observation of the adult world was that it was a world full of puppets that dangled on strings. But by the time I reached adulthood, I, like most of us, had developed a kind of amnesia. The knowing that children bring with them into the world comes from the purity of Being; their minds are unadulterated in that they're not yet entangled with misinterpreted experience or poisoned by the distorted thinking of the adults who educate them. As we grow older, that knowing is buried as the collective shadow of mankind engulfs us and becomes our own.

During our conversations, I shared my experiences of childhood abuse, rape, and the later experience of spontaneous union and forgiveness with the doctor. I had many questions. I asked him about the moments after the rape in which my body took over while my mind remained mostly blank. He explained that there is a connection between psychological shock, trauma, and disassociation. His simple explanation was something like "when a person experiences trauma, the person can be so stunned by psychological shock that they're too stunned to stay in their body." This raised even more questions for me. "Okay, that sounds rational, but what do you mean *in their body*? Where else could a person be?" I had a clue, and the clue was in a spontaneous, transcendent experience at a pizza restaurant! The borders that delineated my *Self* from the *Self* of another had dissolved, but instead of shock or disassociation, I experienced absolute clarity, knowingness, and unconditional love.

Immediately following the rape, I hadn't felt *out* of body, I wasn't observing from above. What I experienced was a drastic minimisation of thought and a lack of any conscious direction of the body's actions. Immediately after the rape, the body seemed to move on its own but I wasn't *outside* of it. The self that I normally experienced had definitely checked out in a dissociative state (which is, in itself, very telling), however, at one point, when I became more lucid in the backyard, I began observing the whole scene without much, if any, thought. I could observe but I couldn't *feel*, and that is key.

I had so many questions. I wanted to understand.

If the Self could disappear, even for a moment, *who* was performing the actions of the body and who was later clearly observing the scene as it unfolded? Where in the hell did the self *go*? Why did I later see the Self looking back at me from another's eyes? Why couldn't I create the same experience with everyone and thereby forgive? Years later, in the depths of depression, why did my will to survive activate the night before I called a psychologist for help? If I was incapable of controlling my mind when it was being assailed by thoughts of suicide, *who* exactly controlled the will that saved me? Why were some experiences more painful than others and just what *is* pain, anyway?

I went into therapy in a haze of suffering but came out with a bright, burning desire to explore.

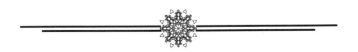

Human beings have a tendency to recoil from suffering. We avoid both our pain and that of others because we fear we may find no solution to it. There's a fear that if we contemplate the true scope and depth of human suffering, it could swallow us up, and make the whole of life seem like a futile attempt at optimism. Despite our aversion to suffering and our efforts to avoid any true intimacy with pain, we remain ardently devoted to the dramas portrayed in literature, theatre, and film. The tragedies of fictional characters serve as both entertainment and catharsis. We watch and hope. Perhaps the plot will reveal the meaning of suffering and purpose of pain.

Physical pain is an unconscious response that warns an organism that something is either causing acute damage to the body or that something in the body is chronically out of order. Physical pain is the perception of discomfort that can range from mild to debilitating and can be localised at one focal point or spread throughout the body. It hurts, but would you want to live without it? Without pain as a warning signal, we could cause irreparable damage to the body.

Much of your pain is the bitter potion by which the physician within you heals your sick self. —Khalil Gibran

Our well, that reservoir from which we constantly drink, provides a space for our unique, individual experience, interpretations, feelings, and personality. Emotions and feelings are meant to bubble up, surface, and be processed, not to linger, held below the surface of the water. The reservoir contains all of our unprocessed painful experiences, but it can only hold so much it. Pain stirs the waters and pushes impurities (suppressed negative emotions and feelings) to the top. The more unprocessed pain a person has, the more frequently and more easily negative emotion will surface. We have all known people who are easily offended, quick to anger, and easily brought to tears. When you see a person like that, you can realise that they have overwhelming, chronic, psychological pain that is the result of their beliefs, interpretations of their experiences, and unwillingness to embrace suffering. It's not all conscious, much of it is repressed.

Both pain and depression are our inner physician's way of letting us know that something is out of order, it's telling us, "Your way of thinking and being in the world is out of alignment with Truth." Sometimes it says, "Open your heart," and forces us to accept unavoidable human suffering. Suffering can only be transmuted if it's embraced. It's not the past itself that causes our current pain; it's our *current* thinking and current human condition that is causing our *current* pain. But it can be difficult to change our thinking when so many of our thoughts arise in response to unexamined, subconscious feelings and beliefs, and those repressed and/or suppressed emotions are creating internal pressure to which pain is a response.

The Truth doesn't hurt, it's our interpretation, attachment, and distorted thinking that pains us, and older, *unquestioned, unprocessed* painful interpretations that chronically ail us.

We are meant to enter into dialogue with our Pain, not to ignore it.

During my time in therapy, I began to experience a transformation of consciousness. It was gradual and was followed by new insights. Those insights were the result of one primary cause: My willingness to ask new questions and look within. Compassion was also key, compassion for myself, and the suffering of those I had previously believed to be the source of my pain.

As I healed, I regained access to joyful memories. My mother was no longer the cold, manipulative woman that refused to console me when I was alone and vulnerable. I was now able to conceive of the idea that, upon hearing that her daughter had been assaulted, she felt such an immediate and overwhelming pain that she was incapable of responding from a place love. I allowed myself to imagine that after that call from her daughter, she wept, and perhaps regretted her response. I was also able to conceive of the idea that the abuse that she was also subjected to as a child limited her ability to respond compassionately at that moment.

Memories of staying up late with mom to watch Hitchcock films, memories of making caramel popcorn, laughing, and gleefully running through the house when she chased us making monster sounds…all of these things reminded me of the joyful states of childhood and how our mother had held that space for me and my sisters to be curious, adventurous children.

I only saw her once during those first five years in Europe. The memory of our last day together before I left the U.S is a lasting one. We spent the day together at her house, watching old episodes of the British series *Are You Being Served?* and making sweet, iced tea and guacamole. The memory is crystal clear because of the last thing mom did before I left the house that day.

Stuffing my mouth with copious amounts of guacamole on tortilla chips, I told her that I would love to have my own avocado tree, and asked her if one could grow in the Georgia climate. She answered, "Why don't we find out? Come here." I followed her to the kitchen. Mom took an avocado pit and two toothpicks. Inserting a toothpick into each side of the pit, she then placed the pit in a small glass with a little water in the bottom. The toothpicks held the avocado pit by resting on the rim of the glass, only the bottom of the pit was submerged in water.

"It will grow roots down into the water and can then be planted to grow," she said. "Once the roots grow, the shell will crack, and it will sprout from the top." My response was something like "Oh! I didn't know you could sprout an avocado pit like that." That was the last time I spent alone with my mother. She passed five years later, at the age of sixty, too young to die.

In a way, it was her own resistance to pain that killed her.

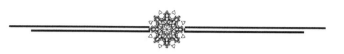

At one level of awareness, pain is suppressed and avoided until it becomes so pronounced that we can't ignore it anymore. Pain in the physical body is often caused by inflammation and pressure. Psychological pain is similar, it exerts constant pressure on the psyche. Pain is not the bad guy. Pain is the warning system that sounds the alarm when too many harmful beliefs and negative feelings have accumulated without being examined, consciously experienced, and released. This is the mechanism through which we process our painful interpretations of experience. In reality, what we are doing is acknowledging our pain and entering into a dialogue with it; we're asking it, "*What are you trying to tell me?*"

The body is a reflection of the mind. If we continue to avoid psychological pain, it will begin to manifest in the body as chronic illness. Pain is trying to get our attention, but we still won't acknowledge it.

When asked about how they see their pain, some people visualise their pain as a dark entity that follows them around. That's not pain. That's the energies of negative emotional (physiological) states that have accumulated in a magnetic field. Eckart Tolle refers to the magnetic field of accumulated negative emotions as the "pain body." I see pain a bit differently.

Pain is a message, a signal, an alert. Pain is Truth's formless, eternal Sentinel.

Not all pain is the product of negative emotion or psychological distortions of reality. Some pain is built into human life and is experienced as mourning, grief, and other forms of unavoidable human suffering. Our most profound suffering is a response to loss. When our loved ones pass away, we feel a gap. What was once immediately available—our loved one's smile, touch, scent, voice, and presence, tangible proofs of their unique existence—now find life only in our memories. Grief is a range of emotions. Your grief is unique to you; it's your unique constellation of feelings when you've experienced loss. We can grieve over the loss of anything: a person, a relationship, a job, a way of life, an object, and even a belief system.

Mourning is the process by which we allow our grief to work on our being. As we mourn, our pain accompanies us, she sits with us.

My older sister died suddenly at age fifty. One year ago, my biological father died. At first, I found it impossible to cry. My mind couldn't grieve but my body did. After some time, there was release and tears. Not long before I began writing this book, around the anniversary of my father's death, I felt struck by the grief of another potential loss. Walking in the forest with our dogs, I became aware of grief as a fog and shifting into a state of deep presence; I walked in that fog without resisting it.

After an hour or so, I saw something emerge from the trees off of the path, a deer and her fawn. The deer in this area of Brittany are smaller than those in North America. The mother wasn't much taller than our dog, a massive Bernese named Ben. Ben saw the deer before I did, and he ran towards them, at full speed before I had time to react. As I ran behind him, yelling for him to stop, I saw the mother dart away but the baby, barely larger than a very small dog, seemed to be having difficulty walking, and was left behind. I was unable to catch up with Ben. He caught the baby deer by the throat and shook her. By the time I reached them, he had released her and gave me a perplexed look as I scolded him.

The small fawn was still alive but barely moving. He must have crushed her throat because there was no visible bleeding. I picked her up in my arms, not sure what to do as we were deep in the forest. She was dying; her eyes stared at nothing. Placing my hand over her beating heart, I held her in my arms and spoke softly. She couldn't have been more than a few days old, and if she was going to die, I wanted her last moments to be of love and tenderness, not instinctual predation. I kissed her forehead, spoke softly, and kept my hand on her heart until it beat no more.

Now holding her with just one arm, I managed to leash the dogs (who were obediently sitting as they watched me intently) to a small tree. They stayed on the edge of the path as I walked deeper into the trees towards the direction that the mother had run. Unsure of how far the mother had gone,

I wanted to leave her fawn where she could find her and mourn. About fifty feet into the trees was a small patch of grass. I lay the fawn down on the grass and sat down for a moment.

It seemed like a senseless loss of life, and I felt the mother's loss. It was heartbreaking. How long would it take her to mourn? The grief fog I had allowed myself to walk through had now cleared, and as awareness shifted, I realised that, because of my spiritual approach to life, I had, to a degree, over-rationalised not only death but all human suffering. One doesn't often associate the rational with the spiritual because there is an assumption that those things are somehow opposites, but they aren't; they're extensions of each other and coalesce on a spectrum of awareness.

By over rationalising, I had failed to fully embrace the pain, and mourning the loss of loved ones had been somewhat unconscious. As I walked out of the forest that day, I walked out in clarity. While no one is ever really gone (they live *in* us, *as* us), engagement with the tangible is just as sacred and real as our engagement with the spiritual. The people who embrace us, and the physical world that we can touch, see, smell, and taste are not strictly illusions. They are aspects of the Absolute, made manifest. The world and the people in it are the *surface* of that thing we call *God*, and loss is a stripping away of that surface. When the stripping away occurs, a presence arrives. That presence is an invitation to embrace our pain, and through that embrace, allow the intangible to embrace us.

Our approach to pain makes a huge difference in how we move forward and heal. Pain sounds the alarm when something is out of order. Does that sound like a negative, dark entity or a friend who is trying to help us?

Marie von Ebner-Eschenbach said, "*Pain is the great teacher of mankind. Beneath its breath, souls develop.*"

Pain is indeed the Great Teacher, and she works in concert with Truth to purify consciousness and allow transmutation.

Pain never stops sounding the alarm; she never falls asleep on the job. At the moment we shut down our hearts, or begin entertaining harmful beliefs as ultimate truth, or interpret our experiences in a way that hinders our evolution, Pain starts poking us…just a little at first but if we ignore her, she'll start clanging cymbals in our ears until we acknowledge her presence. When you go from seeing your Pain as a scalded, screaming baby or a dark, morbid entity of despair, to seeing her as a dedicated, helpful assistant, you can begin the dialogue. Take a walk with your Pain, or sit with her over a glass of wine and ask, "What are you trying to show me?" That's when we realise that more than a great teacher, Pain is a true and loyal friend.

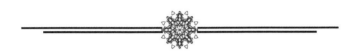

In January of 2005, my mother passed away. Daniel and I flew to the US for the funeral. I was a very different person than the one who had left more than five years earlier. The poet Kahlil Gibran wrote, "*Your pain is the breaking of the shell that encloses your understanding.*" My pain had cracked me thoroughly like an egg on stone. It had been work and required will and inquiry but a new way of being had unfolded within, as it catalysed total forgiveness for family, the past, the church, and especially my mother. Only love remained.

After the funeral, everyone gathered at my parents' home. It was a small house and packed with even more food than family, and we have a large family! I was navigating my way through cousins and second cousins as I navigated my way through different pitchers of sweet, iced tea. I took a sip of one tea that was so sweet that I ungracefully spit it out in the sink, much to the amusement of one of my second cousins. "Is southern tea too sweet for you now?" she teased. "It was always too sweet, there's more sugar than tea in that!" I replied. It was a moment of lightness on a sad day.

Dad approached us and asked me to come downstairs with him for a moment. I was too tired, too jet-lagged, and too sad to have the energy to even wonder what it was about. Once downstairs in the lower level of the house, he pointed over to an area full of his disorganised things. I wasn't sure what he was pointing at. When I looked in the direction that he gestured towards, I saw his workout bench, boxes of tools, a table, and some house plants. The ceiling in the lower level of the house was at least nine feet high. He pointed again, this time more distinctly, to a plant that reached the ceiling.

"You don't recognise that?" he asked. "What do you mean?" I replied. He walked up to the high plant and said, "Your mom has been growing this thing since the week you left. She always made me water it, even when she became too sick to do it herself. She thought you might come back home one day, and wanted you to have it. This is your avocado tree, Dana."

As it turns out, the leaves of the avocado tree are used for their ability to reduce pain.

Chapter 10
REALMS OF IMAGINATION

Don't ever let anyone tell you that imagination is mere fantasy; it's nothing less than the foundation of reality. Imagination is a realm, not an activity. *Envisioning* is the activity and faculty unique to human beings that allows us to enter realities that have not yet manifested and imbue them with life. It's through the act of envisioning and the willingness to enter the imaginative realm that we can inhabit the life of another and empathise. It's in imagination that all experience can be shared, matter rearranged, circumstances altered, minds changed, and hearts transformed.

Physics and the Imagination

In physics, the observer effect is the theory that the observation of a phenomenon changes that phenomenon. The "double-slit" experiment is part of a class of experiments referred to as "double path," this describes when a wave splits into two separate waves that will later merge again into a single wave. The double-slit experiment was first performed in 1801 by Thomas Young. He used light. In essence, the experiment demonstrated that light has both a wave nature and a particle nature. The original double-slit experiments were part of classical physics but with the emergence of quantum physics, scientists began offering different interpretations of the experiment. The double-slit became a useful thought exercise for quantum physicists.

The most famous interpretation is the Copenhagen interpretation, which states that within quantum systems, no definitive states (for example, 1 or 0) exist. They exist as potentialities before measurement. In other words, they exist in an imaginative realm. Some physicists argue that the observer effect is misrepresented by some of their peers and other researchers, like parapsychologist, when they claim that consciousness (the observer) can alter matter. They argue that *to observe* in scientific terms doesn't just imply that a human being is there to make an observation of the event. To scientists, *anything* that takes measurements or recordings (like a machine) counts as an observation. Technically, no human is necessary. The experiment can easily be performed automatically with machines.

But here the dissenting scientists are missing something vital: Ontology. Are the machines separate from the humans that create and use them? Machines are an extension of the human being. They perform both physical and computational functions on behalf of the humans who designed, built, and programmed them. You can't separate a computer's 'intelligence' and actions from the consciousness of those who created it any more than you can separate your own being from *beingness*. The experiment has demonstrated two truths: an imaginative realm exists and human consciousness, either via an organic portal (the human) or inorganic portal (a machine created by human consciousness), *does* alter matter.

The universe is a never-ending revelation, and no branch of scientific inquiry has made that more evident than quantum physics. John Archibald Wheeler was an original maverick. He liked to say, "If you haven't found something strange during the day, it hasn't been much of a day." He was a Professor Emeritus of physics at Princeton and the University of Texas. It was Wheeler who coined the terms "black hole" and "wormhole."

Wheeler worked with Niels Bohr in the late 1930s on a theoretical treatment that applied Gamow's and Bohr's liquid drop model to explain the mechanism of nuclear fission. He went on to do much more throughout his long life. He passed away at age ninety-six. Wheeler coined the term "geometrodynamics." Geometrodynamics was his effort to reduce the general relativity of Einstein to a more fundamental geometry. Of this, Wheeler said, "There is nothing in the world except empty, curved space. Matter, charge, electromagnetism—are only manifestations of the bending space." He also said, "Space tells matter how to move, and matter tells space how to curve."

The general view that most people have of space is that of a large, empty nothingness just waiting to be filled with objects. But quantum physics has now demonstrated what mystics have long known: Space and matter are entangled, space is not an empty void, nor is it dependent on matter. We know this intuitively, and this is why we find ourselves saying things like, "I need space" and "a space opened within." Space is not limited to physical, mental, or emotional phenomena. It can be all of those things. Space can expand, bend, ripple, and do a kind of acrobatics.

Isaac Newton argued that space is the Absolute Entity. English philosopher Samuel Clark, a close friend of Newton, argued that space is divine. Being precedes space. Space is both an emanation of Being and exists within it. This is why imagination is a realm: **Imagination *is* space**. We move around in imagination, we expand our vision of the world and ourselves, in imagination, and we transform in imagination. **Imagination is consciousness itself, and we reside within it.**

Perhaps this is why the poetic soul quoted in Acts 17:28 states, "In Him we live, and move, and have our being." Perhaps this is also why Neville Goddard said, "The imagination is God," and perhaps this why William Blake wrote, "Man is all imagination."

Wheeler also expressed this ontological approach to space and the universe when he said: "Today I think we are beginning to suspect that man is not a tiny cog that doesn't really make much difference to the running of the huge machine but rather that there is a much more intimate tie between man and the universe than we heretofore suspected...The physical world is in some deep sense tied to the human being."

Psychology and Imagination

Carl Jung is perhaps most known for coining the term "archetypes," but what's not widely known is that Jung was the second person to identify archetypes. William Blake was the first. Blake referred to them as "unnamed forms." Jung acknowledged this after discovering Blake's cosmology. The human psyche is unparalleled in its complexity. Blake was uncovering and revealing that complexity in his work. Blake's, *The Four Zoas* and *The Book of Urizen*, are full of archetypal allegories that Blake used to symbolise man's divided being.

Jung coined the term "active imagination." In this regard, envisioning (or imagining) became an organ of understanding but both Jung and Tolkien referred to imagination as a realm. Imagination as a realm is not new. In Islamic tradition, it's called *Alam Al-Mithal*. Avicenna, the Persian polymath, said that the imagination unified human reason and the divine realm. Blake, Jung, Goddard, and others have said the same.

Imagination is a Bridge

William Blake and Neville Goddard insisted that Jesus Christ is the personification of awakened (i.e., enlightened) human imagination (reminder, imagination in this context *is* consciousness).

Carl Jung also held that the imagination, specifically active imagination, is the bridge that gaps the conscious and unconscious mind. Jung's exercise of active imagination was intended to bring about a state of hypnagogia. Hypnagogia is a state that exists between wakefulness and sleeping. In this state, the person remains lucid and experiences imagination as a lucid dream, in which they can either take control or, while remaining aware that they are in a dream-like state, allow the experience to unfold.

Neville Goddard taught the same technique, and William Blake used it as well. But both Goddard and Blake had even more profound visionary experiences, including the bi-location of their awareness and body. Visionary states are the more extreme and sudden version of hypnagogia in which the person enters the state spontaneously, without warning, and remains lucid during the experience. While Jung is primarily known for his work on archetypes and active imagination, he also spent decades in engagement with alchemical texts. Jung recognised that the Medieval alchemists were using meditative techniques on par with his active imagination in an attempt to unify the fragmented psyche and coalesce opposites. Jung was particularly interested in establishing that the Great Work was dependent on the comprehensive use of the imagination.

To be fully actualised and fulfilled as a human being, imagination must flourish.

This use of active imagination was beneficial to the psyche because it promoted psychological purification and healing by relieving psychological and emotional pressure that would otherwise cause injury to body, mind, and soul. When shamans give patients plant medicines that cause visions, they are doing the same thing that the alchemists were doing when they went into an altered state and had visions of salamanders, dragons, and other strange creatures. They were projecting the contents of the unconscious mind outward onto the screen of space. All of the 'woo-woo' sounding practices of Alchemists, Hermeticists, and Shamans are, in actuality, psychological operations performed in an effort to resolve repressed psychic conflict, relieve psychological and emotional pressure, and unify the mind and spirit.

While we're thinking about Jung and the imagination and unification of mind—let's take a moment to look at a symbol. We'll consider this symbol in more detail in chapter fifteen.

The symbol above is one that Alchemists use to represent the earth element. Years ago, while in a quiet state, I found myself staring at this symbol. In my relaxed, non-questioning state, I suddenly understood that this symbol is the representation of the four aspects of the Divine Being (Blake's *Four Zoas*) beginning to unify and create equilibrium in the individual. I immediately understood that this symbol represents the KRST/Christ poured out in perfect equilibrium upon and within an individual. The symbol is used to represent earth, but remember, the human is the *earth* of *God*. Blake's Zoa, called Urthona, represents Divine Imagination. His name means "earth owner." Blake names Urthona's emanation in the outer world, "Los," a reversal of "sol" (sun) and equates Los with Christ, the initiative catalyst of reunification.

This symbol reminds us that superconsciousness is entombed *within* Man and that when it unfolds, it *begins to unify* the fragmented mind. This symbol shows that unification is not complete but the process has begun, and that process eventually leads to restoration. This symbol represents the moment when the individual recognises their own fourfold nature and consciously begins to work to move into a state of equilibrium.

I was so thrilled by the sudden insight that I immediately shared part of it with an acquaintance. Three months later, he made it part of his work. I didn't realise it at the time but Carl Jung, and other psychologists had also used this symbol for decades to represent psychological states. That's the thing about insights; they're meant to be shared. All human beings have access to the same wellspring of insight, when we share our insights with others, we may find that they also had a related insight or they may find the missing link that they've been looking for. I can't tell you how many times I've had what I thought was an original idea, only to discover that it's not original at all. I dropped the notion that any idea is original." There is nothing new under the sun." Everything arises from a field.

All of our insights and ideas were seeded by the insights and ideas of other people, and our ideas will seed and germinate in others as well. Ideas reside in imagination and draw life from human engagement with them. Our insights don't belong to us alone. They come from a universal source: the human imagination.

So why isn't society encouraged to use imagination more intentionally?

The answer is simple: it's a threat to the Containment System.

Those Who Control Imagination, Control the World

The exercise of imagination is dangerous to those who profit from the way things are because it has the power to show that the way things are is not permanent, not universal, not necessary. —Ursula Le Guin

A hierarchal control system that gives the few control over the many is by the very nature of its intention, reliant on systems of commodity, ownership, oppression, and manipulation. For the few to control the many, they need more than brute force and large armies. Control starts in the mind.

Julius Caesar noted that the Celtic belief in an imaginative Otherworld, through which an immortal soul passes after death, made the Celts a formidable enemy because, as he noted, "They were more willing to go to war, having no fear of death." The Druid imagination represented a threat to the Roman Empire because their philosophy and scientific inquiry contradicted Roman orthodoxy, an orthodoxy that was created for the sole purpose of controlling the people. The Roman view was materialistic; humans were utilities, not conscious, potentially divine beings. All property was in the hands of wealthy men. Women and slaves were part of that property. To maintain the status quo, the Roman State needed to extinguish any thought in the minds of its subjects that things could be different or that one could imagine and move into new ways of being in the world.

The imaginative and creative impulses are virtually impossible to annihilate. Realising that the Celtic peoples throughout Europe would never fully surrender their imagination to the brutal machine of Empire, the Roman State set about to create a mechanism through which they could effectively manipulate and control human imagination while guiding people into predetermined, state-sanctioned, modes of living: State sanctioned religion.

Jean Markale and other historians have pointed out that, as Christianity was forced on the tribes of Europe, some Druidic beliefs were brought to bear upon the religion. So that in the end, Catholicism can truly be said to be a hodgepodge of actual truth mixed with ancient philosophy, so-called pagan celebrations and rites, and mysticism—all combined with state-sanctioned dogma. Truth mixed with untruth. Because of the insertion of the pre-existing symbols, beliefs, and practices from the ancient world, deep truths are woven into the tapestry of Catholic thought.

Earth history is nothing like what we've assumed. The myths of the Bible are not secular history, but within those myths, you'll find a circular history (or a map) of consciousness. Many of the ancient books are copies, forged, and manipulated to support a certain narrative.[2] Upon the discovery of ancient mystery school symbolism in religions like Catholicism, some ex-

---

[2] For more details on this, see the work of Anatoly Fomenko and that of Dr. Alexander Koltypin, a geologist and director of the Natural Science Research Centre at Moscow's International Independent University of Ecology.

Christians and conspiracy theorists have unfortunately thrown the baby out with the bathwater by claiming that the pagan roots of religion nullify its usefulness as an aid to human evolution. Forming such an emphatic and final view of organised religion, one fails to acknowledge the complexity of the collective human experience, the manner through which consciousness evolves, and truth reveals itself.

It's through **direct, personal revelation** that an individual makes contact with truth. Personal revelation and social structures (like we see in organised religion) are not mutually exclusive. Sometimes, social structure offers a framework within which the individual can do the inner work that catalyses personal revelation. As the individual evolves, they drop the dogma and eventually find that religion is no longer a necessary component of their intellectual and spiritual life. Their focus turns to the deep, inner work of the soul.

Throughout human history, individuals who have evolved into a stratum of illumined awareness have shared their insights with the world within the structure of various world religions. One such individual was Meister Johann Eckhart. Like our 20th century messenger Neville Goddard, Meister Eckhart's theological view was one of radical *panen*theism, "All in God, God in All." Both Eckhart and Goddard stated unequivocally, and from their own, direct experience, that the *true* identity of every soul is Divine Spirit itself. This may seem a startling declaration but mystics throughout all of human history and in every culture, have come to the same realisation. Eckhart was eventually charged with heresy by non-mystics who found his teachings inconceivable. Meister Eckhart's message may never have been heard if it weren't for the audience that the Church gathered together (control systems always contain the seeds of their own destruction). An audience will always include people who are evolving from a fractured, immature view of themselves and reality, to an awakened existence.

Meister Eckhart was not the first nor the last who could be labeled as "panendeist" (not to be confused with pandeism), there have been others. Marguerite Porete's views appear to be panentheistic. She was burned at the stake one year before Eckhart arrived in Paris. Before that, there were individuals like John Scottus Eriugena (c.800–c.877), a philosopher born in

Scotia Maior, the 9th century name given to what is now called Ireland. Like some of the Eastern Christian Fathers, Eriugena, a philosopher, expressed the view that, "God became man so that man may become God."

While official Church doctrine declared the Church to be the only legitimate channel between humanity and the Divine, there have always been enlightened individuals within the structure of the church, who kept the conversation about the sacredness and primacy of individual human experience alive. No religion or tradition is immune to truth. Even Buddhism, a beautiful philosophy and yet still attached to dogmatic beliefs (like reincarnation), loses its hold on any human that has experienced true awakening. Speaking of the theory of reincarnation—which is the theory of the transmigration of souls from one body to another—what if life is more like the film *Groundhog Day* than the game *Musical Chairs*? Just a thought.

Amidst all of the debate of the early Christian period, the Empire, through the arm of their church, took good care to create a "spiritual" and earthly hierarchy that kept the priestly caste firmly at the top and in control, with Rome acting as the central authority. Over time, many verses were intentionally mistranslated, and others were added to their "holy" texts, that were very convenient for the State. Verses like, "*All of you must obey those who rule over you. There are no authorities except the ones God has chosen. Those who now rule have been chosen by God. Whosoever opposes the authorities, opposes leaders whom God has appointed*" and "*pay Caesar's things to Caesar.*"

Above all else, the texts of the Bible are books of imagination, and like all human imagination, some of it is transcendently beautiful, and some of it is nightmarish. It's a powerful example of the breadth, depth, and magnitude of the human imagination. The remarkable thing about Catholicism is that the individuals who helped develop it over the centuries managed to encode some of the mysteries and truth into Catholicism's iconography. They also pay homage to the mysteries of the cosmos and express reverence for Divinity through the architecture of magnificent European cathedrals.

The Holy Roman Church was created as part of an overarching strategy of state craft and expansion of empire. Ultimately, the Inquisitions (there were more than one) were about stamping out any remaining vestiges of authentic, independent, imaginative impulses left in the people. They sought to "put an end to heresy." The creation of *heresy* as a concept is, in itself, a crime against and an attack on, the imagination. Any opinion or view that differed from church dogma was heresy. The word *heresy* is derived from the Greek word *hairesis*, which literally means to "choose for oneself."

Fast forward in time: An examination of the 20th-century reveals that the individuals and groups at the top found new and clever ways to maintain control over the population. Heresy and blasphemy are still with us, only now the inquisition ensues on social media, where the masses, frothing at the mouth, gather to view the latest human sacrifice.

The Catholic Church coined the term propaganda in the sixteenth century to describe the propagation of the religion but propaganda (as we use the term today) is as old as humanity. Plato argued that the art of persuasion (rhetoric) was in contrast with, and opposed to, philosophy, the love of wisdom. He makes it clear that the aim of rhetoric is domination, not elucidation. In the Republic, Plato argues that myth-making is an essential part of state-craft.

Propaganda is, at its most fundamental level, the strategic application of archetypal symbolism, linguistics, and programming methodologies in order to exploit the power of human imagination to create sub-realities, i.e., social constructs, that suit the agenda of the propagandists.

Propaganda isn't limited to wartime and state craft. After witnessing the effectiveness of propaganda during WW1, Edward Bernays, an Austrian-American and relative of Sigmund Freud, observed that propaganda (which he coined "public relations") was a necessary part of democratic, social life. In his book entitled *Propaganda*, published in 1928, Bernays writes:

> The conscious and intelligent manipulation of the organised habits and opinions of the masses is an important element in democratic society. Those who manipulate this unseen mechanism of society constitute an invisible government which is the true ruling power of our country. We are governed, our minds are moulded, our tastes formed, and our ideas suggested, largely by men we have never heard of.... It is they who pull the

wires that control the public mind.

Bernays referred to the process by which the few gain control over the minds of the majority as "the engineering of consent," and this engineering wasn't limited to any particular media. *Engineering of consent* could be accomplished through entertainment, education, advertising, journalism, religious and spiritual movements, control of academic and scientific organisations. It can also be accomplished through direct threat. By making examples of people whose careers and reputations were destroyed because they said the 'wrong' thing, even while trying to do the *right* thing. The more absurd and irrational the example, the more effective the psychological operation is; people feel insecure, destabilised, and become paranoid, and the Machine says, "Gotcha!" Propaganda is about controlling not just the minds of the people but their hearts and souls as well.

Nothing has held our imagination quite like television and movies over the past century. Children are exposed to scenes of violence in cartoons as soon as they're old enough to watch a screen. Around 90% of all movies and 60% of television shows contain some form of violence. The influence of both stories and moving images on children is profound. The average child sees 12,000 acts of violence per year on television and in movies. The average adult can see up to 3 times that amount. Regardless of the content, whether it's violent or inspiring, the stories we engage within our imagination have the power to alter our perception of the so-called *real* world.

Experiential Crossings

A recent study made by Durham University has revealed a fascinating psychological phenomenon. As part of this study, researchers interviewed readers of literary fiction. Both authors and readers reported hearing the voices of fictional characters in their heads. Researchers at Durham University surveyed more than 1500 readers, and around 20% of them reported that the unique voices of fictional characters stayed with them after reading. Some of them reported vivid experiences of hearing the characters' voices in their heads, which included auditory properties like volume and pitch. Some readers admitted that a fictional character began narrating the reader's world and influencing their behaviour. This phenomenon is called

"Experiential Crossings" by psychologist Charles Fernyhough, one of the original researchers who studied the phenomenon. In an interview with The Guardian newspaper in 2017, Fernyhough said,

> One respondent described 'feeling enveloped' by (Virginia Woolf's) character Clarissa Dalloway – hearing her voice and imagining her response to particular situations, such as walking into a Starbucks. Sometimes the experience seemed to be triggered by entering a real-world setting similar to one in the novel. In other situations, it felt like seeing the world through a particular character's eyes and judging events as the character would.

There might be more to this phenomenon than the reader's inner experience of a fictional character's voice, viewpoint, and personality. While it hasn't yet been researched, authors, the very people who imagined the fictional characters that cross over into the reader's inner experience, have reported even more striking examples of experiential crossings. Neville Goddard once shared a story from a letter that he received from a writer who swore that his fictional character had come to life. The author claimed that he had created a wholly unlikely character with a history, personality, unique living conditions, and a very specific and unusual appearance that couldn't possibly exist in the real world, or so he thought. When the author came across a man who matched his character down to the last detail, he feared for his sanity and wrote to Goddard.

Other authors have reported seeing their fictional creations cross-over into the real world and act independently. Writer Alan Moore, creator of the Hellblazer series, reported in an interview that he saw his character John Constantine in a sandwich bar in London. Moore said,

> One interesting anecdote that I should point out is that one day, I was in Westminster in London -- this was after we had introduced the character -- and I was sitting in a sandwich bar. All of a sudden, up the stairs came John Constantine. He was wearing the trench coat, a short cut -- he looked -- no, he didn't even look exactly like Sting. He looked exactly like John Constantine. He looked at me, stared me straight in the eyes, smiled, nodded almost conspiratorially, and then just walked off around the corner to the other part of the snack bar. I sat there and thought, should I go around that corner and see if he is really there, or should I just eat my sandwich and leave? I opted for the latter. I thought it was the safest. I'm

not making any claims to anything. I'm just saying that it happened. Strange little story.

In an article entitled, *I Saw My Novel's Protagonist Walking Across the Street*, author Dana Czapnik discusses the experiential crossings of her character, Lucy Adler. Czapnik estimates that if one were to interview enough writers, a high number would report varying degrees of experiential crossings of their characters into the author's physical world. In his book *Mutants and Mystics: Science Fiction, Superhero Comics and the Paranormal*, Jeffrey Kripal describes an experience that made a lasting impact on the successful comics writer Doug Moench. Kripal provides background by explaining that Moench had been writing a scene for one of the *Planet of the Apes* comics. The particular scene revolved around a gorilla named Brutus. In the scene, Brutus, wearing a black hood, invades a human's home, grabs the man's mate by the neck, and puts a gun to her head. When describing the chain of events, Moench says that he had just finished writing the scene when he heard his wife call for him in a strained, odd voice. He says he stood up, walked across the house and entered the living room where he saw that a gunman, in a black hood, had one arm around his wife's neck with the other holding a gun to his wife's head. To quote Moench:

> It was exactly what I had written…it was so, so immediate in relation to the writing and such an exact duplicate of what I had written, that it became an instant altered state. The air in the room congealed, became almost like fog, and yet, paradoxically, I could see with greater clarity. I could see the individual threads of his black hood.

Kripal reports that Moench was so emotionally shaken that he obsessed over the black-hooded intruder for years. Moench developed a temporary fear of writing, and Kripal quotes him, saying, "It really does make you wonder. Are you seeing the future? Are you creating a reality? Should you give up writing forever after something like that happens? I don't know."

There is an aphorism among modern esotericists that goes, "If you want something to happen, write it down *as if it already has*."

Movies, television, literature, and theatre allow us to inhabit the life of another and to tell stories that would otherwise never be heard. Storytelling can either promote human dignity or diminish it. Sometimes we need to tell those stories of diminishment and share how we found our way back to dignity. Like all tools, our stories and the media through which we share them, are an extension of our Being. Being becomes entangled with the mind, and the mind holds on to its story as a means of ego survival. Our story can act as a bridge between two states, or it can trap us within a state and cause stagnation. When we become conscious of Being's entanglement with experience, we begin to look at stories, both our own and those of others, through more enlightened eyes, we can see stories for what they are: **Engines of Imagination**. An engine converts one form of energy into another to create movement, and so the question arises, in which direction are our stories taking us? Where is our imagination leading us, and what kind of world will we find there?

"Imagination is more important than knowledge. For knowledge is limited whereas imagination embraces the entire world, stimulating progress, giving birth to evolution." —Albert Einstein

It's what we imagine to be true and/or possible that drives our choices, behaviours, and emotions. Imagination is the fabric of our world. When claimed and rightly used, it becomes the ultimate human freedom. When manipulated for agendas, it can create a world of monstrous shadows and enemies to fight, or leave us feeling lost in a dream of randomness and insignificance.

What Neville Knew

In your own bosom you bear your heaven and earth,
And all you behold, though it appears without,
It is within, in your imagination,
Of which this world of mortality is but a shadow. —William Blake

Do not become so completely anchored to the outer garment which you think is
yourself — it's only a garment — and forget the Inner Man, the Imaginative Man,
who is the Immortal You. That Imaginative Man is God Himself! And the day will
come that it will be born, for his whole vast drama – I could break it into three pat-
terns: Innocence, Experience, Imagination. And when you reach that stage — the
third stage of imagination, you are going towards the end, for we came out of a
world of innocence into the world of experience, and move towards an awakening
imagination, which is God Himself! —Neville Goddard

Goddard told those who attended his lectures, "The body is a subsection of soul as perceived by the five senses. It is not separate from the soul. The soul emanates the body and as soon as the body "dies" in one reality, the soul can project another one, brand new and whole, in another reality just like this one." To Neville Goddard, the *fallen* reality was not just the one realm that we call earth but many versions of the same fallen reality. The focus on his work shifted from his earlier lectures about the power of imagination to something far more important. Goddard didn't identify with the soul or mind. He identified with Spirt, The Absolute Self. Like many before him, he called this Absolute Self, "The Father."

He experienced the Absolute as his (and your) True Being. What Neville called "The Promise" was the promise of transcending the illusion of our relative selves and the distorted realities that are created through our misidentification with the *relative creations of Mind* and the only way to transcend the lower realms of false-self was to learn and embody what I call, "right imagination." *Right imagination* aims to treat life like a lucid dream. It treats the people it encounters in the dream, not as foreign, separate objects but as manifestations of the Absolute Self, with which it identifies. Imagination is powerful, you're constantly imagining with every thought, mental image, and interpretation. It's our passive use of imagination that births ignorance, darkness, and suffering.

Years before I discovered Neville or his ideas, I had inner experiences that caused me to completely shift my perception from the limiting belief of reincarnation. My experiences are too many and too personal to layout in this book but they can be summarised as a collection of direct experiences that strongly suggest that there are indeed many copies of this reality we call *earth* and that we are bound to this multiplex of earths until we fully identify with the Absolute Self, also called "The Great Spirit." Goddard also believed in what modern scientists call the many-worlds theory. For him, the many-worlds theory was not a theory but a confirmed fact. That probably seemed like an extraordinary claim to the people who came to listen to him speak in the 1940s.

In the mid-1950s, a young Princeton student, Hugh Everett III, broke from the Copenhagenists view and postulated a new radical possibility. Everett imagined that at the moment of observation, a bifurcation occurred: The wave would continue its evolution by means of *branching*. These branches would each require a *version* of the same observer (otherwise, they would remain existent only as potentialities within an imaginal sphere). Each branch would evolve independently of the other branches and have its own unique future.

Hugh Everett faced only ridicule and criticism of his theory. Other physicists, mentally trapped in their belief in the primacy of materiality and unable to imagine a holographic universe, even went so far as to admit that while they believed Everett's theory to be the most reasonable, they just couldn't believe it in everyday life. When physicist Leonard Susskind proposed the holographic universe theory in the 1990s, some scientists began reconsidering Everett's theory and thinking of it as parallel universes. In order to even begin contemplating parallel universes in which other copies of ourselves are living different potentialities, we have to suspend our rigid belief in the supremacy of physical reality but also entertain the idea that the relative self that we so rigidly identify with is not an absolute.

A hologram is both encoded information and a projected image. Think about this: Unless you have entered into the living 'no-thingness' during meditation, all you have ever known is imagery. During all of your waking hours, all you see and think about is imagery. When you sleep, you are either totally unconscious or dreaming, and when dreaming, you are once again experiencing imagery. Beyond the universe of images, there is a silent, supreme state of Being in which no *thing* exists and yet from which consciousness arises. That consciousness is infinite imagination. The infinite imagination is unified with infinite love, and that unified awareness gives rise to infinite power, as Creative Will. A Creative Will would create correspondent realities.

These realities are perceived as *places* but are in reality, *states of being*. In this regard, the not-so-physical world we call *earth* is a spiritual state of being.

The Imaginal Body

William Brown is a biophysicist and research scientist at the Resonance Science Foundation and Hawaii Institute for Unified Physics. In addition to his theoretical work in unified physics, he's a cellular and molecular biologist, and he has a Master of Science degree in Applied Recombinant DNA Technology from New York University. Brown's work with DNA is focused on the study of non-local, morphogenetic fields that extend beyond the physical body we can perceive and through which we use the portals of our five senses. These morphogenetic fields are multi-dimensional, and because they exist at multiple levels, a means of communication between fields is necessary. DNA is that means of communication.

A group of scientists, including Brown and Rupert Sheldrake, put forth that as the field is multidimensional, so is DNA. Because of this, scientists who are trying to create synthetic DNA will never succeed in creating any true replica. DNA is part of a non-local, holofractal communication system that can only be influenced but never reduced by human consciousness. Nobel Prize winner Max Planck, a theoretical physicist, believed that all matter originates and exists as a projection of *a creative force that is both conscious and unconscious*, which brings the particles of an atom into vibration.

A creative force that is both conscious and unconscious = The Imagination.

Speaking of our bodies and DNA, how *do* our bodies know to maintain a certain form?

In the spring of 1962, Vittorio Michelli, a soldier in the Italian army, was admitted to the Verona Military Hospital due to complaints of severe pain in the left hip. Examinations showed that Michelli had a malignant tumour and other severe damage. The medical report submitted to the Canadian Medical Association by Dr. Marie Salmon detailed the following regarding his diagnosis:

> There was a tumorous mass in the left iliac region, a shortening of the left leg and limitation of motion of the left hip. His pain increased and he had difficulty walking. An X-ray of the left hip (May 22, 1962) showed structural alteration of the bone with osteolysis involving the lower part of the ilium and the roof of the acetabulum. An open biopsy revealed an infiltrating neoplasm that had partly destroyed and replaced the inferior gluteal muscle. The osseous iliac surface was covered with irregular, friable nipple-like, spreading overgrowths. The pathology report showed fusiform cells of a sarcomatous character.

The staff at the Verona Military Hospital deemed the case hopeless and decided not to even bother with radiotherapy or chemotherapy. Less than two months later, Michelli was transferred to Trento Military Hospital. He had osteosarcoma. Cancer treatments in 1962 were nowhere near as advanced as they are today. In 1962, some doctors considered the stage of Michelli's osteosarcoma as a death sentence and completely incurable. Multiple radiographs made in June of 1962 demonstrated the complete destruction of the left hemipelvis, only part of the iliopubic eminence, and the superior third of the ilium remained. In August, he was transferred to Borgo di Valsugana Centre for Tumours to receive radiotherapy but once he arrived, the doctors determined that radiotherapy would not be useful, and sent him back to Trento Military Hospital. In constant pain, he required a full hip-leg cast to walk.

Eventually, in May 1963, examinations of his hip showed that his bone had disappeared. The report states, "The left leg was joined to the pelvis by a few sheaves of soft tissue, no bone. No bony elements could be detected on palpation, only an amorphous, doughy mass. He was unable to move his left leg."

The bone had dissolved.

Vittorio Michelli came from a Catholic family with a mother who believed in the power of healing. She passed her strong belief on to her son, and she encouraged him to go to Lourdes, France, a place that holds power in the human imagination of our times. Many people strongly believe in the healing power of the water that runs into the Lourdes baths. Michelli went to Lourdes because *he imagined* it had the power to heal him. It was a journey he wouldn't have needed to make if he knew that the 'water' that healed him was his very own consciousness.

After he went to Lourdes, he stopped taking pain medication and began walking again. Medical examinations between 1964 and 1971 showed that there was no longer any muscular atrophy. Radiographs showed that the bone had grown back! It was reconstituted in structure—the trabecula had reappeared, and calcification was said to be excellent. The bone had completely dissolved and then grew back again. All tumorous cells disappeared. How did the bone know where, how, and in which form to grow back?

The current view of biophysicists is that there is an energetic structure to which our physical bodies conform. This energetic blueprint is holofractal DNA, which receives and transmits energetic coding. In this paradigm, the body is a holographic projection of consciousness, and it's that consciousness that tells the body what form to take and how to behave.

Reclaiming Our Imagination

I know of no other Christianity and of no other Gospel than the liberty both of body and mind to exercise the Divine Arts of Imagination,
Imagination, the real and Eternal World of which this Vegetable Universe is but a faint shadow, and in which we shall live in our Eternal or Imaginative Bodies, when these Vegetable Mortal Bodies are no more.
—William Blake

The book of Genesis is a purely esoteric text. When it says, "In the beginning was the Word (Logos), and the Word was with God, and the Word *was* God" it's referring to the Logos as the creative fire of superconsciousness. Plutarch wrote that the Logos is the intermediary between superconsciousness (God) and human consciousness. If the Logos is the creative fire, i.e., the creative aspect of superconsciousness, what is the human equivalent of that? Human imagination.

We don't create a damn thing without imagination. We can't even *understand* or *perceive* anything without using imagination. Imagination is not fantasising. To *imagine* is to conceive an idea, either abstract or concrete, and create a corresponding image. The language of consciousness is, at its highest level, what we humans would describe as *feeling* because it's vibratory. As consciousness 'steps down,' it becomes *symbolic and analogue*, as it steps down further, we perceive it as geometric and mathematical. As it steps down even further, it becomes corrupted and limited through binary *digitalisation*. Reality is analogue, not binary. The point is, without imagination, we might as well be dead. Human imagination is the creative fire at work in humanity. Therefore Neville Goddard insists that the imagination *is* God.

Regardless of what one chooses to believe about the power of imagination and the nature of the universe, it's clear that imagination plays a vital role in human life. Beyond all ideas of quantum physicists, philosophers, poets, and mystics, what matters to you is what you choose to believe about your potential and imaginative power to transform your life. We can't and don't do anything without imagining it first. Every action we take first began as an imaginative act. All of our beliefs and thoughts reside in the imagination. They're the scripts we run. The *feelings* that arise when we believe our presumptions and interpretations to be true are the 'run command.' Who controls your imagination? Are you a conscious operator or a programmed puppet?

What would happen if we took back our imagination in radical, new ways? What would happen if, instead of waiting for politicians, scholars, journalists, television, experts, celebrities, and movies to tell us what to imagine, we recognised that we *are* all that we behold, and got serious about our personal understanding of the self and reality? Most importantly, what kind of world would we create if we practiced *right imagination* throughout our lives?

Right imagination is the conscious, **intentionally loving,** *and* **coherent** use of all of our faculties as we move through the world, not as puppets but as consciously creative beings.

Do we, as a group, hold back from truly reclaiming our imaginative powers because we fear uncertainty? It seems so. It's much easier to rely on authorities to tell us how things are than to make a conscious effort to engage in and operate from, a willfully directed imagination because doing so would require that we hold ourselves accountable for the world we create.

Uncertainty can feel paralysing at times, and the world can seem like a big, wild, and random place to be in when we approach life as something that is happening *out there*. But as Margaret Drabble posited, when nothing is sure, everything is possible. Someone once said you are in no way obliged to remain the same person throughout your life, or even from one day to the next. To flourish as a human being and to create lasting fulfillment is, in itself, an exercise of the imagination. Imagination is not an alternative, fantastical reality; it *is* reality. More than that: We truly are *All Imagination*.

As William Blake proclaimed: **"The imagination is not a state: it is the human existence itself."**

Chapter 11
THE MAGICAL LIBRARY

Strange and wondrous things happen in Paris, especially in tiny studio apartments at the end of long corridors. Having directly experienced these wondrous things on numerous occasions, I wasn't at all surprised when a random woman approached me in London a few years ago and handed me a small strip of scented paper on which was written "What we do in Paris is a secret." As it turns out, that's a perfume with an astute name.

Paris isn't a city; it's a Magical Mind, a labyrinth full of unexpected corridors, stone angels, watery dragons, an underworld of bones, and at its metaphoric centre, a heart with a rose window; Our Lady, *Notre Dame*. The ghosts of alchemists, courtesans, servants, writers, artists, and saints can be seen at cafés. If you get on their good side, one might trip that rude guy who just pushed past you to get in the metro first. If he was handsome, they might prompt him to apologise and offer to carry your bags. Parisian ghosts are constantly playing matchmaker. They thrive off the energy of love-making, licentious or sacred; they're not picky.

There are two Parises. One, anyone can visit and live in. To enter the other, hidden Paris requires a rite of passage akin to a magical blow to the head that knocks some sixth sense into you. No one ends up living in Hidden Paris by accident; it's more of a "Don't call us, we'll call you" situation.

Next to Notre Dame is Place Saint Michel with its famous fountain of the Archangel Michael, battling with the Dragon. Place Saint Michel is the best-known public square in the Latin Quarter. I ended up living directly on the square at #6, a building with a copper roof and a facade that has the appearance of golden sandstone.

Initially, finding the studio seemed like a lucky accident, but after moving in, I began to wonder if anything is an accident at all.

One day at work, I received a message from a total stranger in a forum for

German residents from other countries. His username was Mad Axe Murderer. Nice start. He told me that he noticed from my messages that I'd relocated to Paris and asked me if I could help him with a dilemma.

His real name was Francis. He was Irish and so far, seemed axe-free and quite safe. Francis told me that he owned a studio in Paris but was having difficulties with a business partner who was renting the flat out illegally and pocketing the money. He wanted to get in the flat but his shady partner was refusing to return calls and had changed the locks on the door. According to Mad Axe Murderer, the business partner's name was Monsieur Roux (his real name), he was a seventy-something, retired professor of philosophy. Francis told me that Monsieur Roux preferred to rent the studio to pretty, young ladies. He asked me to contact Monsieur Roux and ask him if the studio was available. While the story was getting stickier by the minute, Francis seemed genuinely distressed and in need of help.

As promised, I contacted Monsieur Roux but he didn't immediately agree to an appointment. Instead, he wrote back and requested to know my height and weight. This was very strange and in a moment of paranoid regret, I told a friend, "What if this 'Mad Axe Murderer' is some kind of serial killer and his accomplice wants to know my height and weight because he's building a wooden box to lock me in?! What was I thinking? There's no way I'm going through with this!" I wrote to Francis and expressed my regrets that, contrary to what I had promised, I simply couldn't help him. He called me immediately and sounded crestfallen. "I've arranged to come to Paris so that I can be there when he shows you the apartment. Then I can burst in and get my keys back. I've already booked travel. Please help." This was one of those moments when your intuition and conscience tug at you. A small voice inside said, "As crazy as his story sounds, you gave your word, and you need to keep it." I reluctantly agreed to help but wished there was another way to do it.

I called Monsieur Roux and told him my weight and height. He informed me that it was important for him not to "waste time with big girls because they won't feel comfortable in such a small place." Only in France.

Place Saint Michel is always lit by the light of surrounding cafés, shops, and a few streetlamps. I had agreed to meet with Mr. Roux in front of the apartment door and had planned to meet Francis in front of the fountain on the square, to briefly liaise beforehand because we had never met, and he wanted to be sure that I was in the building before entering himself. I arrived in the early evening and stood in the crisp, February air, watching people. The dusky light of evening mixed with the artificial lamplight. I watched the undulating movement of the passing crowd, unsure how to identify Francis. I needn't have worried.

I spotted a pale man. He was coatless. Wearing only jeans and a sweat-drenched, white t-shirt that was pulled up on one side, exposing his round belly. He darted through the crowd with an odd sort of sideways gait, his glasses askew, his eyes darting to-and-fro, looking for someone. Instead of walking up to me directly, he walked beside me, leaned sideways a bit, and spoke out of the corner of his mouth, "Are you Dana?" I replied, "Francis?" He had a bloody scratch down his forehead and another on his cheek. "Follow me," he said. It was like being in a Mr. Bean spy adventure.

As we walked across the square, Francis gave me an update of the situation. "I've already been in the apartment. I waited until the kitchen light came on. I knew he was there, so I knocked on the door. When he opened it, he saw me, screamed, and tried to slam the door, so I blocked it with my foot. I pushed my way in, and we struggled because I was trying to get the keys from him. He scratched me up pretty bad, we fell on the bed, and my elbow caught him in the eye. I would never hit an old man, but I'm sorry to say that Monsieur Roux has quite a shiner. I've got the keys but just to warn you, he's still in the building, and he's on the phone with the police."

I almost walked away but felt compelled to follow Francis into the building. Sure enough, as we entered, there was Monsieur Roux. His nose was a bulbous ball of red caused by too much alcohol, his swollen eye was indeed bruised to a deep blue, and his hair was dyed to match his name (*roux* is another word for red in French), it was the brightest, most unnatural red I'd ever seen on anyone's head. He slobbered and cried in unintelligible French as he spoke with the police over his phone. As we walked by, neither man acknowledged the other. I felt for him as we passed. He needed a hug. So did Francis, his hands were shaking. The whole scene was surreal, and yet I felt compelled to see this through.

There was no elevator in the building, and the studio was on the seventh and last floor. When we made it to the top, Francis turned down a dark corridor. I followed him to the end. In France, the top floors of old buildings were used to house servants. They're called '*chambre de bonne.*' In the second half of the twentieth century, most of these living quarters were converted into studios.

Francis opened the door, and we entered. The place was fully furnished. The main room had a bed, a built-in desk, and custom-made bookshelves built into the walls that ran from floor to ceiling (eight feet high) and wrapped around the room. Adjacent to the main room was a small hall, a bathroom, a closet with a washer and dryer, and at the end, a small kitchen of about four square meters. The window in the kitchen overlooked Place Saint Michel. For such a small studio, the space was laid out perfectly. Francis showed me around the studio. I kept returning to the main room because the bookshelves held hundreds of books, all in English. I started scanning the shelves. There were books on philosophy, history, spirituality, mysticism, and alchemy. It was remarkable.

Noticing my amazement and interest in the books, Francis said, "They belong to Monsieur Roux. I let him store some of his surplus books here. He's a retired professor of philosophy. He worked in the States for a while. That's why they're all in English. I estimate there are between 600–800 books crammed in this place. If you look, they're in double rows."

I was in awe.

We spoke for a few minutes, and then Francis asked me, "Do you, by chance, know anyone looking for an apartment?" A light went on in my head. I had been so preoccupied with work and my personal life, that I hadn't even noticed the connection when, just a few days prior to meeting with Francis, my roommate with whom I lived in the 16th arrondissement told me that his mother would be moving in with him in four months and would need my bedroom. Since I had plenty of time and was going to look for something close to my office, it had slipped my mind until Francis asked me that question. I told him that I would need a place in a few months and could be interested. I kept glancing at the books like a kid in a candy store. "I'd like to get someone in here as soon as possible because I don't trust that old toad downstairs. He might have other keys made and try to put someone in here. Could you move in sooner?"

Everything worked out perfectly. The police sided with Francis, and ultimately the two men worked out their differences. Mr. Roux said that he had no place for the books, so they remained in the studio. I was elated and moved in a few weeks later. Moving into number 6, Place Saint Michel was like entering another dimension. It felt like I'd entered some in-between realm in time-space, a place between worlds, a magical inner library. Not long after moving in, I found myself without work. Instead of trying to find a job, I chose to live off my savings for a while and immerse myself fully in the books, meditation, and a hidden Paris that was starting to bleed through everyday reality.

The selection of books was extraordinary. There was something from, or about, every major philosopher in history, and a few more obscure philosophers as well. There were Egyptian funerary texts, *The Tibetan Book of the Dead*, books about Zen Buddhism, Taoism, grimoires, books on alchemy, tantra, runes, the esoteric, poetry, Gnosticism, Celtic lore, Druidism, Nordic myth, sociology, shamanism, the Trivium, physics, rhetoric, history, geopolitics, mysticism, American transcendentalism, Hermetics, and classics from the 18th to the 20th century. I read over three hundred of them in my time at Place Saint Michel. The universe had somehow conspired to bring a Frenchman and his books together with an Irishman and his flat, who then found an American, with a striving soul.

The apartment had no phone line, therefore no internet. If I wanted to get online, I had to go down to a café with free WiFi. What's a voracious reader going to do with no job, no internet, and her own personally curated library? Read. Constantly.

I began to meditate and seemed to have beginner's luck. Meditation came rather easy, especially once I worked out the best time of day and position. The more I absorbed from the books, and the more I meditated, my dreams began to change. As previously mentioned, I'd been lucid dreaming since early childhood but now I found that I could 'travel' and evoke individuals and places in dreams. Soon, people and places started coming to me in dreams, without any conscious intention on my part. My dreams turned instructive. I spent my nights partially unconscious in a deep sleep and partially conscious in lucid-dream constructs. There was a whole other world within. An Otherworld populated with people and lands that have a life of their own, *seemingly* wholly independent from the dreamer. Sometimes the dream landscapes were as solidly real as waking reality, literally solid, not ethereal dream wisps.

I meditated for two hours every day. Sometimes it would take an hour or so before I would enter a silent void. Thoughts were still streaming in the background but they were of no consequence, like background noise at a café when you're immersed in a book. You tune it out. My daily waking experience changed as well. It was as if a universal clock that had been a few seconds off my whole life finally synched up. Everything *just worked*, nothing required effort. If I had a thought about something I needed, it would show up. Sometimes things showed up before I needed them.

Everyone was friendly. The universe was a perfectly timed play. I sometimes slipped out of time. I walked everywhere, and there were times when I knew I had been walking at least thirty minutes from one part of the city to another and yet it felt like no time at all. Life slowed down, and yet I could walk thirty minutes, and it would feel like sixty-seconds. Often, I would know when my phone was about to ring and who would be calling. I'd dream about someone telling me some news, and the next day that person would write or call and say the same thing they told me in the dream. Sometimes, when on the telephone with someone, I could perceive what they were wearing, how they were physically feeling, and sometimes perceive things that they were thinking but didn't say. On one occasion, while visiting a friend, he said something that shocked me. I replied, and he went very still and then said, "I didn't say that. I *thought* it. How could you hear what I just thought?!"

This kind of thing might be easy to ridicule, and the world is indeed full of charlatans that pretend to be 'psychic' and who take advantage of the gullible. I'm definitely *not* a psychic and have no desire to be. So, what was really going on? The faculties of expanded perception have a name, Hindus and Buddhists call them the *Lower Siddhis*. Eastern Masters and monks have always insisted that *Lower Siddhis* are a by-product of contemplative practice like meditation. They warn that the *Lower Siddhis* are not to be strived for or even desired. Both Eastern and Western masters have stressed that so-called psychic sensation is no more advanced or desirable than a normal sensation.

The *Siddhis*, both lower and greater, can be an instrument of Maya (illusion) and are said to cause the downfall of those who seek them. Blake also stressed that intuition and psychic sensation are actually fallen modes of perception. The aspirant is working towards *spiritual* sensation, like *Tharmas and Urthona,* in their transcendent states. The siddhis are a distraction, and I eventually switched mine off (as much as I could) through the use of will. Some stopped on their own when I stopped meditating every day and got back to 'normal' life. The greatest siddhi (power) of all is to *become* love, to *become* wisdom, and to *become a fully causal*, creative, consciousness.

Neurological studies have proven that meditation changes the structure of the physical brain. What we can't measure directly is how meditation changes the *holographic* brain. In her book, *Stroke of Insight,* Harvard trained neuroanatomist Dr. Jill Bolte-Taylor describes what happened when, at age thirty-seven, she had a massive stroke in the left hemisphere of her brain. She describes what it was like to have her left brain chatter stripped away. She experienced the world as an interconnected sea of energy. She experienced expansiveness and knew herself to be the life-force power of the universe; All was One.

The brain is a receiver. When meditation changes the brain, we receive (perceive), not only more, but *differently*. We shouldn't, however, try to understand reality through the narrow lens of the hemispheric view of the brain. The Far Eastern traditions have a lot to teach us about the universe as perceived through just one side of this binary lens, in which the irrational is considered liberation, and the rational is considered an undesirable limitation. Reading Bolte-Taylor's book is like reading a Buddhist description of the universe and Nirvana. Believing this to be the ultimate goal is the Eastern blindspot. Rational materialism is the modern Western blind spot, what some consider a fully 'left-brain' construct. But we did, and do, have a tradition in the West that is just as deeply spiritual as that of the East.

During my time at Place Saint Michel, living above the fountain in which the Archangel Michael battles the dragon, I was not just meditating, I was also using my faculties of reason and analysis to study. Both hemispheres were active and changing. I believe that there are a few reasons why the outer landscape I moved through (Paris, in this case) seemed to sync up. One reason is that meditation was causing my *physical* brain hemispheres to synchronise. I suspect that the reason I developed *Lower Siddhis* was because my *holographic* brain was also syncing. It was like coming online with the universe. This balance of rational and irrational opened a portal in the soul. The outer world is a dream. It corresponds to your state of mind. You're *meant to find meaning* in it, that's what all dreams are for! Synchronicity is a sign that you are finding and creating a *meaningful dream*.

Goddard's insistence that the world we perceive is a projection of our own making but that this projection mingles with a shared, consensus reality. This consensus reality, because it's holographic and responsive to consciousness, has a measure of plasticity, just like the human brain. Synchronicity validates that idea. If we carry on through life without ever awakening to this power, the world within us is dead and without vision (Blake's dead realm called *Ulro*). To transcend the fragmented state, East must meet West in a marriage of the irrational and the rational. Even then, the story isn't finished. What of North and South? We'll explore this in a few chapters. It was during this time in my life that I understood that, as powerful as the present moment is, there is much more going on in the human story than temporal confusion or the yin/yang dichotomy.

The altered, holistic state that I experienced became my normal way of being while living among Monsieur Roux's books. I felt like I was on another frequency. I could talk to regular people living their lives as they regularly do, but I noticed that the presence that flowed through me (I was just a vessel) often affected them. I spent a lot of time alone, but when I occasionally met with a friend, she or he would show up in a whirlwind of thought, chatter like a bird for the first few minutes, and then suddenly calm down. Their whole appearance would shift as they became more present and relaxed.

One morning, after months of daily meditation, I sat on my bed, closed my eyes, and focused on the bones in my face. As I put all my attention on the structure of my face, breathing became deeper and slower, and the bones in my face began to feel heavy. They grew heavier and heavier until it felt like they were made of the heaviest substance. Eventually, the weight grew so much that I felt a *swoosh*, like oil separating from water. I was no longer aware of having a body at all. I wasn't in the void, because the void still feels like a place, albeit empty. This was pure no-thingness and no-place. There was no 'I' and therefore no questions or concerns about a 'where.' I'm not sure that I can call it an experience because to have an experience, you need an *I*. This was pure being, and the state lasted for an indeterminate time. There must have been an *I* to bear witness to the 'no-thingness,' perhaps it just stepped into the background for a while.

At some point, the *I* arose again. I became aware of having an *I*, and so I asked myself, "What is this?" The moment I asked that question, I opened my eyes and returned to normal consciousness. I now understood that images are all we ever know as humans. Our five senses create imprints. We *think* in images, everything we *see* is an image, and our dreams are images. But there's another realm, an existence devoid of any image, and that's the ground of our Being. I don't know how long I stayed in the flat after that. I was blissful. When I eventually went outside, I walked around in this state and noticed, for the first time, that everything moves in a pattern. Even millions of people who seem to move in random patterns through the city are moving in ways that create curvature and, in addition to that, some kind of pulse. We don't notice these patterns in our normal state of awareness.

Everything was alive, even the stone of buildings and bridges. Nothing was separate or even independent. There was something like a Great Hand moving the universe and everything in it. Nothing had a life of its own. All life belonged to the will of that Great Hand, and this Will was Love. I couldn't separate the two, Will and Love. There was no way of differentiating them. A universal Will was *breathing me*, I wasn't breathing for myself but when I consciously focused on my breath, that will was my will, and that Love was both my form and life force.

Everything seemed clear. It was so obvious now. There was only one Being and one mind that was doing all of this. Nothing was random. This doesn't mean that everything has a highly relevant meaning, some of it *just is*. The meaning is *in* the existence *as* existence. Everything that I saw was a crude copy of something that existed in a higher realm as part of a higher-order of organisation and structure. I understood why the Buddha laughs. Who would have thought that a sweet man called Mad Axe Murderer and a lonely, curious, perhaps alcoholic Frenchman would be the signposts that the Universe put in place to lead me to this moment?

Judge not lest ye be judged.

Enlightenment is an ancient human concept that some 20th-century players, fatigued by the grinding machinations of the Industrial Age, plucked from the sacred, mystic waters of Contemplative Life and paraded around as the latest shiny thing to attain, a last feather in Ego's hat.

The mode of perception and quality of awareness that the world refers to as "enlightenment" is a realisation. It's an ongoing process of integration of superconscious awareness and states of transcendent being into the experience of the relative self. Who is the enlightened one? The Absolute, True Self requires no enlightenment, it transcends all knowledge and exists as pure awareness. When we speak of someone being enlightened, we're referring to the transient, relative self of an individual. There's an attempt to label their internal experience, awareness, and state of being with something that we can categorise. Enlightenment is most often spoken of as if it's an end state, the final result, the ultimate aim, and the highest attainment. It's none of those things. It's simply a first realisation of many successive realisations and personal revelations. In other words, it's a process. The first glimpse of timelessness and connectedness is just the beginning of a process that demands humility, surrender, practice, and *a willingness to go dark*. Darkness isn't something normally associated with enlightenment, perhaps that's part of the problem.

Towards the end of my time living in the tiny studio, I went for two months without seeing anyone I knew. I could have gone longer, I enjoyed the anonymity and the feeling of being an invisible observer of the world, and I never felt alone.

After seven months at Place Saint Michel, I arranged to meet with a friend from the Congo who I hadn't seen since before I moved to the Latin Quarter. We arranged to meet in Le Marais, an area on the other side of Notre Dame full of shops, restaurants, and cafés. He and his partner were waiting for me outside of the restaurant. As I approached, he looked right at me without recognising me. I paused, looked at him, and his eyes widened in recognition as he said, "*What* happened to you?!" Before I could respond, he said, "You look so peaceful," his eyes still wide. I was deeply peaceful, but it wouldn't last. I hadn't learned to stabilise this state or insights that arose from it. This was just a pause, an embrace, and a period of rest and recovery before an intense inner work began.

I lived among Mr. Roux's magical library almost one year before returning to Germany for a while. Damn Germany, I loved it but it was a place of work for my soul. Not long before leaving, I had a dream, in the dream, a gentle presence spoke and said, "Why are you withholding your love?" I felt full of love, so the suggestion that I may be withholding love confused me. I didn't understand what the question meant, but I was about to find out.

Chapter 12
THE QUEST FOR LOVE

Imagine that you're a cosmic anthropologist from another realm who's arrived on earth to study the human race. You're able to study humans from the inside out. You can experience all of their memories, feelings, and thoughts. How would you study human love? Would you start with infants and monitor them as they grow? Or would you begin with the elderly and work backwards through their experiences? How would you define and measure human love? Where would you say it originates? How does it impact human life? What *is* it, exactly? Feeling? Emotion? Action? Behaviour? All of the above?

The word *love* can be ambiguous. To examine love from an ontological perspective means to enquire into the nature and reality of love. Is love just a subjective phenomenon, or something else? In The Four Zoas, when Luvah, the Zoa of Love falls, the *definition of love* falls as well! It fragments and loses its true meaning. We see this fall and division of meaning in the language that the ancients used to describe love and in our conditional approach to love today. The ancient's concept of love was very different from that of our modern society. The pre-Socratic view of love was one of a universal, undeviating principle. Love was the uniting force that held the four elements together. In the beginning, all was contained within a love-filled sphere. During the Platonic period, love was not something aimed at another person, love was a *spiritual anchor* within the individual. It anchors one to eternity and its qualities: truth, beauty, and goodness.

The Greeks used six different words to describe human love: Eros, Philia, Pragma, Philautia, Storge, and Agape. Philautia is the love of self. It can be helpful if it causes us to strive towards higher principles and harmful when it leads to seeking self-gain. Pragma is the love that endures, such as in a marriage or friendship that lasts a lifetime. Storge is the love between a parent and a child. Eros is the desire for something that we don't yet possess. This desire is not evil, quite the contrary. Eros is an intermediary between gods and men. Desire makes us *strive*.

Socrates said that because Eros makes us strive for beauty and goodness, it leads to a longing for immortality. Eros is the first phase of the journey back to eternity. The interesting thing about Eros is that it acts as a catalyst that forces us to confront our shadow. This is what makes romantic relationships so challenging. They force us to confront ourselves.

Philia is the mutually beneficial love between friends. These friends could be anyone—a lover, parent, child, sibling, neighbour, and even a stranger. Speaking of Philia, Aristotle said that the only reason to end a friendship is when you can't do anything to contribute to the goodness of another. This means that we don't end friendships because the other doesn't do good for us, but because it is absolutely impossible to do good for the other. That's something to ponder. Is it ever truly impossible to contribute to the goodness of another? Someone once asked me what friendship means to me. Even though I hadn't really thought about it until that moment, the answer came automatically. I answered, **"True friendship is witnessing the *becoming* of another, without judgment."**

By "without judgment," I mean without condemnation, not without discernment. Blake said that friendship requires constant, repeated forgiveness. I believe that love means realising that there was never anything to forgive in the first place. How could there be? Sometimes, we step back from a person's immediate sphere because they've fallen into a state that makes being intimate with them a very draining experience. But be aware; there are times in which we feel the impulse to step back from someone because they force us to confront our own shadow. Perhaps this is why Blake said, "Opposition is true friendship."

Whether you step back or remain in regular contact with someone, you are always intimately connected to them. You can still contribute to their good, by imagining the best *for* and *of* them, and by having faith in your vision of their well-being. People suffer, distort, and fall. True friendship means loving each other through those states, even if we choose to step away, or end contact, we don't condemn. We love them from a distance because we recognise that fundamentally, it's *our* human condition, not theirs, that requires us to step back. Truly it is, and that's okay.

Agapé is unconditional love. It's the only human love that even comes close to Divine Love. One could go so far to say that, if love isn't unconditional, it isn't love at all, it's a weak imitation of it.

Love played an important role in Blake's myth of fall and redemption. His cosmology has four realms: Great Eternity, Beulah, Ulro, and Generation. Ulro is the fallen world of experience in which we pass through the "Furnaces of Affliction." Beulah is a resting place, a place that one can enter to recuperate from the trials of life. Generation is the second fallen level and the way out of Ulro. We enter Generation when we began the ascent up the spiral of awareness. Generation is like a ray of light that wakes us up from the deep sleep of Ulro. It's the way out of Golgotha, the tomb of our skulls.

Within time (within Beulah, Generation, and Ulro), love is a unifying force. But for those who enter Generation and Beulah, love becomes a state of being. The more consistently one remains in this state, the closer one is to Great Eternity. Love is a *state of being*, not a feeling, emotion, or good works. Our ideas of familial, romantic, and brotherly (friendship) love are faint adumbrations of Love's true body.

William Blake said that if a thing loves, it is infinite, but for Blake, the love of Nature was the cause of the fall of Man. I disagree with this causal sequence. The two faces of Nature, her beauty and her violent predation, seem to me to be the *result* of fallen consciousness, not the cause of it. Nevertheless, it could go both ways, and like most things, it probably does. Blake wrote, "Nature teaches nothing about Spirituality but only Natural Life." He criticised the Druids for getting lost in, and worshipping the natural world. Blake personified Nature as the female emanation of the Zoa, Luvah.

For Meister Eckhart, God was (is) separated from Nature and from all symbols. No symbol could ever represent the unknowable God. Blake's view was that everything in the fallen world of Ulro is a symbol of something else. Ulro is a dream state. All states have corresponding spaces, or realms. Therefore, Ulro is a dream *realm* as well.

In 1914, Pierre Berger elucidated the Blakean view in his book *William Blake, Poet and Mystic*:

> Familiar symbols will help us to understand Blake's conception of the visible world. We have only to apply the same procedure to every case. The world of matter has no existence of its own: it is only a symbol of the invisible universe, something shown to us in order that, through it, we may gain knowledge of what we cannot see.

> The earth, the sky, the sun, are all symbols, each at once a portion and a visible representation, as elusive as a mirage, of some eternal spirit. Trees, animals, nay more, even men, are only symbols. History is a symbol: revolutions are symbols of some great change actually taking place in the invisible world.

> The American Revolution, for instance, merely symbolised the revolt of the angels of liberty against the powers of tyranny in the eternal universe. America itself is only symbol, standing for the part of the human spirit not yet subjugated and bound down by tyrannical laws. Blake is a symbol, a mere transitory form of the prophetic spirit: his wife is a symbol for the internal joy felt by that spirit, and for its softer emotions.

> And so we pass through this little life of ours, unknowing, unsuspecting that we are but reflection, metaphors in action, symbols and representations of eternal beings, who dwell outside of time and space, and whose life is the only real existence.

Beulah is a *threshold* state. Blake says of this state of being:

> In this country the sun shineth night and day; wherefore this was beyond the Valley of the Shadow of Death, and also out of the reach of Giant Despair, neither could they from this place so much as see Doubting Castle. Here they were within sight of the city they were going to, also here met them some of the inhabitants thereof; for in this land the Shining Ones commonly walked, because it was upon the borders of heaven.

Beulah is a place of rest and repose where the "contraries are equally true." Gender exists in Beulah and it's understood that these contraries are equally true and divine, two sides of the same coin. Beulah is the state in which one is "within sight of the city." This city is Eternity. In this state, we can interact with some of the inhabitants of the land of Eternity, Blake's "Shining Ones." The state of Beulah borders heaven. Remember, heaven isn't a place we go, it's something we become.

During my time at Place Saint Michel, I was in Beulah. Beulah is an evanescent state. The metaphoric sun did indeed shine day and night. All I knew was rest, peace, and love. I could sense a small thread of eternity, not as another place but as a state—the state of timelessness. It's easy to love in Beulah. It's not so easy in Ulro, and that's the point. It's common to oscillate between Beulah (which is called relative Bodhicitta in the Buddhist tradition) and Generation. Beulah is not Eternity, and Blake warns that remaining in Beulah can lead to pity.

The Absolute and the relative need each other. We pass through Beulah to get to Eternity, but we also pass through Beulah to re-enter the everyday life of Generation and Ulro. Beulah is not a state in which some ultimate truth is revealed. In Beulah, our subconscious distortion can blur the lines between what is ultimately real and what is an unconscious projection. In Beulah, we get a bit of both, so it's important not to take our transcendent experiences literally. We also shouldn't ignore them. It's about striking just the right balance and learning to use our insight gained from transcendent states of awareness as a tool for self-learning and discovery.

If we mistake Beulah for absolute reality, we confuse the *part* for the whole. In other words, we're still experiencing and perceiving in a fragmented way. You may be wondering, what do Eternity, Beulah Generation, and Ulro have to do with love? We're getting there, stick with me…

At the beginning of chapter 3, I said that I'd like to take you on a journey in which we travel together through streams of thought, layers of self, and realms of imagination. Let's do that now.

Blake said that to those who dwell in immortality, he appeared as one sleeping on a couch of gold. How did he get that way?

Imagine that you're standing at a precipice, a large window of a mountainside castle. You're an androgynous, non-materialised being who desires to fully understand and embody Absolute Love and Wisdom. You're prepared to give up spiritual innocence in order to bring individuated consciousness into a dark world of duality and linear time, and allow the dark world to teach you more about the nature of the ultimate reality, which is God. You know that the way up, is down, and the way out, is in. You also know that once you fall, there's no escape until you transcend the illusion. But you're willing to do it, your brave…it takes courage to be a human being.

As Blake said, without contraries, there is no progression. Individuation requires *differentiation* as we chart polarities in duality. It's a reconciliation of the many levels of the transient self with the Absolute Self. When I experienced seeing my self in another's eyes, I didn't cease to have a self, I was in two places at once, both unified and individual. This is what that ultimate reconciliation is like when the small self merges with the Big Self.

Reflecting on that, and on the journey you're about to take, you look outwards to the limit of Eternity, where you observe many people in a deep sleep. They appear to be fast asleep on couches. You see that Thel, Clod of Clay, and a myriad of other characters are going about life. Extending your sight, you're able to see the mid-realms known as Beulah and Generation. Peering even farther, you see darkness, the dark realm of Ulro in which all vision is lost. Here you see not androgynous beings, but men and women, going about their lives like automatons with no awareness of the existence of Beulah or Eternity, like ghosts in a machine.

You turn now, your heels at the edge of the threshold, your back to the open air. Extending your arms and surrendering, you fall backwards but not *all* of you falls. You fall *backwards* which signifies forgetfulness; the part of you that is 'fallen' must forget. Otherwise, the journey isn't much of an adventure. A part of you remains eternal and out of the stream of time; the Daimon.

You fall first to the edges of Eternity. It's a place of peace, serenity, and beauty at the border of Beulah. You meet Thel, the eternal virgin who, like many others, refuses to incarnate. Thel points your attention to a meadow full of couches. On these couches are sleeping royals, all wearing crowns. You're watching them and wondering what they're dreaming about, when from behind comes a voice, "They're dreaming of men and women in the realms of Generation and Ulro."

Turning, you come face-to-face with a beautiful female.

Recognising your curiosity, she introduces herself, "I am one of the daughters of Beulah, come to sit with and sing to the royals who sleep. I travel beside them in their dreams, creating spaces in which to shield them, and balms to heal them, lest they dream themselves to death."

Thel then leads you to a temple where you meet with a High Priestess who, you are told, is responsible for the spatial aspect of a fallen world. She's also a poet, weaver, and mystic, and represents receptive imagination. She's wife to Urthona, the Zoa of Imagination. You learn that it's she who weaves the garments of flesh, and she who assigns gender to the inhabitants of Generation and Ulro. Blake calls her Enitharmon. Enitharmon tells you that you can turn back if you choose. The offer is tempting, but you choose instead to continue your journey.

Thel leaves, and you journey on alone. You walk eastward. After a while, you enter a forest of dense oaks from which orchids hang. Maples radiate with the promise of sweetness, pines exalt your senses with their perfume, and magnolias cool the air with their low, broad canopies. The forest is alive. You feel its heartbeat pulsing in the beat of a bird's wings, the frog's croak, and the bubbling streams of clear water. You're wandering through nature's skirts, mesmerised by the feel of her green petticoats against your skin.

Suddenly, as if out of nowhere, a being appears. His appearance startles you. He's elegantly beautiful and very tall, with deep auburn hair, and eyes the colour of tiger stone. "I have a gift for you. Before you go any deeper into this forest, sit and speak with me for a while."

You sit across from the strange being, this messenger who seems so familiar. Have you met before? He radiates love, and you wonder if this isn't some old friend in disguise.

He holds out a wooden box, "Take it."

You accept the gift but are reluctant to open the box. "What is it?" you ask.

The stranger smiles and says, "It's a very special instrument."

Opening the box, you find a beautiful orb of undulating light. It has a measure of solidity to it. As you pick it up, it reacts to you. It radiates joy. In curious amazement you turn it over in your hands, unable to take your eyes off it.

"What kind of instrument?" you ask.

"It's a human heart," says the stranger.

"What do I do with it?"

"Hold it up and look through it," he instructs.

Holding the instrument slightly above your head, you peer into it, and are amazed by what you see. It's like looking through a looking glass; you catch a glimpse of someone standing at a threshold. A sense of melancholic longing makes you want to turn away, and so you quickly shift your attention to the forest. The forest that seemed so solidly real looks very different when seen through your new instrument; it now appears as a veil—a shimmering, transparent veil of beauty.

"You'll need this if you choose to go any deeper into the wood," says your new friend. You're still not quite sure what this instrument is for. Noticing your perplexed expression, the man says, "Press the heart into your chest." You obey.

Everything shifts instantaneously. You're filled with joy and remembrance. All is connected. The universe is enlivened and nourished by a stream that flows out of eternity. You know that if you turned around and left the forest, you could pass through Eternity's gates, and return home.

Tearing your eyes away from the radiant prize in your hands, you look into the stranger's face and ask, "You say that I will need this instrument if I choose to go deeper into the forest. What do you mean?"

"I mean," he says, "that if you were to lose your way, the heart could be your compass…*if* you know how to use it…which you won't."

"Then tell me how!"

"That I can't tell you. I can only tell you that, in the dark lands, having a heart is like waking up in the wilderness with a survival pack that you don't know how to open." His statement is enigmatic because you don't know what a wilderness or a survival pack is. You look at him skeptically and ask, "If I don't know how to use this instrument, what good is it to me?"

"You'll learn if you try."

"Why don't you just tell me how to use this heart thing?"

"I can't tell you because I don't know. Every heart is unique to its owner. Only the owner can learn to use his particular heart. But I warn you. A heart in Beulah is like a child at play. In Beulah, the heart is always open and radiant. In the dark realm, it becomes more mysterious. In the beautiful land of Beulah, it radiates like all things here, but its power is limited. In the dark realm, Ulro, the heart may grow dim. It may go dark, and may close altogether. But it may also be opened, and if it is, its power grows beyond any power found in Beulah. The maker of every heart is provided with a spark of wisdom and power to place within the heart. The spark may stay dormant, or it may light a fire. If it lights a fire, the heart becomes an open gateway. Just remember, your heart is not only here,"—he points to your chest, "A heart is also a vast window at a precipice, on the side of a majestic mountain, through which those in Eternity can look down into the lands below. For those within the fallen realms, it appears as a star in their sky."

He pauses for a moment, considers, and then says, "You must understand that in Ulro, those who own hearts often misuse and misunderstand them. They believe their hearts can be broken, they believe the heart makes them vulnerable. In truth, all hearts are indestructible. They can be closed, ignored, shrunken, and darkened but no heart can be totally destroyed. Only the one who crafted it could destroy it. The one I'm giving to you was made by a very talented designer."

"By you?"

"No, never by me, I'm just a messenger. There are other Watchers, but The Watcher at the Window only ever peers through the window that he himself has designed."

The stranger rises to his feet and turns to leave. "Keep it close," he says before disappearing among the green vines.

What beautiful instrument. What a strange conversation. You sit on the knoll a while longer, intoxicated by the scent of nature. Finally, unable or unwilling to leave, you venture deeper into the wood, finally reaching the centre of the forest. At the centre of nature resides a woman, a priestess more alluring than Enitharmon. Her name is Vala. She first appears as a tree, a massive, mysterious tree at the centre of Nature, which is her own body. She then appears as a woman. What you don't yet know, is that while Vala is the epitome of beauty, she has two sides.

One side is the irresistible, golden-haired goddess standing in front of you, so beautiful that you're happy to forget all about Eternity. The other side is her Silver Twin, a predacious, treacherous, wild, and untameable goddess. She can heal and harm. She creates the poison and the antidote.

The more immersed you become in Nature, the drowsier you grow. Until overcome by her beauty, you fall into a deep sleep. While you sleep, a stream bubbles up from the ground and runs through you. The stream merges with you, extracting one of your two primordial essences, either male or female. According to which essence Vala extracts and possesses, Enitharmon weaves a garment for it. Like any non-lucid dream, you are unaware that you're dreaming. You've now entered another realm as either male or female. Welcome to fallen realms of Generation and Ulro. You remain asleep as the Daughters of Beulah carry your body back to the couches where, placing a crown on your head, they lay you down, to dream among the other sleeping royals of the realm.

Will you ever wake up?

William Blake was not 'enlightened' by today's standards; prophets don't need to be. To be frank, he had difficulty mastering unconditional love. He was a product of his time, occasionally sexist, egotistical, and financially irresponsible. He despised others like Newton and Swedenborg and had a tendency towards resentment and suspicion. But we don't expect our poets and prophets to be perfect; we expect them to inspire us, and make us see the world differently.

If anything, Blake's faults serve as a reminder that no one is without fault. We all get things wrong and bring our distortions into our work. We should forgive him, ourselves, and others for this faulty perception.

Blake's work was so symbolic and dreamlike (he describes dreams within dreams), that if we take it at face value, we miss the finer, esoteric threads. For Blake, the Divine Man is a protean, androgynous being, and the many individuated Eternals who make up that body are also androgynous. The Eternals can create emanations (forms) that can become physical male or female bodies.

Parallel to this use of gender, Blake also uses gender as a representation of energies and consciousness at work in all levels of the universe, even in Ulro. In this context, the consciousness that imagines and projects is 'male' and the consciousness that receives, shapes, and manifests that imaginative vision is 'female.' Feminist critics lament that Blake is subordinating actual women to men because of his insistence that the female is subordinate to the male and has "no life of its own." Blake was indeed biased and influenced by the age he lived in, but in this case, he's not being sexist at all. All esoteric traditions describe the consciousness that *projects* as 'male' (physically projecting semen, spiritually projecting images) and the consciousness that receives and gives shape and life to images, 'female' (the physical and spiritual womb of life).

When Blake said that the "female has no life of its own," he's referring to another level of meaning—to the way consciousness creates. In this instance, he's not referring to the physical, human female because for Blake, the physical human being, both male and female, are both emanations. Blake's work is multi-dimensional and has enfolded meanings that express truth at different levels of perception. For instance, at the level of what he calls "Twofold Vision," he insists that life is a dream, and the men and women of Earth are but *symbols* of something else. What they're a symbol of varies according to the individual.

Blake says that the body is a portion of the soul as perceived by the five senses. Neville Goddard said the same thing, as did Michael Talbot (author of The Holographic Universe), who wrote that, "The body is the most solid section of the soul, not separate from it." The panendeist, Meister Eckhart, described all souls as 'female' in that they are receptive to God (what receives is always described as female). He wasn't suggesting that the soul is literally a female person. Mystics, philosophers, and poets constantly employ metaphor.

All metaphors are imperfect, they economise word usage but don't substitute it. Metaphors enrich conceptual understanding by making us aware of the intricacies of life. We must be cautious not to take them literally, which seems to be the tendency of those who see metaphor as purely substitutional. The character Jesus spoke in metaphor precisely because the authors of the gospels wanted to share the process of illumination without "throwing pearls before swine." In other words, they knew that literalists wouldn't understand their message. Literalists who are drawn to dogma and organised religion, are most often one-dimensional thinkers who think metaphor is mere substitution.

Which leads us to love…

Is human, conditional 'love' a kind of imperfect, lived metaphor for an incomprehensible truth we long for but never fully grasp while human?

Blake provides us with two images. One is the Human Image, which he equates with experience. The other is the Divine Image, which he equates with true innocence. Remember, he said that true innocence *requires* experience. Those, like Thel, who are unwilling to incarnate remain innocent, but it's an embryonic innocence, not *true* innocence.

The Human Image is described as one that creates poverty through pity. Instead of using imagination to envision the poor as prosperous and then having faith in that image through works that we do to lift up others, we just feel pity for them and do nothing. This human image, because it's inauthentic, is unfulfilled and unhappy, and due to this we have imperfect mercy for others who are in the same lot. In this human image, peace is the result of mutual fear. In other words, we create peace because we fear mutual destruction. This kind of peace is, in reality, a selfish impersonation of love. "I'll be nice to you if you're nice to me"—"I'll love you if you accept me"—"I'll love you if you love me"—"I won't blow up your country if you don't blow up mine."

The Divine Image is also one of pity, mercy, peace, and love. But the cause of these attributes is different. Blake says that the Divine Image is the *true human form*. Blake's Divine Image is the image of true innocence. We've entered the realm of experience, separation, and spectres, and passed through the furnaces of affliction. We forget who we really are. When we do come out on the other side, we've learned to truly love because we understand that we are one, protean body.

Henry David Thoreau wrote of our recovery of innocence in *Walden:*

> Through our own recovered innocence we discern the innocence of our neighbours. You may have known your neighbour yesterday for a thief, a drunkard, or a sensualist, and merely pitied or despised him, and despaired of the world; but the sun shines bright and warm this first spring morning, recreating the world, and you meet him at some serene work, and see how his exhausted and debauched veins expand with still joy and bless the new day, feel the spring influence with the innocence of infancy, and all his faults are forgotten. There is not only an atmosphere of good will about him, but even a savour of holiness groping for expression.

I once read about a judge who, upon facing a violent murderer in court, looked into the murderer's eyes and saw himself. He recognised himself in the other and knew himself to be capable of the same violence. Brushing his momentary lucidity aside, he sentenced the murderer to death by hanging. By ordering the man's death, the judge was also condemning himself, the part of himself that he didn't want to face.

The Divine Image is one of true mercy because we're **willing to face ourselves and see ourselves in others**. Mercy is the closest humans come to imitating divine grace. The Divine Image is one of *active* pity that works imaginatively and literally, to lift another out of their suffering. To do this, you refuse to see the other as someone who *needs* your pity, you recognise their strengths and potential, and remind them of their self-agency by *believing in them and making sure they know it. You don't do it for them. You help them do it for themselves because you respect the sacredness of each human, and acknowledge their divinity.* The Divine Image is one of mutual love that recognises the truth: we are all connected. **We are *in* each other *as* each other.** This is the ultimate peace. Divine Love has no opposite.

I am in you and you in me, mutual in divine love. —William Blake

Ludus Amoris

There are very few human beings who receive the truth, complete and staggering, by instant illumination. Most of them acquire it fragment by fragment, on a small scale, by successive developments, cellularly, like a laborious mosaic. —Anaïs Nin

"Why are you withholding your love?" The question was posed by some other part of my psyche in a dream. It stayed with me, lingering in my mind for months. I started to keep a more thorough journal of my dreams and the insights they provided during my time in Paris. Looking back, it's clear that I had been living in Blake's Generation all my life without realising it, even during a deep depression.

Alchemists used the Latin term *Magnum Opus* (The Great Work) to describe the process of creating the philosopher's stone. The objective of this work is to unify opposites and achieve mystical union. The Great Work is a quest for love, and God plays 'peek-a-boo' with the questing hero.

The game is called *Ludus Amoris*. In 1911 Evelyn Underhill wrote the following about Ludus Amoris:

> The mystics have a vivid metaphor by which to describe that alternation between the onset and the absence of the joyous transcendental consciousness which forms as it were the characteristic intermediate stage between the bitter struggles of pure Purgation and the peace and radiance of the Illuminative Life. They call it Ludus Amoris, the "Game of Love" which God plays with the desirous soul. It is the "game of chess," says St. Teresa, "in which game, Humility is the Queen without whom none can checkmate the Divine King." "Here," says Martensen, "God plays a blest game with the soul." The "Game of Love" is a reflection in consciousness of that state of struggle, oscillation and unrest which precedes the first unification of the self. It ceases when this has taken place and the new level of reality has been attained.

> Thus St. Catherine of Siena, that inspired psychologist, was told in ecstasy, "With the souls who have arrived at perfection, I play no more the Game of Love, which consists in leaving and returning again to the soul; though thou must understand that it is not, properly speaking, I, the immovable God, who thus elude them but rather the sentiment that my charity gives

them of me." In other terms, it is the imperfectly developed spiritual perception which becomes tired and fails, throwing the self back into the darkness and aridity whence it has emerged. Such prolonged coexistence of alternating pain and pleasure states in the developing soul, such delay in the attainment of equilibrium, is not infrequent.

So how was I withholding love? By trying to remain in Beulah, while ignoring the shadow. Love is no *artifact* of the light. Nor is it absent in the darkness. By focusing solely on the light, I remained unconscious of my distortion and how it shaped my choices, behaviour, and relationships. I wasn't withholding my love from the light, I was withholding it from the shadow. This darkness (that which we are unconscious of) is within each of us. As wonderful as my time in Beulah was, *becoming* requires that we integrate what we learn from higher states by bringing it back into daily life and allowing it to transform us. Experiencing transcendent states does not mean we are permanently enlightened.

After experiencing what I did during my ten months at Place Saint Michel, many people run off to Ashrams in India or monasteries. Some begin presenting themselves as enlightened and putting on a persona that supports that claim. Some become celibate because they say they can't find another enlightened person with whom to have a relationship. They can't find an enlightened person because they aren't enlightened themselves. **We attract what we are**.

Avoiding intimacy with the outside world by hiding in an ashram won't lead to enlightenment. Focusing on the light of enlightenment while avoiding the shadow will only prolong the work. The foundations *are* the work: Processing painful interpretations of experience, transforming personality, facing what lies in shadow, and transforming our relationship to every-thing and everyone is a long process. It doesn't happen instantaneously.

Suffering twists a person. While therapy saved my life and catalysed transformation, it was the early stage of a greater process. Suffering and survival had twisted me up into a tight knot that no amount of meditation could unravel. Meditation certainly loosened the knot, but unraveling it is an act of will. It requires a willingness to face the dragon, a confrontation that requires a very special instrument, and no small measure of grace.

The Heart is an Instrument

Do you remember that instrument that your mysterious friend gave you? What is it? Something to pump blood? The seat of all emotion? Something with which to feel? Remember, feeling plays out in the theatre of the mind. When you read that statement in chapter seven, did you think of the brain?

I learned about the heart and its manifold purpose from a dream. When you advance in lucid dreaming, you'll find that you can shift into visionary states from within a dream. If you take hold of the dream, as so many lucid dreamers do, it becomes a kind of self-directed movie. Things will appear from the subconscious. Because you're lucid and aware that you're dreaming, you take conscious control of the dreamscape.

If, on the other hand, you realise that you're dreaming, but choose to go along with the dream, *some* of the dreams can shift into visionary experiences in which you can journey and learn a thing or two. It will always be personal to you and coloured by your psyche. *Look for the metaphorical meanings enfolded within your dreams and use lucid dreaming as a means of radical self-inquiry and evolution.* These visions are *soul visions*, but they don't occur in a vacuum. The inner realms are interconnected and interdependent. You'll feel things, know things, and remember things that you wouldn't in normal, waking consciousness.

Here is the dream that, instead of taking control of, I allowed to play out. It reminded me of what the holographic heart is:

I awoke within a dream standing on a grassy hill. I looked down at my body and saw that I was a tall woman in the clothing of a Knight. I knew a few things instantaneously: 1. I was a female Knight of an Order that was similar to the Japanese Samurai, but my garb and sword were Western. 2. I had just arrived on earth along with other comrades. We weren't together because we'd been assigned to different locations.

I unsheathed my sword to get a better look. It was a broad, double-edged Western sword. I re-sheathed it in its scabbard and stood still. Somehow, I felt worried that my heart could compromise my mission, so I drew an ornate dagger from my side, cut open my chest, and removed my glowing heart. It wasn't a bloody affair. I thought I was being practical. I put my heart in my pocket for safekeeping.

The moment I pocketed my heart, I felt a powerful tug. Following the pull, I walked through the land until I reached a mountain. The pulling sensation guided me to a large door of stone in the base of the mountain. The dark stone door opened automatically. As I entered, a tall, male being was there to greet me. I can't remember now whether I got a good look at him or not. We went deep into the mountain until we reached a massive, circular hall. There, I could see very well; it was lit with some kind of light that wasn't electric and wasn't the light of the sun. Now I could see the beings very well. They were human-looking, very tall, with dark hair that was pulled back tightly. The females were as tall as the males, and they all had widow's peaks. On their backs they had wings that looked like dragonfly wings. The moment I saw them clearly, I knew that while I didn't belong to their kind, we were working together.

In the centre of the room was a dais with columns around it. The beings stood around the circumference of the room, each at their station. They each had a round, egg-shaped stone in their hands. Their stations were stone-carved podiums on top of which was some sort of crystal receptacle. The one who had met me, led me to the dais in the centre of the room. There was a much larger apparatus that looked like a command centre made entirely of crystal. I was also given a larger, egg-shaped stone and told to stand in front of what looked like a docking station in the centre of the dais. With everyone else encircling me, one of them said, "We're going to put our stones in our cylinders. When we do, we want you to put yours in this,"—he pointed to the crystal docking station that seemed to be the primary one because it was larger than the rest.

They simultaneous docked their stones, and a second later, I did the same, as commanded. Nothing happened. Then a female among them said, "You need to put your heart back in." Pulling my heart out of my pocket and reinserting it into my chest, we went through the process again. This time, when I placed my stone in the crystal cylinder, a vast window or screen (as large as an iMax theatre screen) appeared high up on the cavern wall. On this screen appeared the earth, all flattened out. I could see all of the land-masses. On the earth, many lights appeared with lines of light connecting each dot. "You see," said the female, "you have to keep your heart in because otherwise we can't observe humanity through you."

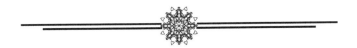

We associate the heart with love because the heart is a looking glass through which we glimpse eternity, the *State of Timeless*. Timelessness and love are inextricably bound to each other. The heart also connects us to each other, a much wider universe, and the intelligences found in it. The world is so much bigger than our surface story of nations and continents. The heart is not just a chakra, nor is it limited to the figurative concept of the spiritual heart through which one finally experiences divine love. The heart is a gateway through which the unifying force of love flows into this world and creates coherence.

For those in Eternity, the heart is a window through which they can observe us Time-Dwellers. Your Daimon stands in that window and observes his player in the game, *you*—the version of himself/herself in Ulro or Generation. Remember, the Daimon is androgynous, and only appears as female or male depending on your psychological and emotional needs. If you unshield and open your heart, he/she can communicate more clearly with you. Eternity is the state of timelessness through which love, as a unifying force, flows down into the realms of time: Beulah, Generation, and Ulro. The heart is the only instrument through which that force can enter the dense realms.

We are, as Blake poetically represents, living a dream within a dream. Waking up, we find ourselves in a stage play and realise, "Oh! The Absolute Self is playing all of these parts! How funny!" This is what Blake means when he says, "I am in you and you are in me, mutual in divine love."

Love has no anchor except in understanding. —Meister Eckhart

Intimacy teaches us about love because, through deep connection, we discover, often for the first time, how alike we really are but the **intimacy didn't** *create* **the love;** *it unveiled it*. Once we know it's there, why withhold it from the world?

We understand that the relative self of the other person is not who, or what, they really are. There's an innocence that remains at the core of every person. We can never know *why* a person is the way they are. We forgive the surface, love the core, and have compassion.

Remember Blake's quote:

> *Eternity exists, and all things in eternity, independent of creation, which was an act of mercy. By this, it may be seen that I do not consider either the Just or the Wicked to be in a Supreme State but to be every one of them, States of the Sleep which the Soul may fall into, in its deadly dreams of Good and Evil.*

The quest transforms the way we see others. For me, God is my favourite atheist, Ricky Gervais, and my favourite theologian, Meister Eckhart. He's definitely Bill Hicks. He's the president you like, and the one you don't. He's every assailant and every victim. He plays the role of the oppressor and the oppressed. God is the Jester and the King, the comedian and the heckler. He's Mother Theresa and at least one of the Kardashian sisters.

To refuse to see everyone as an embodiment of God is to withhold our love. Whether he be sleeping or waking, he's there in everyone. The ancient Egyptians didn't associate the brain with the mind, that association is recent. Egyptians saw the *heart* as the mind. It's the heart, not the brain that understands. **Love is where striving and allowing coalesce**.

By using our hearts to anchor us in eternity, we begin to feel more at home in this strange world. Fulfillment comes with a feeling of being home no matter where you are.

Home is in you.

'It's only the **Red** King snoring,' said Tweedledee. 'Come and look at him!' the brothers cried, and they each took one of Alice's hands, and led her up to where the King was sleeping.
'Isn't he a LOVELY sight?' said Tweedledum.

Alice couldn't say honestly that he was. He had a tall red night-cap on, with a tassel, and he was lying crumpled up into a sort of untidy heap, and snoring loud—'fit to snore his head off!' as Tweedledum remarked.

'I'm afraid he'll catch cold with lying on the damp grass,' said Alice, who was a very thoughtful little girl.

'He's dreaming now,' said Tweedledee, 'and what do you think he's dreaming about?'

Alice said, 'Nobody can guess that.'

'Why, about YOU!' Tweedledee exclaimed, clapping his hands triumphantly.' And if he left off dreaming about you, where do you suppose you'd be?'

'Where I am now, of course,' said Alice.

'Not you!' Tweedledee retorted contemptuously. 'You'd be nowhere. Why, you're only a sort of thing in his dream!'

'If that there King was to wake,' added Tweedledum, 'you'd go out—bang!—just like a candle!'

—Lewis Carroll, *Through the Looking Glass*

Chapter 13
WILL AND AGENCY

As children, the highlight of our year was a religious convention that the Watchtower Society referred to as the "district assembly." A district assembly is when four-to six-thousand proselytising evangelicals gather together to listen to lectures and eat sandwiches. I loved the opportunity to socialise with kids outside of our congregation, even if it meant being forced to sit for eight hours of Bible lectures over three consecutive days.

It would be an understatement to say that, when I was a girl, I loved the colour red. I more than loved it; I lived it. One day, in expectation of an upcoming district assembly, I begged our mother to sew a red dress with white trim for me to wear to the event. She agreed but my glee dimmed when she presented me with the finished dress. Mom's idea of red was burgundy. Seeing the disappointment on my face, she said, "Burgundy suits your skin tone better, sweetheart." I wanted fire-engine red like the colour of mom's lipstick, not a subdued burgundy. Exasperated and yet still happy to have a new dress, I threw my head back, put on my strongest southern drawl, and proclaimed, "Red is my signature colour!" Mom laughed until she cried and told me to stop being a ham.

The saying stuck, and so did my love for intense reds. Throughout my teens and even into my early twenties, I'd occasionally pull the "red is my signature colour" line (always with the strongest possible southern drawl) to make mom chuckle. When I finally earned a decent income, the first nice outfit I bought for myself was fire-engine red dress suit for work. And yet, something happened in my twenties, something that I didn't even notice. This something happens to a lot of people. The vibrant colours of our youthful beingness begin to fade. I became colourless, a sort of grey woman. It took a few years and required me to cross an ocean but a serendipitous meeting with a German man, almost sixty years my senior, would not only remind me of the colour I'd forgotten, but forced me to ask *why* I ever loved it in the first place.

Der Rote Mann

We should never forget that Germany was hijacked by the National Social-ists Party which had just over eight million members at its peak. Approxi-mately sixty-two million Germans were *not* members of Hitler's party. More than sixty-million innocent, German civilians suffered the horrors of a war they neither wanted, nor believed in.

Seventy-five percent of the Munich Old Town was destroyed during WWII. Other areas of the city were left in total ruin. The traumatised people of Munich awoke every morning to the sight of rubble as a constant reminder of the misery of war. The reconstruction efforts only brought more conflict. Architects, politicians, and citizens fought vehemently over two starkly different visions of what Munich should become, now that the war had ended. Germany was now an occupied nation. The allies took control of the education system, administration, court system, and military, effectively bulldozing the will of the people. Perhaps this is why Müncheners were so fierce in their resolve to decide for themselves how their city should look.

Everything-should-be-modernised activists wanted Munich to be a bold example of modern architecture, high-rises, and broad streets. The tradi-tionalists argued that a traumatised people needed to see their home city restored to what it had been. They believed that the Renaissance, Ro-manesque, and Gothic architectural aesthetic was not only pleasing to the eye, but a balm for the injured soul of the German people. In cities like Hannover, the modernists won, while in Munich, the champions of tradi-tion prevailed in the Munich Altstadt. Other areas of the city weren't so lucky. Neighbourhoods like Neuhausen and Schwabing were restored par-tially to what they had been but also allowed for the construction of new, modern buildings, commercial centres, and parking garages.

In addition to the emotional and psychological post-war fallout, there was also the practical issue of thousands of German refugees, all in dire need of shelter. This need for speed, combined with a massive growth boom in the 1950s (and then again in the 70s), resulted in the construction of some of the ugliest, utilitarian, modern architecture one could imagine. These buildings of concrete and metal are soulless offences to the eye and spirit of man, and thanks to WWII, they're scattered all over Europe, the scabs of war that we can't pick off.

We lived in one of these tall, grey boxes right next to Rotkreuzplatz in the Neuhausen area. Our apartment was on the eighth floor of a concrete high-rise that was punctured by boring, rectangular windows framed in metal. The ground floor consisted of an entry hall and two doctor's offices.

One morning, as I exited the elevator, I came face-to-face with an elderly man standing in front of one of the offices. He appeared to be in his mid-to-late 80s and stooped slightly as he held onto a walker with wheels. He was dressed in traditional Bavarian attire: green *Hosen* with suspenders, a red shirt and red socks that reached his knees. We smiled at each other and I said, "Guten Morgen." He looked at me with a mischievous grin and said, "What a wonderful way to start my day, greeted by a beautiful woman." Older men are the most accomplished flirts.

I laughed and asked him if he needed help getting down the ramp. He shot down that offer in no uncertain terms, but then offered to help me with my bags because, he said, "That's what gentlemen do." I told him that it wouldn't be necessary because my bags were empty. I was on my way to the market. He insisted that I hang my bags on the handle of his walker and offered to walk me to Rotkreuzplatz, as that was his destination as well.

As we walked very, very slowly out of the building, he told me that his name was Herr Günter Kraft but that most people in the neighbourhood called him *Der Rote Mann* because he had worn red every day of his life since his twenties. At that moment, I might have looked a little stunned. It was one of those moments in life in which you realise that you've completely forgotten about something you used to love, and perhaps someone you used to be. He continued, "I love red so much that even the carpet in my apartment is red!" Looking at his smiling, weathered face and his bright eyes was like looking at a beautiful flower you weren't expecting to see in the winter, a small, defiant bloom of colour contrasted against the white snowfall of age. We continued our extremely slow march towards the square.

"I used to love red too," I told him. "I'd forgotten all about that! I haven't worn red at all in the past few years but I used to adore it." He just shook his head and asked, "Are you English?" "No, I'm American," I replied. This won more approval from him, and then he asked me, "And why don't you wear red anymore, Fräulein?" I didn't have an answer. I'd simply forgotten all about my old preference. Then Herr Kraft said something that didn't mean much to me at the time but later made a lot of sense, "Red is the colour of the living. It's fire! You're a living woman. You should wear red."

Herr Kraft then told me his story, a story that I'm going to attempt to relay, to the best of my ability. I might have some details wrong but I'm hoping that one of his relatives will read this one day and correct any mistakes in the details. I'm only unsure of the exact decade (I'm not sure if it was the late 40s or early 50s) and of the city that he mentioned. The rest of the story is as he shared it with me almost twenty years ago now. Here it is, in his voice:

When I was a young man, I worked in men's tailored clothing, suits, jackets and the like. This was after the war and the fashion of the day was very boring! All of the men's clothing stores carried only greys, blacks, and the occasional dark blue. I wanted to bring some colour into the world. I wanted to sell colourful jackets for men, things that would make a man stand out, but people just weren't having it. I traveled for my job, attending men's clothing salons and trade shows. One day, upon arriving at one of these events in Berlin, I found myself stuck in a terrible traffic jam. It was a mess!

They were doing construction around the trade show building, and the traffic was completely blocked. No one knew what to do. As I sat in my car, looking at all the lost, confused people who couldn't even manage to figure out how to enter a parking area without signs or leadership, I got an idea. I had brought some of my red blazers to present at the trade show. I grabbed one of them, put it on, and walked out into the middle of the traffic. I directed the traffic, and everyone automatically obeyed! In the sea of grey, one man in a red jacket stood out and people obliged.

That was the moment that I realised that people sleep through life and that I wasn't one of them. From that day forward, I wore red every single day of my life, and now the people in Neuhausen call me "The Red Man."

This was the beginning of our friendship. On our third meeting, he called me "Die rote Frau." It felt like a big compliment coming from such a man. I would eventually move away, and Herr Kraft would disappear from his normal perch on the square. But until then, he would sometimes meet me on the street in front of my building and escort me to Rotkreuzplatz, where he perched for hours and watched the people pass by.

He taught me to yodel, and I taught him the words to the song *Edelweiss* from *The Sound of Music*. We would walk, talk, and yodel and sometimes I would sing to him. The stereotype about Germans being somewhat severe is unfortunately based on truth. It's especially true of old Munich women with an axe to grind. We caught our fair share of disapproving looks as we yodelled gleefully in front of the Karstadt but we didn't mind. We were The Living, and they were the sea of Grumpy Greys. I was still recovering from depression, and I couldn't help but notice that Herr Kraft felt a bit like a messenger, offering a clue to where I might find an elixir for my revival.

Herr Kraft sent me a letter, written in red ink along with his photo and a small, ivory edelweiss. Looking at the envelope, I'm struck by his address, he lived in Nibelungenstrasse, another hint. I've had his letter for almost twenty years now. I will always keep it as a reminder that, when life wants us to understand something, it sends exactly *who* and *what* we need. Our only job is to be open enough to receive it, and lucid enough to catch the clues.

The German language has three words that can be used to denote power: *Macht*, *Kraft*, and *Stärke*. *Macht* is used to indicate bestowed power, such as military might, as in the word *Wehrmacht*. *Stärke* means strength, which normally references an inherent power. Herr Kraft's name was meaningful because, in German, the word Kraft not only refers to inherent, primordial power but also potency, virility, vigour, and *agency*. In many cultures, these words are associated with the colour red.

Personal agency is defined as a state of *being in action* as one exerts one's inherent power. True power is an essence. We don't often associate power with essence because the power that we're confronted with, and obliged to acquiesce to, is the bestowed, externalised force of institutions: That of the State, the Church, the education system, the corporate machine, etc. The power of these institutions is coercive, not intrinsic, and has no true essence.

Your will directs an essence. Will is true power, and agency is *how* you put that will to work in the world.

We find it difficult to conceptualise the will because it's so foreign to the mind. Will isn't part of the contents of your well, the reservoir of thoughts, feelings, memories, or personality construct. Will is the *directing force* that moves those contents, and it's that force that makes transformation and transmutation possible. Blake called Tharmas "The Parent Power." Tharmas is Will.

The will exists only in the present moment; there is no future or past will. Will is not desire. Will is the *energy of deciding*, and demands an automatic, unassailable *faith* that, what was once unseen, unknown, or existing only as potentiality, shall now exist, be perceived, and known. I'm defining *Faith* as consciousness in the act of confirming its own ability to alter the world by means of its creative faculty and will. Will is not the *decision*; it's the *deciding*. Deciding, *willing*, is a faculty of Being, not a construct of the rational mind. The rational mind can think, plan, and design, but if deciding were left up to the rational mind, we'd never achieve our goals. When we make *deciding* a mental activity, resolutions are never kept. This is why Tharmas threatens to starve Urizen on one occasion, and when he does, Urizen backs off because, without Tharmas, Urizen (as intellect/reason/mental control) would be nothing.

The will exists beyond the psyche and its particular use of rational, mental faculties. The soul essence, before any content is added (via experience), is purity. It's what Meister Eckhart referred to as "the ground of being."

Your will flows from this ground.

There is no *try* in will. The will is never passive. Fundamentally, your *personal* will to do, or not do something, is the same *impersonal* will that causes a flower to bloom. There is only one will in the universe. Personal, free will is paradoxical. Your will is "free" because it's an endowed faculty, made available even to the transient, ultimately illusory self, but it doesn't belong to the relative self. Will exists at the level of the Absolute, and its power is given *freely* to the transient self to use, but the small self doesn't own the will, it borrows it. The small self can exercise a measure of so-called "personal will" but it can't limit the Will's true power. It can only limit its personal use of it, which it always does. The Divine Will is an inexhaustible source of power, but you get to freely decide how much of that power you access by deciding how much you're willing to surrender your personal "will" to God's Will.

Eventually, every devoted spiritual seeker realises that the personal will is an illusion. The esoteric statements, "All power is Will Power" and "All will is Divine Will," are true. Will is the power by which consciousness accomplishes anything. Consciousness envisions an image, but the will is the *directing* **power** behind psychological, emotional, and physical *movement*—all of which is energetic. To understand how will both directs, and *is*, the animating power in our world, we must know that it's the *inherent* power behind movement, not just the externally applied force. If you decide to move a chair from one side of the room to the other, the will was the animating power and the director that *decided* to move the chair. It was also the force that commands the bodily functions to obey, as you physically move the chair.

Imagination is the realm. Envisioning is the engine. Faith is the binding agent. Will is the director, and is inseparable from Pneuma. It's the inexhaustible, animating power that catalyses and completes the process of transmutation.

Externally applied force is exhaustible but will directs an *inherent*, inexhaustible source of power.

Why does this matter? It matters because changing our lives, and ultimately the world, must be an act of *will*, not an effort of applied force.

Personal Responsibility is a Signal

Fools regard themselves as awake now—so personal is their knowledge. It may be as a prince or it may be as a herdsman but so cocksure of themselves!
—Chuang Tzu

If you will accept this as your philosophy of life, and not turn to the left or the right, but claim you are solely responsible for the phenomena of your life, you will find it much easier to live. But if, at times, life seems too hard to bear, and you find a secondary cause, you have created a devil. 'Devils' and 'satans' are formed from man's unwillingness to assume the responsibility of his life.
—Neville Goddard

When Goddard said, "and not turn to the left, or the right," he was referring to what it means to take the narrow path instead of the broad path that the gospel, and some Egyptian texts, say leads to destruction. If you're like every other human in the world, there have been times when you haven't taken responsibility for the conditions of your life and state of being. We've all been there, done that.

When tracing the word, *responsible* back through the etymological tree, we're led to the idea of one taking an oath, as a witness-bearer of truth. The "re" at the beginning of the word denotes a reversal of direction, such as to turn something back towards the self. Accepting responsibility is essentially saying, "I bear witness that I am the causal power." Or, as my grandfather used to say, "The buck stops here." Personal responsibility is *willingness*, and because it's *will*ingness, it automatically connects us to the Universal Will. It's a sign that we're prepared to consciously participate in the creation of our life and the world, not as puppets operated by some cosmic fate but as sacred co-creators.

It's hard to take responsibility for something when you've been conditioned to believe that your perception, thoughts, and feelings have no impact on the *outside* world. This illusion of separation also makes it easy to believe that things just *happen* to us; it refuses to acknowledge the complex, interconnectivity between all of the phenomena of life.

Refusing self-responsibility is easy. All we need to do is any of the following: complain, blame, take things personally, succumb to fear, hide behind ideologies, refuse to self-inquire, procrastinate, or remain locked in rigid subject/object dualism. Over the past ten years, it's become trendy to refer to oneself as *awake*. For some, this means that they know about conspiracy. For others, it means that they're *socially conscious* (whatever that means when it comes from unconscious, blame-mongers).

In the quote above, Chuang Tzu is referring to individuals who become so entrenched in their personal worldview and delusions of "knowing the truth" that they believe themselves to be awake when, in reality, they still slumber on through life. This isn't to condemn anyone, because we've all been there. If we point out this behaviour and tendency in others, it should only be so that we can turn inwards and examine ourselves. We might ask, "To what degree have I accepted responsibility for my life and the state of the world?" That is a huge question because it implies that we do indeed play a part in the world in which we live.

Think of personal responsibility as a valve. A valve is a device for controlling the passage of air or fluid through a pipe. The more personal responsibility we accept in life, the wider the valve opens, which allows more power to flow from the inexhaustible source. We can only access that source via personal responsibility, which then directs that power towards us, for our use. It's this power that fuels your agency.

Being informed about government corruption, researching conspiracies, or learning about how the Machine operates does not mean we're awake. Wakefulness is the awareness of those things *as they exist in one's self.* One will ask, "How am *I* corrupt in my thinking or behaviour?" "How do *I* perpetuate the existence of the Machine?" "Is my disavowal of self-responsibility the primary cause of my dissatisfaction with the state of the world and my life?"

Neville Goddard showed us what it means to be fully *woke,* and he gave up wealth, prestige, and social acceptance to do so.

Personal responsibility is the foundation of wakefulness.

The system isn't afraid of guillotines, yellow vests, or pussy hats. The energy of protest is in resonance with the energy of the externalised force and control (both overt and subtle) of the containment system. What it fears is mass peaceful non-compliance and a humanity that flourishes from the inside out. It fears billions of people who have opened that valve wide, the valve through which true power flows.

Revolutions are examples externalised force, not inherent power. They destroy one tyrant who will eventually be replaced with another one, but the containment system stays firmly in place. Inherent power *implodes*, it doesn't explode. Female orgasm is a perfect example of this. The study of sexual Tantra shows us that while male orgasm and the female clitoral orgasm are explosions of energy, the vaginal orgasm is an *implosion*. Explosion exhausts but implosions provide even more energy. We all know that men fall asleep after orgasm but a woman, if she has a vaginal orgasm, can go on, and on, and on.

Any sufficiently advanced, clean, and limitless energy source is an *implosive* one. The ethos of empire runs on combustion. The Divine uses implosion. Women are vessels for an implosive, inexhaustible energy. Hint, hint. Maybe this explains why the Abrahamic religions actively suppress the female, and tried to wipe out so-called pagan knowledge (which they didn't mind appropriating when it suited them).

Revolutions happen when the collective shadow (combined with a fair share of social manipulation by those who use revolution as a power-grab) *explodes*. What we seek is an upward spiralling *evolution* but we keep getting revolution. Why? Because we haven't learned our lesson yet. We allow ourselves to be imprisoned by a machine mind and acquiesce to the agendas of its agents, those who Tolkien referred to as "servants of the machine." Our world will evolve when individuals do—by virtue of our inherent power. Until then, humanity will continue a circular motion through the revolving doors of lower consciousness, stuck in a time loop like a dog chasing its tail.

The Sword and Scabbard

The world we think we live in is a construct; a multi-headed mental hydra of appropriated, primeval myths that we've been sold as 'history,' Roman law, the philosophy of elites who still believe in the "divine right to rule," and a cult of rational materialism. It's a vicious net that serpents itself around our minds and imprisons us in a poisonous narrative. The filaments of this net are strong and burn into our minds as they quite literally rewire our neurological pathways. Only a sharp blade applied with utmost precision can cut through that net.

Hindu myths and Arthurian legends speak of a sword. The sword represents the humanisation of divine power. When divinity bestows the sword, it signifies an outpouring of power into the individual. As we open the valve wider, via radical self-responsibility, that influx of power shines a light. This illumination gives us access, via direct experience, to deeper layers of Self.

Direct experience can come in the form of vision, personal revelation, expanded perception, and synchronistic signs. The universe is alive and fully conscious. It's constantly communicating with us. We may perceive, but the perception of a thing doesn't guarantee that we'll understand what we're witnessing. That's why the Great Work lasts a lifetime, and is utterly and deeply personal.

This is the next stage of radical responsibility. Reality is revealed to each individual in response to, and as a reflection of, who they currently are. It's an intimate dialogue between the individual and the Divine. There's also a constant awareness that we know nothing at all, and so humility demands a measure of silence, deference, and reverence for the mystery.

The Sword has a companion; it's called the Scabbard. The sword appeals to people. They love to pull it out and wave it around, and they always end up injuring themselves or others. Here is a truth: The scabbard is just as important as the sword; at times, it's more important. Some might say that the importance of the scabbard should be the first thing we learn, but that's missing the point. We're stubborn, foolhardy creatures who need to cut ourselves occasionally to understand how deadly sharp the sword is. Knowing when to sheath it in the scabbard is a sign of wisdom. Keeping it in the scabbard requires lucidity and self-control. Learning balance and measured self-containment is also part of the process, the scabbard needs to be able to hold the sword. We become the scabbard but the sword belongs to a higher-order. While this higher order seems to precede our existence, it also surrounds and permeates it. Both the sword and the scabbard are artifacts of the will, not of the intellect. It's the _will_, not the rational mind, or the heart that spiritualises and animates matter. It does so by directing spirit into matter.

Learning to accept responsibility is a process. We begin our lives learning about responsibility by observing the adults around us. They're not always the best examples, but if we have some good role models, we learn to keep our rooms clean, get to class on time, and turn in our completed homework. With time we take on more responsibility for our choices; we lead projects, take care of animals, pay our bills, and eventually have children, which is the ultimate responsibility for any human that decides to become a parent.

The highest level of responsibility is to accept responsibility for our thoughts, feelings, interpretation, and imaginative acts. Ultimately we accept responsibility for the world we help to create. Mastering movement is a big part of that.

Movement—An Animated Life

Consciousness is only possible through change; change is only possible through movement. —Aldous Huxley

No one wants to drink swamp water. It's murky, opaque, and a veritable Petri dish for harmful bacteria, but swamps teach us about movement. If you'll recall, spirit is often associated with wind. Wind is a current that moves through air. These same currents move through water and our bodies. Some move as electricity through the brain. Lack of a water current creates a swamp. The water becomes putrid but it's not dead per se. It's full of micro-organisms. Even a human corpse is full of microscopic life as it decays. Without movement of the heart, lungs and blood, we would die.

The Hellenistic mystery tradition distinguished between spirit and psyche. A person could be alive and yet dead at the same time. A person without spirit is like Blake's *Clod of Clay* or the Gnostic *hylic*. They seem to be alive but they're rather swamp-like. There's some life in them, but it's *putrid*, the current of spirit is extremely weak.

Vibration is movement. Everything vibrates. We see various degrees of vibration in the world. The vibration of rock is so low that it can't move itself, think, act, dream, or create.

At the next level, vegetation—there is movement as a plant germinates, sprouts and grows. Trees are miraculous, awe-inspiring plants that can strategise, feel, react, and communicate. Then there are animals—they can move, feel emotion, have a sense of self (anyone with a dog knows that), dream, love to play, fight sometimes, and feel connection. We humans do all of the above. But unlike the other animals, we have the ability to use active envisioning to access the realm of imagination. We can lucid dream. We can investigate the mysteries of the cosmos. We can reason and develop powerful intellects. We can also learn to love selflessly and unconditionally. In a human, higher reasoning and will can triumph over instinct. The difference between each successive level is *movement*. The more spiritualised the matter, the more creative, willful, individuated, and actualised it is.

Decay is a diminishing of spirit. In human life, we call it "stagnation," we're not dead but we're not really alive either. Everyone, theist and non-theist alike, uses the phrase "He's in low spirits." We also refer to people as being "highly spirited," and use the phrase, *spirit of the times* (Zeitgeist). When we use these terms, we're referring to *movement*. At the social level, when ideas are catalysed by will, change is set into *motion,* and we call it "a social movement."

A person of will is never stagnant. This doesn't mean that he or she moves house or country all of the time, or that they constantly change jobs or friends. They might change those things but that externalised movement is the result of an *inner movement*, an inner change…transformation.

An animated life is a transformational life, a life through which a powerful current flows.

The Enlivening

Between 1300 and 1700, alchemy could be described as an underground counter culture of the age. In their work to produce the philosopher's stone, alchemists described four phases. In an earlier age, Heraclitus named the phases as:

MELANOSIS—blackening: confrontation and purgation.
LEUKOSIS—whitening: further purification as the soul is illuminated with conscious awareness.
XANTHOSIS—yellowing: associated with solar light and pure, creative intelligence.
IOSIS—reddening: fusion of lunar and solar and creation of a golden, liquid essence.

The last stage, the reddening stage, is also called *the enlivening*. While the reddening is the final stage, it's not the final goal. Remember, the alchemists wanted to make metaphorical gold. For the alchemists, the enlivening is the resurrection of an immortal energy and consciousness that appears as a golden 'blood' at the base of the spine. Neville Goddard described his experience of fusion many times in his lectures. Here Goddard describes his own experience of the golden liquid light (at other times he refers to it as 'golden blood') that the alchemists many often sought in vain:

Your body, which is split from top to bottom, from east to west, as one side moves northward as the other side moves southward, revealing liquid, molten gold at its base. As I looked at this living, liquid gold I knew it to be myself; I fused with it, and up I went into my skull—into the kingdom of heaven, for the kingdom is within. At that moment, I departed the world of generation and returned to the world of regeneration, as the heavens reverberated like thunder. Having returned to the molten state, I cast myself into the mould which was prepared for me before this world existed and I became the Living Image that radiates.

160

This golden 'blood' is our eternal self and our life force. There's a long road between the life of a youthful soul who blames others for his or her circumstances and the light of an elder soul who has reached the point of fusion.

The 'yellowing' is the process of 'coming into consciousness'. Blake envisioned Eternity as a realm of pure intellect. Pure intellect isn't the same as the rational mind; it's much more than reason. It's *true* intelligence, and creative consciousness, often referred to as Buddha Nature or Christ Consciousness. This represents the Inner King in all of us, who has transformed through purification and remembered his true identity.

The next stage, the 'reddening,' is a rebirth and awakening of the Red King as he shoots up the spin and into the skull where he reverberates like thunder. It can seem like an impossible dream, but we must start somewhere.

Put on that metaphoric red blazer, and direct your life, thoughts, emotions, actions, and imagination like Herr Kraft directed traffic. Will ensures that reality will obey, it just depends how wide you're willing to open the valve.

What a wonderful way to live; at peace with the impermanence of this world, in love with something greater than ourselves, and yet fully responsible for our interpretation of experience, our imagination, our actions and our choices. Not slaves to a machine. Imagine what it means to be disciplined and creative, instead of conforming to cultural norms; to be vigilant, and lucid, instead of fabricating saviour narratives as compensation for a life not fully lived, and a will left untapped.

Der Rote Mann—Herr Kraft on his perch at Rotkreuzplatz (Red Cross Place)

Chapter 14
A LIVING PHILOSOPHY

In this age the word philosophy has little meaning unless accompanied by some other qualifying term. The body of philosophy has been broken up into numerous isms more or less antagonistic, which have become so concerned with the effort to disprove each other's fallacies that the sublimer issues of divine order and human destiny have suffered deplorable neglect. The ideal function of philosophy is to serve as the stabilising influence in human thought. —Manly P. Hall

Philosophy is the love of wisdom. But what is wisdom? What does it mean to be wise?

The word wise comes from the Proto-Germanic *wissaz* as well as the Frisian *wis* and Old Norse *viss* and from the past-participle adjective *wittos*, which comes from the Proto-Indo-European root *weid*, which means "to see." The Old English *witan* means "to know." But what is being *seen*, and what is being *known*?

A wise man has no extensive knowledge; He who has extensive knowledge is not a wise man. —Lao-Tzu

Philosophy is the *love of wisdom,* and that love is the driving force behind our search for truth. In our hearts, we all know this. The search may take you outside of yourself for a while, but it will always end within your very own being. We're not merely searching for truth. Deep down, we feel an overwhelming desire to *merge* with what is true. We become what we revere. Therefore, if we really mean it when we say that we "love wisdom" and that we wish to grow wise, we must revere truth by *living* it. Which means that we become a truthful person in all aspects of our lives.

Philosophy has asked questions about truth such as, "What is the nature of truth?" and "Does truth require correspondent facts that exist as entities?" The philosopher Joachim asserted that, "*Truth, in its essential nature, is that systematic coherence which is the character of a significant whole.*"

Joachim insisted that anything true must be "wholly and completely true." This stance on truth places coherence over consistency. Facts that are accepted as true today can be proven false tomorrow. So, is there a truth that can never be proven false? If such truth exists, can we ever hope to encounter it?

In his *Annotations to Bacon*, William Blake wrote:

> Self-evident Truth is one Thing, and Truth the result of reasoning is another Thing. Rational Truth is not the Truth of Christ but of Pilate; it is the Tree of the Knowledge of Good & Evil.

In chapter eight, we examined three hypothetical strata of consciousness. The lowest level is the level of polarisation, labelling, and literalism. Both William Blake and Neville Goddard equated the act of "Eating of the Tree of Good and Evil" with the lowest level of human awareness. At this level, people think in binary terms of positive and negative, good vs. bad or left vs. right. They label everything and identify with those labels. They have little to no capacity for subtlety, insight, or understanding. They live as victims of life and perceive the events of their life as happening to them without taking responsibility or acknowledging that they are part of the cause. Emotionally and mentally unstable people who operate at his level, become a danger to themselves and the world because they invariably believe that they're gatekeepers of some unquestionable truth. If you challenge them, they either grow distant and avoid you or label you immediately as one of the "bad guys." They might even become agitated and violent.

Discussing the nature of truth requires patience, delicacy, and humility. We have to constantly check ourselves and be careful that we're not also eating apples from that tree by thinking *exclusively* in terms of *good* and *evil* or *right vs. wrong.* Creating a world in which humans, as imperfect, flawed beings can flourish means that we master the ability to perceive, think, and feel along a much broader spectrum of awareness. We know that some things are indeed always wrong without exception, such as child abuse, sexual violence, and torture of any living creature. We feel the wrongness of those things. But there are ethical and moral questions that require more wisdom and insight.

Should a serial-killing cannibal be executed? Is killing wrong without exception? What exactly constitutes a killing? Is it wrong for a starving child to steal a piece of bread? Questions like these are examples of awareness asking itself questions about the nature of love and truth in a world of suffering. In a world in which a large portion of the population lives at lower levels of awareness most of the time, who can we entrust to make these kinds of decisions about social life? Corrupt politicians, social media companies, or biased, ideological scientists? Shouldn't we be able to trust ourselves? How can we manage things of such magnitude if we don't even know ourselves or take responsibility for our feelings, perception, and choices? Within the body of the Absolute, humanity exists as a single cell. In this state, we're neither omniscient nor omnipresent. We can never know the totality of truth; we can only catch glimpses of it.

Some have suggested that the key to happiness is to live authentically, but for them, 'authentic living' is an ongoing reaction to circumstances: If you're feeling dissatisfied in your marriage, they say, "Leave it." If you hate your job they'll say, "Walk away." In some cases, this might be perfectly reasonable. There's no need to remain in a job you detest or in an unsalvageable, miserable relationship in which neither person is growing but is this *truthful* living?

Courageous, personal responsibility is just the beginning of the wisdom path. To live truthfully requires that we go deeper than our reactions to life and our default perception of the world. One can spend decades studying philosophy, psychology, and the esoteric and never fully accept that one's world view is always a mix of accurately perceived truth, mixed in with misinterpretations and projection based on limited understanding. Blake referred to our limited understanding as "the ratio." The *ratio* is the totality of all that we know, or *think* we know. It's naturally limited and subject to change and yet we constantly filter reality through our ratio.

Living authentically generally infers that you're being true to yourself, but which *self* are you being true to? And what does being "true" even mean in this context? The immature relative self occupies itself with relative "truths," like its assumptions, opinions, feelings, and longings.

As the relative self matures, the individual begins to view the circumstances of his or her life, as external creations caused by an internal state. The individual stops reacting and begins to do more self-inquiry. At this early stage, they begin responding with more self-awareness rather than reacting unconsciously. If a woman hates her job, she doesn't just walk away. If she feels dissatisfied with her marriage, she doesn't just walk away. A truthful woman tells herself the truth *about herself.* To do that, she needs to see herself for *who* and *how* she really is.

She'll ask herself *why* she's dissatisfied, and the answer will never be, "My boss is a jerk" or "My husband is inattentive." She'll ask herself whether her dissatisfaction is based on truth or unexamined beliefs that might be false. **An honest person is a self-inquiring person**. She'll ask, "Am I creating my own dissatisfaction in some way?" Going deeper, she might begin examining her motivations, her values and her unprocessed painful experiences that might be clouding her vision. Instead of blaming her husband, boss, or the patriarchy, she'll always turn inward. Regarding her career she may ask, "Am I doing what brings me joy?"—"Do I even know what I love?"—"Do I feel a calling?"—"If I begin an entirely new career will I still bring my attitude and inner-distortions into my work?" Regarding her husband she'll ask, "What kind of wife am I?"—"Am I truly present, patient, and understanding with my husband?"—"Do I even know what love is?"—"What does it mean to love a man as his partner through life?"—"Is my fulfillment dependent on my husband?"—"Could I grow wiser in the way I communicate?"

And all of that is only the beginning of self-awareness and truthful living.

Authentic, truthful living isn't about circumstances, preferences, opinions, or beliefs. Authentic living is about telling the truth of ourselves: how we feel, what we fear, why we fear it, our weaknesses, our hopes, our dreams. It's the first step towards contact with an Absolute Truth, which transcends all of those things. Authentic, truthful living means that we align our speech, actions, thoughts, and imagination with our values and our true, inner self. With time, the *self* as an object begins to fade, and one begins experiencing *self* as a presence, as an Awareness that is wavelike, rather than a fixed entity to be perceived as an object.

The Eastern Traditions are often misinterpreted in a way that treats everything relative as unimportant, illusory, and without intrinsic value. When the Buddhist teachers use the word *illusion*, they're not implying that it's of no value, but some people interpret it as such. This leads to metaphysical solipsism, which isn't what the Buddhist masters teach. Buddhism asserts that it's impossible to perceive an objective reality independent of the perceiving mind. The original Western Tradition treats the relative experience of the individual as sacred while considering passive inaction as a disavowal because the West recognises that humans are divine, co-creative creatures. The Eastern and Western traditions, when pruned of dogma, are perfect compliments of each other.

In the esoteric teachings of both the East and the West, the consciousness that we call *God*, is *in* his creation, *as* his creation. He hid himself in us wee little humans so that he can find himself again. Finding and acknowledging our divinity leads us to a life of inquiry, honesty, responsibility, and alignment. Again, philosophy is the *love* of wisdom, which is ultimately a love of truth, but it's not the truth itself. Living philosophically is not a life based on awareness of the totality of Truth. A philosophical life is an honest, sincere life that is steered by the love of wisdom, and a love of a Truth that we can never completely grasp, but can catch glimpses of, and participate in, by **making Truth our compass.**

To love is to *merge*, and to merge requires a form of *surrender*.

We can't divorce Love from Truth or Truth from Love; without one, the other is suspect. As stated before, love is a state of being, and that state is one of harmonious unity. Therefore, philosophy, as the love of wisdom, is a harmonious, unfragmented unity with what is true. Truth is not a collection of facts; it's a *direction*. The only way to live wholly is to reunify our fragmented way of being. A philosophical life is not defined by our subjectively truthful way of living.

A philosophical life is a commitment to learning how to live our individual experience as *fractals* of the whole, rather than fragments of it.

Chapter 15
TRANSFORMATION

When you begin to understand what you are, without trying to change it, then what you are, undergoes a transformation. —Jiddu Krishnamurti

Lasting transformation is the result of *un*becoming. Transformation doesn't occur when some new activity begins, or a new belief is adopted, but when old patterns unravel, and things fall apart. We must *unbecome* before we can become. Perhaps this is why so few people ever really change, they're afraid of the unraveling. Friendships may end, relationships with family members may change, a marriage could dissolve, you might find yourself unemployed after walking away from an unfulfilling career or, the most fearsome of all, *identity* may be challenged as the ego is diminished. "My whole life could fall apart? No, thank you!"

Many people have experienced the unraveling described above, and not only lived to tell the tale, but thrived as they moved into new states being, and created fulfilling lives. The good news is, it doesn't have to be so drastic. As we change from the inside out, so will our situation and *how we experience it.*

It's not guaranteed to be a pain-free process, but through presence, right use of imagination, faith in oneself, integration, and mastery, a person can navigate the potential stormy weather of transformation to such a degree that the process feels like sailing on smooth seas, with only the occasional bump. Having help along the way is crucial. You have much more influence over the conditions of your life, and on the people in it, than you might realise. That realisation is one of the aims of this book; it's about *how* we make use of the foundations of fulfillment to live a fulfilling life.

How We Transform

You have brains in your head. You have feet in your shoes.
You can steer yourself, any direction you choose. —Dr. Seuss

It's common for people to think of transformation as a sort of reconfiguration of components. I see it very differently. In my experience, how we view something, even if we haven't given it much thought, greatly influences our experience of that thing. Have you ever played with a Rubik's cube? Did you secretly wish you could just rearrange the stickers and be done with it? If we view transformation as a Rubik's cube, changing our lives can feel like a disjointed, frustrating puzzle that we'd rather throw out the window than spend another second on.

I see transformation as a wave, specifically a *sine* wave. To be even more specific, a sine wave that arises from Euler's formula. If this seems foreign to you, just bear with me and I'll explain.

In mathematics, *e*, a.k.a. "Euler's number" is a transcendental number and a mathematical constant that's not defined by geometry. It's a constant that's related to *growth* and *change*. *e* is the base rate of growth shared by all continually growing processes and systems. Euler's *formula* is a mathematical formula that describes two, equal ways to move in a circle. The first way is through exponential growth; the second way is via imaginary growth. The imaginary growth shouldn't be thought of as unreal, it's just as real as the exponential growth. Imaginary growth is about *rotating*, while exponential growth is about a *linear* increase in the same direction. What do you get when you move up while rotating? A spiral.

If you combine real growth (moving forward or upward) with imaginary growth (rotating yourself i.e., changing your direction), you get what is called "complex growth." Remember, Euler's formula describes two ways to move within a *circle*. Speaking of that imaginary growth, mathematician Kalid Azad said, "When I grow, don't push me forward, or back, in the direction I'm already going, rotate me instead."

In other words, change my perspective and direction.

Ok, so where does the sine wave come in? Earlier, I said that transformation doesn't have to be bumpy and disruptive; it can be smooth. A mathematician will tell you that sine is the epitome of smoothness. Sine is the motion of a pendulum. It's the thing that makes a circle, circular, a triangle, triangular, and the strings of an instrument vibrate. Sine is *smooth movement*.

A sine wave emerges from Euler's formula, and this sine wave does something very interesting in that circle, it pulls you towards the centre.

Remember this symbol?

The image below represents Euler's formula and the sine wave that emerges from it, pulling you back towards the centre, to the axis point of the vertical and horizontal lines.

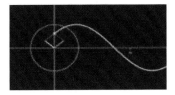

This pull towards the centre will be important in chapter sixteen. For now, let's return the idea of transformation as a smooth wave.

Meister Eckhart said that most people find it difficult to understand that they are both creature and creator. I sense that between creature and creator, there is a wave, and that wave *is* transformation. The entirety of human existence can be seen as a wave of transformation that takes the transient, unfinished creature to the integrated, transcendent, existential self.

Transformation can be painful and disruptive when we insist on holding to our subjective, negative interpretations, and when we fail to acknowledge and lay claim to our inherent power. The power inherent to every person is the ability to do radical self-inquiry and change our circumstances, and felt experience of life by altering our mode of perception. One mode sees the outer world as something that is happing *outside* of oneself. The other mode sees the outer world as what Goddard described as "The self, pushed out."

Does that sound impossible? Test it for yourself. When you change how you perceive other people to *be* and begin to imagine the best *for* and *of* them, they begin to transform before your eyes. It's then that we realise that we never saw them for who they really were; we saw our version of them, which is a projection. In reality, the others aren't transforming, *we* are. To see the world and the people in it differently, we need to become more compassionate, understanding, forgiving, loving, peaceful, patient, hopeful, kind, and wise. Each of those traits has its own way of looking at the world and oneself.

When we use our imagination in the right way, develop mastery, are present, perceive imaginatively, have faith in our potential, and practice letting go...transformation is like riding that smooth wave.

The business of the mystic in the eyes of these old specialists was to remake, trans-mute, his total personality... to bring it out of the hiddenness, and unify himself about it as a centre. —Evelyn Underhill (1875–1941)

Psychology did not suddenly spring into existence, one could say that it is as old as civilisation itself. —Carl Jung, ETH Lecture I, Page 11

Esoteric means *within* and also means *belonging to the inner circle*. Exoteric means *belonging to the outside*. Mysticism is concerned with the esoteric. "As within, so without" is the axiom of mystics. The word *mystic* carries with it many misconceptions and prejudices, especially in a society full of people who try to elevate rational materialism by disparaging the irrational. It's also not helpful that too many of the people who aim to promote the mystical, do so by disparaging the rational. By failing to develop their rational and contemplative faculties simultaneously, and without any true self-knowledge, these kinds of 'mystics' have little to offer beyond fantastical conjecture, and sometimes paranoid delusions. These are the people who might claim to channel space aliens or Jesus, talk to the dead, be in touch with hidden masters on Mars, and to have full access to the Akashic records.

The mature mystics of the world, individuals like Rumi, Akbar the Great, Meister Eckhart, Hildegard von Bingen, Mechthild von Magdeburg, Khalil Gibran, Lao Tzu, Najmuddin Kubra, Plotinus, and even Pythagoras, all sought union with the *unfragmented, Universal Mind* and with the *Beingness Beyond Mind*. All of these mystics understood that the journey began with one, universal requirement: Self-knowledge—but it didn't end there. The aim was to know thyself so that you could then fully surrender the transient self to the Absolute as you cross the abyss.

The esoteric could be said to be the original psychology but with caveats:
1. It's not all "in the head," and 2. It wasn't *called* psychology, and it didn't exist as an independent discipline. The roots of Western philosophy and psychology are anchored firmly in the ancient world that thrived long before the Greek philosophers were born. Egyptologist and historian James Henry Breasted (1865–1935), researcher and writer Gerald Massey (1828–1907), and Dr. George G.M. James (1893–1956) all demonstrated that Greek

philosophy was not just strongly influenced by, but was an actual replication of the knowledge and philosophy of the Egyptian Mystery Schools. The only issue with Massey's and James' work is that they never asked, "*Where did the Egyptians get it?*"

A hint to the answer is found on the walls of an Egyptian temple in Edfu, known as the Temple of Horus. The temple walls are covered with enigmatic hieroglyphic inscriptions. Some of the inscriptions refer to "Seven Sages" and describe them as being "The only divinities who knew how the temples and sacred places were to be created."

The secret rites and mystic observances were not peculiar to the Eastern nations alone, nor to particular races of human beings. They existed everywhere.
—Alexander Wilder

Interestingly, other cultures around the world have ancient texts that also speak of seven divinities. Ancient Babylon had the Seven Apkallu, the Saptarishi are the seven Rishis (sages) of ancient India, China had the Seven Sons of Heaven, Zoroastrianism has the *Amesha Spenta*, the seven divinities that were individuated emanations of Ahura Mazda, Zoroastrianism's highest deity. Tolkien's work, *The Silmarillion*, reflected the same concept. In Tolkien's cosmology, the divine emanations of Eru Ilúvatar were divided into masculine and feminine counterparts, so seven became fourteen, the fourteen Ainur.

"There was Eru, the One, who in Arda is called Ilúvatar, and he made first the Ainur, the Holy Ones, that were the offspring of his thought."
—First words of the Ainulindalë

What does any of this have to do with transformation? Take a look at what each of the seven divinities represented in each of the cultures listed above. The seven divine ones are philosophical abstractions and *aspects of the universal mind and states of being,* personified. These archetypes are not to be considered in a strictly psychological sense. Plato believed these archetypes are not the projections of human minds, but the other way around. They project into us and take possession of our mind. To evolve beyond them, we must overcome their influence. This is the exact opposite of Freudian psychoanalysis. Blake took a similar view but believed that the projection went both ways.

Upon examination of the myths, rites, and symbology of the ancient world, it becomes apparent that the ancients used an esoteric psycho-cosmology by which the cosmos could be mapped to the human being in its entirety, psyche, heart, and soul—as without, so within, as above, so below. Psychology and mysticism apply a similar framework and process for self-analysis and transformation. There's been a plethora of research into Eastern mysticism and its correlation to the development of the psyche, but in this regard the mysticism of the West has been mostly ignored.

Humanity has sought to understand, transform, and unify the soul for many thousands of years.

A return to unity and wholeness through identification with the Absolute Self was the objective.

Transformation vs. Transmutation

Alchemy has performed for me the great and invaluable service of providing material in which my experience could find sufficient room, and has thereby made it possible for me to describe the individuation process at least in its essential aspects. —
Carl Jung, *Mysterium Coniunctionis*, Paragraph 792

Mind (as well as metals and elements) may be transmuted from state to state, degree to degree, condition to condition, pole to pole, vibration to vibration.
—*The Kybalion*

The alchemists of the Middle Ages represented the evolution of man's consciousness as a three-phase process: Transformation, transmutation, and transfiguration.

Transformation means to change at the level of form and function, while transmutation means to change at the level of both form and substance. The metamorphosis of a caterpillar into a butterfly or a tadpole to a frog are examples of transformation. They transform not only in form, but in capability. The caterpillar can't fly, but a butterfly can, and the tadpole can't live out of water, but a frog can. Transformation allows us to live in and move through an entirely new environment (strata of consciousness) in new ways.

The term *chrysopoeia* was employed by the alchemists to describe the process of transmuting one substance, like lead, into another chemical element, such as gold. The transmutation of lead to gold is a metaphor for the transformation of consciousness. Transmutation is a change of both form and substance.

The sun transmutes light elements into heavier ones through a process called *stellar nucleosynthesis*. Philo of Alexandria (c. 20 B.C.E.–40 C.E.) characterised the stars as souls in De Gigantibus 8:

> The stars are souls; through and through immaculate and divine. Wherefore also they **move in the circle**, which is **the motion most akin to intellect**, for each is an **intellect of the purest type**.

Note that he didn't specify that they are *human* souls, only souls. Philo said that what the Greek philosophers called "daimon," the Hebrews called "angel." He took the idea of stars as souls from Plato, who did connect the stars to human beings. Plato said, "The souls of humans are the stars, and return to those stars when they die." The Babylonian mages seemed to be aware of *stellar nucleosynthesis* long before modern scientists coined the term.

Babylonian mages believed that stars could transmute earthly substances through astral irradiation. Plato suggests that the starry realm is a habitation for the human soul, and the soul is imbued with the star's essence, its processes, and faculties. Modern science tells us that we're made of "stardust." This connection would have to go much deeper than the surface level of matter. It would have to extend to the quantum realm. Which leads one to wonder, are we also capable of *stellar nucleosynthesis* at some level?

The ability of stars to transmute substances becomes important in a psycho-cosmological mapping of the human being to the cosmos. What part of the human psyche (soul) and essence (spirit) do the stars represent?

Plato's assertion that each person has his or her own native star, to which he or she is bound in essence, is interesting because it indicates an anchor. This is an anchor to one's True Being, a realm of Self that is accessed by way of a starry gateway. Having access to this anchor, the gate, and one's true essence means that every human has access to their own type of psychological and emotional *stellar nucleosynthesis*. This is the *transmutation of consciousness* that the alchemists were concerned with.

Transformation begins with the realisation that our way of seeing ourselves and reality is imperfect and fragmented. Many people can't accept that, but there are many more who *can* accept it yet have no desire to change. They may not particularly *like* the bubble they live in, but they feel secure in it. They'll go to great lengths to ignore the fact that every human being must experience the *stripping away*. They construct their lives as a means of avoidance, erecting barriers around their emotions and hiding out in mental bunkers.

The bunkers may be ideology, knowledge, glamour, career, social life, religion, the occult, or even spirituality. But if someone suggests that they see a therapist or counsellor, they can't run away fast enough.

The surface of life is vulnerable; it is forever changing. You will age, your loved ones will pass from this world, and anything—be it a circumstance, all of your money, your physical assets, your reputation, your health, your relationships, and even your belief system—can be stripped away at any moment. Would it destroy you to lose those things? Or, can you recognise that you are a creative being with infinite potential? If you created those things once, you can always create them: loving, mutually beneficial relationships, a home, a craft, and your unique way of engaging with life.

The degree to which we weather the storms of loss and change depends on the degree to which we are open to transformation, have faith in our abilities, and have developed inner stability and calm. It might seem paradoxical, but the more we surrender, the more fulfilled we become. Transformation asks us to **let go** so that we can *become*. Becoming means receiving; we receive a new mind, a new heart, and access to a will beyond anything we could have previously imagined.

The Egyptian School

The Egyptian Mystery System was an institution of learning and development and was organised similarly to our modern universities. Candidates had to apply for entry, were tested in various ways and if accepted, were required to submit to many years of preparatory work. The Egyptian system was divided into the Lesser Mysteries and the Greater Mysteries. The lesser mysteries were focused on branches of science, liberal arts, and emotional and psychological development.

The Greater Mysteries were focused on deeper transmutation and transfiguration—evolving from a being of matter to a being of self-sustaining light. Pythagoras, Plato, and Herodotus were initiates of the Egyptian mysteries. They all spent twenty years in preparation before being admitted to the Mystery Schools.

Richard Pietschmann (1854–1923) was a German Orientalist and Egyptologist who is most known for his book, *The History of the Phoenix*. Pietschmann researched the Egyptian system in great detail and described it as a system that required years of preparation before one could even be considered as a candidate. Pietschmann describes the three grades as:

1. Mortals
2. Intelligences
3. Creatures of Light

The Creatures of Light were those individuals, of both genders, who had become one with the light and developed KRST/Buddha consciousness.

This is referenced in the Bible as one who becomes a "life-giving spirit." The Egyptians considered this a resurrection from the material realms. The Egyptians did not believe in reincarnation, which is the transmigration of souls from one body to another. They believed in Eternal Return. Eternal Return means that we live our lives over and over again, as the same individual but with hundreds or thousands of lives in parallel timelines.

As interesting as that sounds, what should be noted about the Egyptian

Mystery System is what most people ignore: The candidates spent many years in preparation as they learned how to learn, how to think, and how to live the Ten Virtues.

The Ten Virtues are:

1. Control of Thought
2. Control of Actions
3. Steadfastness of Purpose
4. Determination to lead a spiritual life and unify with higher ideals
5. Faith in one's ability to perceive the truth
6. Willingness to assimilate the truth
7. Freedom from resentment—Total forgiveness, *no victim mentality*
8. Discernment of what is right (reflects a love of truth) and what is wrong (reflects an ignorance of truth) and, therefore, the ability to distinguish between what is real and what is unreal.
9. Fidelity—confidence in one's ability to learn and transform.
10. Readiness for Initiation—which requires embodiment of the first nine virtues.

In addition to learning how to live the Ten Virtues, the candidates were required to learn grammar, logic, arithmetic, astronomy, and geometry. The purpose of the foundational learning was not to create a conceptional framework for the student to think from, but rather a total reconditioning of the student's consciousness. The initiate doesn't merely study philosophy, mathematics, or astronomy; they *live* it. Not as obsessions with any specific discipline, but through a phenomenological reorientation and becoming.

Contemplative exercises and meditation developed the irrational side of the spirit, while logic, astronomy, and mathematics developed the rational side. As the two sides converged, words like *inner*, *outer*, *rational*, and *irrational* lost their meanings. They were not separate functions of, or realms within, the cosmos or the soul. Each is enfolded within the other to such a degree that they cannot be extracted or separated at all. There is no inner or outer; there is no rational or irrational. Because the rational is, at its core, irrational, and the irrational is, at its core, rational.

The ultimate goal of the Egyptian Mystery School path was to bring the initiate from identification with the relative self and all of its delusions about reality, to identification with divinity, The Absolute. Through this process, the relative self becomes harmonious, self-reliant, healthy, responsibly inter-dependent, and whole.

The Autopsia was the final experience at the Initiatory Rite when the candidate became an Epoptes or Beholder. It was at once a view of one's own interior self and a vision of the Divinity. —Alexander Wilder

Above each Egyptian temple and learning centre was the phrase "Know Thyself." Considering the ultimate objective of the Mystery School, one might ask which *self* that statement is admonishing us to know?

The Topography of the Relative Self

Reading the Bible, but not understanding that it is psychological truth, one mistakenly believes it to be historical fact. When we misunderstand the texts in this way, we cannot understand the word. But when man knows the Bible is the greatest collection of psychological truths and was never intended to be seen as history or cosmology, then he gets a glimpse into this great wonderful book. For man himself is the great psychological earth that must be subdued. In man move all the passions, all the great emotions symbolised as creeping things and animals. In the deep of man actually live the invisible states symbolised as fish. In the deep of man actually live all the unnumbered infinite ideas symbolised as the fowls of the air. It is this man that must be self subdued, for when you subdue it comes The Promise and you will have dominion over this vast wonderful country that is called "Man." If man does not know that he himself is the earth spoken of, he thinks he must go out into the world and conquer it. The outer world reflects the inner work done in an individual. And yet, when he looks upon this wonderful world around him, he imagines himself to be so little. — Neville Goddard

People will do anything, no matter how absurd, in order to avoid facing their own souls. They will practice Indian yoga and all its exercises, observe a strict regimen of diet, learn theosophy by heart, or mechanically repeat mystic text from the literature of the whole world — all because they cannot get on with themselves and have not slightest faith that anything useful could ever come out of their own souls.
—Carl Jung, *Psychology and Alchemy*, Page 99

The modern philosopher, Ken Wilbur, has pointed out that while the Eastern traditions have a lot to offer when it comes to how we connect to, and recognise the existence of an Absolute Self, their approach is fragmented because of a massive blindspot in Eastern tradition: they place a singular focus on the Absolute while demeaning or completely ignoring the relative self. This philosophy demonises the ego. The relative self is a necessary proxy. If one is to live and interact in this world, some degree of ego is operationally essential! The relative self is like a surfer riding a wave, but this imaginary wave-rider is more of a flowering (a process of unfoldment) than an actual entity.

To clarify: The self is a process, and the wave is transformation. The only entity in this picture is the in-dwelling, sleeping deity that the mystery schools and alchemists sought to awaken.

Neuroscientists have been unable to find the centre in the brain that houses the self, but that hasn't stopped people from claiming that since the left-brain is responsible for analysis and interpretation, the big, bad ego must be there. They think that since the ego is a *baddy* and ultimately unreal, everything that the left-brain is responsible for is also guilty by association. Reason, analysis, order, and even *maleness* are now considered disruptive, unnecessary, and need to be "transcended." That's a load of hogwash.

Just a note: The left brain is often rigidly associated with masculinity while the right brain is rigidly equated with femininity, neither of these assumptions is wholly true. The mind, like the human being, is a mosaic. People who focus exclusively on the irrational ('right-brained') become all yin and no yang. This lack of coherence leads to the passivity that Markale criticised, a passivity that both the Celts and Egyptians found inexcusable.

A decoherent, immature, relative self can meditate for thousands of hours and sit on a mountain top laughing all day, but if you put them back in the 'real' world, they can't handle it very well. No lasting, stable illumination has occurred.

A coherent sense of self, although it may be ultimately unreal, is the only means by which the light of the Absolute can flow into the world. An unbalanced relative self can't hold that light; it would tear them apart and sometimes does. People who try to force kundalini awakenings have become psychotic, and spiritual intuitions can lead to delusions and personality disorders in the unintegrated individual. A little bit of this seems to be part of the process. As consciousness rises on the spiral, an individual may experience visions and other experiences that those who apply a strictly materialistic model of reality would say are inexplicable.

Everyone that makes an effort gets a little blinded by the light at one point or another. When this happens, we can either course correct, recover (the effort of which leads to even greater transmutation), and keep going, or give up, and float through life like a jellyfish with flashback syndrome who inks out spiritual platitudes on unsuspecting passers-by. No amount of heightened spiritual awareness can bypass the need to develop a stable, healthy, integrated relative self who can fully function at its highest potential in the world.

Referring back to the quote by Jiddu Krishnamurti at the beginning of the chapter, "When you begin to understand what you are, without trying to change it, then what you are, undergoes a transformation." To understand *what* we are we first must be able to observe *how* we are. The *how* is key to grasping the *what*. It's been established that observation, whether by a conscious human being or through the machines that humans create, has an impact on what is being observed. This confirms that Krishnamurti's statement is true. He's asking us to not just observe (non judgmentally) what we are, but to *understand* it.

In this context, what does it mean to understand?

It's easy to imagine, and perhaps you've met, people who know a lot but understand very little. Understanding is not knowledge and intellect is not intelligence. There are different types of understanding: Objectual understanding as in, "I understand X," where X is a specific subject matter. Then there is understanding *why,* as in, "I understand why my boss is displeased with my performance." Propositional understanding is expressed in individual propositions like, "I understand that my sister's birthday is in April (even though I always forget it)."

The understanding that we're concerned with here is a more complex state in which knowledge coincides with sensing (intuition) and feeling. There's a deeper motivational element behind understanding that isn't found in knowledge. When we desire to truly understand something or someone, we're driven by curiosity, and that curiosity is driven by our desire for truth. The definition that we'll use here refers to a type of penetration. An awareness that is beyond the confines of the relative self, penetrates the layers of the relative self in order to understand it. The word *emperipolesis* describes an active penetration by one cell into and through, a larger cell. Emperipolesis is unlike *phagocytosis,* in which the engulfed cell is killed. In emperipolesis, the engulfed cell remains perfectly viable within the other, and can exit at any time without causing structural or functional abnormalities in either cell.

To truly understand one's self requires a mental and sensory penetration of the relative realm—so that we can know it from within, which leads to understanding. Animal cells have an ultrastructure. Again, to understand *what* we are, requires first clearly observing *how* we are. To do that, we need to penetrate the outer membrane of our relative self and look at the components and determine whether these components create harmony or disharmony. Exploring the topography of the relative self is part of the inner work of the Lesser Mysteries and continues, in an even more intense way, as one journeys through the Greater Mysteries.

The relative self encompasses all of our:

- Feeling and emotion
- Thought patterns
- Beliefs
- Experiences
- Values
- Our unique approach vector (the way we approach the world)
- Shadow

All of these things combined create a self-image and influence one's measure of worthiness and confidence.

Western psychology is perfect for the preparatory inner work needed before one begins to explore the Mysteries. To thoroughly explore the topography of the relative self would require an entire book, or collection of books, and most of those have already been written in one form or another. The following is a brief look at the way Western psychology has developed means by which anyone can begin riding the wave of transformation by exploring and healing the self.

Feeling & Emotion

Some feelings and emotions are so powerful that we try to hold them in check and suppress them because we fear that if we allowed ourselves to fully feel, we would come apart at the seams. While coming apart at the seams is not something we should do on a regular basis, sometimes it's the best thing we could do. The sensation of falling apart isn't your Beingness coming undone; it's patterns that are unraveling. It's the patterns that hold negative emotions in place, patterns of thinking, feeling, and responding.

Emotions are of particular interest because, unlike feeling, they play out in the body without our conscious effort. Something moves through us before we even have time to think about it. Some emotions create disharmony in the body, disrupt the immune system, and damage the heart's electrical system. Learning to master emotion isn't to become an unfeeling robot. Mastering emotions means to consciously allow emotions to move through the body and then dissipate without identifying with them.

One challenge that people face today is society's misunderstanding of what emotion is, what feeling is, and how those two different responses combined create a state of being. Happiness is an emotional response, but joy and love are *states of being*. Hope and gratitude are also not emotions (more on that in chapters 17 and 21). Feeling is a response that arises in awareness as a valuing function. Emotions are involuntary. Surprise, amusement, excitement, disgust, primal fear, gleeful elation, sadness, anger, anxiety, embarrassment, and sexual arousal all play out in the body as automatic responses, and can hijack our ability to discern, reason, respond wisely and connect. Awe, gratitude, hope, confidence, and appreciation for beauty are more complex, *feeling* responses that arise in awareness.

On one hand, emotion is the alchemical fire whose warmth brings everything into existence and whose heat burns all superfluities to ashes. But on the other hand, emotion is the moment when steel meets flint and a spark is struck forth, for emotion is the chief source of consciousness. There is no change from darkness to light or from inertia to movement without emotion. —Carl Jung, *Collected Works 9,*
Page 96

Jung is saying that involuntary emotion was the chief source of human consciousness. Imagine if humans went through life without any response whatsoever. Emotion was the first primal response to the phenomena of life. If you find a list that accurately classifies emotions versus a list of feelings, you'll see that the majority (around 70% depending on the list) of emotions are considered negative. This is because emotions are primal responses in the ancient, neurological structures of the brain that were formed to ensure survival. Emotions do not emerge from the cerebral cortex associated with thinking, feeling, valuing, and planning in modern humans.

Feeling is the secret. —Neville Goddard

As human consciousness has evolved, feeling has come into play. Emotions were the first spark that woke us up, but it is our ability to *feel* that makes us truly human.

Psychologist, Steven C. Hays developed Acceptance and Commitment Therapy or ACT in 1986 as a response to the approach that psychology was taking to human suffering. Up until the mid-eighties, the common belief among psychologists was that pain and suffering should be minimised. Hayes understood that suffering is an integral part of human existence. He wanted to develop a therapy model that encouraged patients to not only accept their pain, but to embrace it. ACT focuses on learning to compassionately accept all our feelings and allow ourselves to feel them fully so that we develop understanding of them, where they originate, and how they impact our lives.

One concept at the core of ACT is *experiential avoidance,* which the ACT model defines as "the deliberate attempt to change or reduce difficult thoughts, feelings, memories, or sensations at the cost of overt effective action." Another concept at the core of ACT is that language shapes reality since it creates the illusion that the world is pre-organised into parts and forces. We see here that the ACT model recognises cognitive fragmentation, which will eventually lead us back to William Blake and *The Four Zoas.*

ACT uses mindfulness practice, acceptance, values exploration, and commitment (goal setting) to help the individual develop psychological flexibility and resiliency that ultimately creates space for value-based choices and actions that lead to well-being.

Thought Patterns

Cognitive Behavioural Therapy focuses on thoughts, feelings, bodily sensations and actions, and how these seemingly disparate phenomena are interconnected and can create complex patterns that can lock us in a vicious cycle, or set us free. CBT tends to focus on the present life circumstances and experience without delving too deeply into childhood experience and trauma.

When we begin to look at ourselves and our patterns of thought, we start asking different questions and making new connections. This change is reflected in our body. The brain is a remarkable organ capable of drastic change. Researchers at Linköping University in Sweden established that after just nine weeks of CBT, the brains of the research subjects physically changed. The magnetic resonance images of the patients' brains showed a decrease in the volume and activity of the amygdala.

Hebb's Rule (1949) states that repeated experience can either strengthen or weaken neuronal bonds in the brain, hence the statement, "Neurons that fire together, wire together." The more you focus on something, the more neuronal connections to that image your brain makes. CBT has been shown to be twice as effective as antidepressants in preventing relapse. Antidepressants dampen the limbic activity in the brain, which is the emotional centre, but CBT creates coherence in the cortex, which is not only the seat of reason—it's also the region where feeling flowers.

Researchers at King's College in London demonstrated that CBT also strengthens *healthy* neurological connections in patients with psychosis and schizophrenia. They recorded an increase in connectivity between dorsolateral prefrontal cortex and post-central gyrus that were predicted to reduced levels of psychotic symptoms. CBT has a transformative effect on the human brain, which leads to a cascade of other physiological changes in the body. We really do transform from the inside out.

Belief

Beliefs are choices. First you choose your beliefs.
Then your beliefs affect your choices. — Roy T. Bennett

Assumptions and beliefs are the lenses through which we look at the world. They can distort, magnify, filter, tint, blur, or clarify.

Willingness potentiates.

Questioning opens.

Belief shapes.

Truth clarifies.

When we're willing to see ourselves for *who* and *how* we really are, a power within us immediately responds to that willingness by opening the door to potentiality, all we have to do is walk through it. Like stories, beliefs are engines of imagination. If we carry too many rigid beliefs, our perception and understanding of life will be drastically limited. If we don't believe at all, our creative faculties are nullified. Beliefs are indeed choices. Whether those choices are conscious or not is another issue. Henry David Thoreau wrote, "Live your beliefs and you can turn the world around." We are **always** living our beliefs, even if we're not aware of it. Any serious self-inquiry demands that we perform a sort of inventory of our beliefs. We retrieve them from the recesses of our mind, unwrap them, and closely examine them: Are they helpful, harmful, neutral, untrue, true?

Conscious use of belief as an engine of imagination is the most helpful tool we have for creating the life we desire. Likewise, a willingness to let go of harmful beliefs is the first step to maximising our potential to heal, transform, and create. We hold beliefs based on models that we've created. Humans develop mental models for skills, knowledge, behaviour, people, nature, etc. The mind is constantly adopting, applying, or rejecting models without us giving it much thought. When we adopt a model for anything, we're adopting a pattern, and those patterns that collect over time, become our habitual perception of experience.

I first encountered Byron Katie's work through her book, *Loving What Is: Four Questions That Can Change Your Life* in 2005, after the death of my mother. Ten years later, I picked up the book again to see if it could help me through some shadow-integration work I was doing; it did. Katie's words are timeless because they point towards truth. She calls it "The Work" and describes The Work as the *how* more than the *what*. On her website she writes, "Great spiritual texts describe the what—what it means to be free. The Work is the how. It shows you exactly how to identify and question any thought that would keep you from that freedom." *The Work* is deceptively simple. It's the most powerful tool for the first step of examining our thoughts, and helps us question the nature of our beliefs.

Our core beliefs are our most basic foundational beliefs about ourselves, other people, and the world. A core belief is a belief that you accept without question. You're convinced that it's true, and you'll insist that experience has proven it to be so.

Some examples of core beliefs are:

People can't be trusted.
Life is random.
Men aren't emotional.
Women are irrational.
I'm unworthy.
I'm unlovable.
The world is dangerous.
Rich people are selfish.
The world is pre-organised into parts.
The world is divided into the privileged and the disadvantaged.
The world is divided into the oppressors and the oppressed.
My agency is limited because the system is oppressing me.
I'm not artistic.
I'm always second-best.
I'm not entrepreneurial.
Women don't like sex as much as men.
All men want sex all the time.

CBT, ACT, and Byron Katie's *The Work* are all highly effective ways of examining our core beliefs and liberating ourselves from them.

It's funny how easy it is for teenagers and adults to adopt limiting core beliefs, and how difficult it can be to fully integrate positive, helpful ones. If you've spent much time around small children, you've probably observed how ready they are to adopt positive core beliefs about themselves and the world. It's easier for children under the age of seven to believe that they can learn to do anything because they're still connected to the vast potentiality with which we're all born. That potentiality is our true nature. On the Wisdom Path, experience is our greatest ally, but it's also the biggest cause of our disconnection from the open state of awareness (innocence) from which children operate.

Experience

William Blake asserted that experience and innocence were two contrary states of the human soul, but that true innocence couldn't exist without experience. The return to innocence requires a journey through experience. As we journey through the experiential terrain of life, we have a choice: We can develop defence mechanisms and hide away in a tower of belief, or we can reach forward and make the most of the impulse we were born with, the tendency to self-actualise, to *become*.

In "Songs of Experience" Blake included a poem called *The Angel*.

> *I Dreamt a Dream! What can it mean?*
> *I was a maiden Queen,*
> *Guarded by an Angel mild:*
> *Witless woe, was ne'er beguil'd!*
> *And I wept both night and day*
> *And he wip'd my tears away*
> *And I wept both day and night*
> *And hid from him my hearts delight*
> *So he took his wings and fled:*
> *Then the morn blush'd rosy red:*
> *I dried my tears & armed my fears,*
> *With ten thousand shields and spears.*
> *Soon my Angel came again;*
> *I was arm'd, he came in vain:*
> *For the time of youth was fled*
> *And grey hairs were on my head.*

In this poem, an Eternal who decided to enter experience as a human being meets her personal angel in a memory (a vision) that she thinks must have been a dream. She remembers herself as a noble one, a Queen in her own right, that is guarded by a higher angel who is another part of her being, that exists in another realm while she journeys through experience in the land of the dead (life on earth).

Insecure and jaded, she doesn't trust her angel. She says, "I wept and he wiped my tears away." Here she's acknowledging that she can't hide her sorrow from the angel. She says that he soothed her, but she can't trust. Experience has made her doubtful. So she hides her heart's delight from the angel, causing him to take his wings and flee.

Without awareness of any connection with her angel, she continues. A new day dawns, and she shields herself with "ten thousand shields and spears" to continue through life. But these shields block her from her angel and her own heart. The angel comes again, but he comes in vain. The time in which he could have helped her make her heart's delight manifest within the realm of experience has passed. She is now an old woman close to the end of her life. What could have been? What is the point of experience if we leave it up to randomness or fate?

Experience Reveals the Self

In his book, *On Becoming a Person* (1967), psychologist Carl Rogers describes how we discover ourselves through experience. He asserts that to find oneself means to find a pattern, an "underlying order which exists in a ceaselessly changing flow" of experience. He says that rather than trying to cling to "experience in the form of a mask," or to make it conform to a structure, being oneself means to "discover the unity and harmony of one's true feelings and authentic reactions."

The real self is something that is comfortably discovered in one's experiences, not something imposed upon it. —Carl Rogers

In other words, don't try to impose yourself upon the flow of experience, *find yourself within it* instead. Anything that we could impose will ultimately be found to be inauthentic, as a mask or a pattern.

Values

Life is a question, and you are the answer. Life is constantly asking us, "What do you value?" We answer that question unconsciously most of the time because we haven't gotten clear on what our values are.

Deep in your heart, what matters most to you? At the end of your life, what would you like your life to have meant? What kind of person do you most desire to be? If everything were stripped away from you, what do you possess that no one and nothing could take away?

Our core values are the things we revere the most; they're the reason we get out of bed every day. Peripheral values are the things that are important to us, but not essential to our motivation for acting. Being aware of, and honest about our values is a step towards alignment. Knowing what you truly value makes riding the wave of transformation smoother and less confusing.

In chapter two, I listed the foundations of fulfillment and clarified that they aren't rigid, universal requirements. You'll see that some of the foundations appear to be values. In identifying them, I couldn't rely exclusively on my own experience. I've been observing and questioning people my entire life. I've worked and connected with hundreds of people and read books from thousands more. My entire life has been a study of humanity and remains as such. While it's true that we start with ourselves, we don't exist in a vacuum. Learning from my interactions with people who are fulfilled versus those who aren't, I did my best to identify the states of awareness, modes of perception, values, and priorities of people who are deeply fulfilled human beings.

You determine which foundations resonate with you. You might add to, or subtract from the list. Some of the foundations of fulfillment are not just values, some are states of being. A value is a treasure and a sort of mental vector. A state of being is vastly more complex. As an approach vector, our values determine how, and from which angle, we touch down in life. A value exercise helps us gain clarity and gauge our level of alignment. Do our choices, behaviours, and circumstances align with our values? If they don't, you can expect a crash landing.

Here is a list of values. You may think of some that aren't on the list, if so, add them. To complete the exercise, go through them and mark each one as E=extremely important, Q=quite important, or N=not important. Then narrow your list down by selecting your top ten E values and top ten Q values.

Once you've done that, choose just three values from the list of twenty. These are your core values, for now. As you transform, your values might change.

There is another aspect to values that people often forget: When we are still in the beginning stages of transformation, our values are the masters we serve and *how* we serve them matters greatly. Drug addicts and Zen monks share the same core value: Peace of mind. One gets there via meditation, inner work, and dedication to a path; the other attains only temporary, unconscious peace via annihilation of awareness with chemicals and damages their life in the process. Some of the wisest people I know are ex-addicts. They recognised that the way they were serving and living their value was destructive; so they turned things around through extraordinary effort and commitment.

It all starts with a realisation.

Once you're clear on what your values are, it's important to discern whether those values are being served in a way that creates equilibrium, health, and brings true fulfillment. Eventually, the journey up the spiral of awareness means that we don't serve values as a master; we master our values—they serve the process of becoming, not the other way around. This is another example of trans*mutation* and the aforementioned phenomenological reorientation of aspirants.

Acceptance	Development	Integrity	Sensitivity
Accomplishment	Devotion	Intelligence	Serenity
Accountability	Dignity	Intensity	Service
Accuracy	Discipline	Intuitive	Sharing
Achievement	Discovery	Irreverent	Significance
Adaptability	Drive	Joy	Silence
Alertness	Effectiveness	Justice	Simplicity
Altruism	Efficiency	Kindness	Sincerity
Ambition	Empathy	Knowledge	Skill
Amusement	Empower	Lawful	Skilfulness
Assertiveness	Endurance	Leadership	Smart
Attentiveness	Energy	Learning	Solitude
Awareness	Enjoyment	Liberty	Spirit
Balance	Enthusiasm	Logic	Spirituality
Beauty	Equality	Love	Spontaneous
Boldness	Ethical	Loyalty	Stability
Bravery	Excellence	Mastery	Status
Brilliance	Experience	Maturity	Stewardship
Calm	Exploration	Meaning	Strength
Candour	Expressive	Moderation	Structure
Capable	Fairness	Motivation	Success
Careful	Family	Openness	Support

Certainty	Famous	Optimism	Surprise
Challenge	Fearless	Order	Sustainability
Charity	Feelings	Organisation	Talent
Cleanliness	Ferocious	Originality	Teamwork
Clear	Fidelity	Passion	Temperance
Clever	Focus	Patience	Thankful
Comfort	Foresight	Peace	Thorough
Commitment	Fortitude	Performance	Thoughtful
Common sense	Freedom	Persistence	Timeliness
Communication	Friendship	Playfulness	Tolerance
Community	Fun	Poise	Toughness
Compassion	Generosity	Potential	Traditional
Competence	Genius	Power	Tranquility
Concentration	Giving	Present	Transparency
Confidence	Goodness	Productivity	Trust
Connection	Grace	Professionalism	Trustworthy
Consciousness	Gratitude	Prosperity	Truth
Consistency	Greatness	Purpose	Understanding
Contentment	Growth	Quality	Uniqueness
Contribution	Happiness	Realistic	Unity
Control	Hard work	Reason	Valour
Conviction	Harmony	Recognition	Victory
Cooperation	Health	Recreation	Vigour

Courage	Honesty	Reflective	Vision
Courtesy	Honour	Respect	Vitality
Creation	Hope	Responsibility	Wealth
Creativity	Humility	Restraint	Welcoming attitude
Credibility	Imagination	Results	Winning
Curiosity	Improvement	Reverence	Wisdom
Decisive	Independence	Rigour	Wonder
Decisiveness	Individuality	Risk	
Dedication	Innovation	Satisfaction	
Dependability	Inquisitive	Security	
Determination	Insightful	Self-reliance	
Development	Inspiration	Selfless	

Transactional Analysis

When you grow beyond the limits that other people would like to confine you to, you may notice that friends fall away, and family members begin to act oddly, sometimes even hostile. It doesn't matter how humble you are, how altruistic you are, or how much you care; you'll still hear things like, "Oh, you think you're too good for us now?"—"Just remember where you came from!"—"Who do you think you are?"—"Ah, you know you're just (insert whatever label they're trying to place on you)."

It can be baffling and frustrating, especially when members of your own family say, "You've changed," and you realise that they never knew you to begin with. You are just a person that they project the unconscious patterns of dysfunctional family dynamics upon.

So, what gives? What's really going on here?

Dr. Eric Berne is the author of the best-selling book, "Games People Play." In the 1950s, Dr. Berne developed a theory called Transactional Analysis, henceforth referred to as TA. TA examines the underlying patterns that influence relationships, communication, and emotional responses.

Berne observed three, key ego-states that most people inhabit and oscillate between:

- Parent
- Child
- Adult

Each of these states represent an individual's model of what they believe a parent or child is like, and how a parent or child perceives and responds to events. In his book, "Transactional Analysis and Psychotherapy," Berne states, "It will be demonstrated that Parent, Adult, and Child are not concepts, like Superego, Ego, and Id, or the Jungian constructs but phenomenological realities." The Parent State consists of internal impressions formed by external events in the first five years of our lives. These are the imprints that the child accepts without questioning. Statements like, "Because I said so," "Don't play with fire," and "Don't trust strangers" are examples of imprints that the child records and accepts as not only true, but an example of parental infallibility.

The Parent State is also influenced by people who are not their parents. Any event that involves an adult with authority can be recorded by the child as an imprint that informs their view of The Parent.

The Child State is also programmed in the first five years of life. These are internal impressions that are emotional and/or feeling responses to external events. Impressions like, "I felt scared when I got separated from mom at the store and couldn't find her" or, "It feels good to be praised for colouring inside of the lines."

TA uses the following diagrams to clarify the first two ego-states:

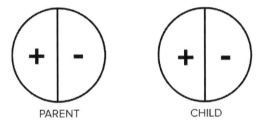

PARENT   CHILD

TA uses the alchemical solar symbol to represent the Adult State:

Adjacent to the binary, Parent and Child symbols, TA theorises that the Parent and Child states comprise functional states as well, each being either negative or positive, as follows:

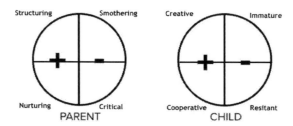

According to TA, until an individual becomes conscious, he/she moves into the various ego-states constantly, without realising it. These states determine our responses and behaviour during transactions with other people. A transaction is defined as any interaction between two people, verbal or non-verbal. The Parent and Child states are reactive and unconscious. The adult state is unique in that, unlike the other two states, it is a state of mindfulness. It's responsive, not reactive, and can tap into the functionally positive aspects of either the Parent or Child states at will.

Transactional analysis goes very deep into how each ego-state functions and the interplay between people as they move between states. The scope of TA is vast to summarise here. It's worth learning more about because it helps one understand how our interactions evolve as we transform and become more conscious.

People are always trying to get their needs met in one form or another. As you change, some of the people around you may notice (albeit unconsciously) that you are no longer playing their games. When we stay in the Adult mode, a state that is actualised, mature, present, and non-reactive, the people around us will either accept our new way of being and respond positively, or reject it. If they choose to reject, they will typically be triggered into the "flight or fight" response. This is where understanding the Drama Triangle of TA comes in.

The Drama Triangle

The Drama Triangle was conceived by a student of Dr. Berne named Stephen Karpman. The triangle models the toxic interaction that occurs when three unconscious ego-states feed off of each other. It's another way that humans seek to have their unconscious, unexamined needs met. There are three roles: Persecutor, Victim, and Rescuer.

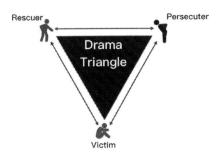

Victim: Blames others, feels powerless, feels incapable, is needy, may grovel, and constantly allows others to do for them instead of doing for themselves. We can move into this state in a fraction of a second and move out of it just as fast.

Persecutor: Criticises, "Who do you think you are?"—"You're just X, Y, Z," and so on. They're insulting, rude, abusive, criticise without offering guidance, and are generally unpleasant. They might often micromanage at home and work, curse people while driving, or if they are especially Machiavellian, they might resort to gaslighting and find more creative ways of undermining and sabotaging others. Persecutors love to knock a person "down a notch" and remind them of their "place." Ironically, like the Victim, they also blame others.

Rescuer: Loves helping others, but does it in a way that actually disempowers the person who is in victim-mode. The rescuer will say, "Here, I know how to do this; let me do it for you" instead of showing the person how to do for himself. Rescuers make themselves indispensable to others as a way of getting a need met, the need to be needed, admired, and appreciated.

In any interaction, people can move between the Parent/Child ego states while playing any of the roles on the Drama Triangle. By now, you're probably starting to understand exactly why some people react negatively to your growth and transformation. You might also be seeing how and when you have moved into any of these states yourself. Now that you're aware of them, you can focus on stabilising in the 'Adult' state and refuse to be pulled into drama triangles and the games people play.

Bypass

Society seems to be built to encourage something called bypass. At one level, bypass is an example of the mind's tactic of misdirection, a tactic that leads people into, and through, a labyrinth. It plasters posters over hidden doors that, if you knew were there, would lead you to an inner sanctum.

John Welwood, a Buddhist teacher and psychotherapist, coined the term "spiritual bypass" in the 1980s. Spiritual bypass is defined as "The tendency to use spiritual ideas and practices to sidestep or avoid facing unresolved emotional issues, psychological wounds, and unfinished developmental tasks." There are more ways to bypass than spiritually. Ultimately, bypass is a means by which one avoids the inner work necessary for self-actualisation. *Spiritual* bypass is the rarest form of bypass. In my experience, there are four primary forms of bypass. In addition to spiritual bypass there are:

- ◆ Cultural/Societal Bypass
- ◆ Ideological Bypass
- ◆ Religious Bypass

Cultural bypass—is the most obvious and most common because it's the easiest. People invest much of their energy to check the boxes of societal conformity: formal education, a diploma, a good job, acceptance by a peer group, an attractive appearance, some degree of conscientiousness, alignment with a political party, religion, a spouse and children. That's it; they stop there because creating that, and maintaining it, demands most of their energy and creates a degree of satisfaction that some call happiness. If you add a little art, cultural savvy, travel, intellectual pursuits, and hobbies, you get a gold star next to your name. If all, or most, of those boxes are checked, society and family let you get away with *a lot*. If you've got a gold star, you get away with even more. A person can be narcissistic, emotionally unstable, chronically depressed, unfulfilled, and even toxic to others, but if they can maintain the above-listed criteria, they're given a pass even if they're hanging on by a thread. Most importantly, they give themselves a pass because radical self-inquiry and honesty are just too painful for them.

Ideological bypass—can be part of cultural bypass or sidestep it completely. Extreme ideologues may completely reject social norms and the culture in which they live. Ideological possession is an identity crisis and one of the most extreme forms of projection. You stop being fully human and become a replicator.

Religious bypass—is also part of cultural bypass. At its most extreme, people who use religion to bypass self-actualisation do so by adopting the belief that as long as they follow the rules, accept theological statements as incontrovertible truth, and confess sin, all is good. On the other hand, religion can be part of a healthy approach to self-actualisation. It depends (in part) on the person, the religion, and how deep an individual goes into the esoteric core of their exoteric faith. Even then, if they don't address their core, and the fundamentals of self-inquiry, psychological health, and emotional maturation, they end up taking the spiritual bypass. It's extremely difficult to resolve emotional wounds, process pain, and foster our *becoming* if we're isolated. We need other people, specifically wise, helpful, and nonjudgmental souls who are understanding, and who know how to support others through the process of transformation. This assistance is especially important as we begin the most challenging part of the process: shadow work.

Dark Wings

Across the midnight sky
Dark wings capture me
Guiding me to oblivion
Releasing the essence of my soul
Sip sweet nectar my dark butterflies
At last your dark wings soar
—Anonymous poet "Basia"

The I Ching is perhaps the oldest known model of the human psyche. Unlike Blake's fourfold representation of the psyche as The Four Zoas: Thinking (Urizen), Sensing/Willing (Tharmas), Feeling (Luvah), and Imagination (Urthona); the I Ching models the psyche as a sixfold construct with the four aspects explored by Blake, plus two unconscious areas of the psyche; the chthonic (the underworld) and the divine (the Daimon), an inner sage living outside of time.

The lines of hexagram 36 called, *Ming—The Darkening of the Light* says:

Not light but darkness,
First he climbed up to heaven,
Then he plunged into the depths of the earth.

This hexagram is referring to what happens to human consciousness as it misidentifies with the light side of the psyche as the totality of one's true self while suppressing the undesirable aspects.

Philosophy, fairytales, mythology, and mysticism have explored the two unseen aspects of our psyche for thousands of years, but it was Carl Jung who made the concept mainstream when he coined the term "The Shadow" to refer to this repression. It's important to recognise that repression isn't limited to the ugly, evil parts of the psyche. It can and does include positive, potentially helpful aspects of the persona as well. The shadow is everything of which a person is not fully conscious, both the positive *and* the negative. Not all of it is repressed, there are parts of the shadow that exist in the collective that haven't entered the personal shadow—yet.

Our shadow is our depth.

Remaining aware of this depth and integrating it into our conscious experience is a lifelong process. Encountering and integrating the shadow is central and necessary to actualisation. Jung describes the three phases of the shadow process as encountering, merging, and assimilation.

When the individual is confronted with both sides of the shadow, they often describe one side as angelic and the other as monstrous. Do you remember the Zoroastrian *Daena* from chapter two? Listen to Neville Goddard's account of his experience of his *Daena* and his own cacodaimon, that he shared in his 1968 lecture, "The Role of the Book."

> Back in the early 1930s I suddenly found myself confronted with two characters. Above me and to my right stood a beautiful angelic being, while below stood a monstrous hairy animal that looked like an orangutan. Speaking in a guttural voice he looked up at this heavenly being and said: "She's my mommy." Repelled by the thought, I struck him and with each blow, he grew in strength. Then, from the depth of my own being, I realised that these two were my creations. Speaking with a human voice and looking like an animal covered with hair, this monstrous being was the embodiment and personification of all of my misspent energies. Every unlovely thought, every cruel, thoughtless act aided its growth. Whispering in my ear, influencing my decisions in order to feed its hunger, it fed on violence, while the angelic being was the embodiment of every kind and lovely thought I ever possessed.
>
> Then I realised *he had the right to live.* By claiming to be the offspring of this heavenly being, he claimed to exist but I knew he did not. He had no power of his own, only my power of awareness. Although he appeared to be detached and completely free of my perception, I knew I was the cause of his life. And as I pledged myself that I would redeem him, he melted and all of the energy I had given to create and sustain that monster, returned to me. He not only dissolved but left no trace of ever having been present. Today I can bring him back in memory but he had no existence outside of myself.

When we were children, we quickly learned that certain actions, thoughts, and speech are unacceptable by our parents, teachers, peers, and God (or so we're told). To avoid being "bad" children, we create an imaginary figure in our psyche that polices our thoughts. Whenever an unacceptable impulse or thought arises, this inner monitor triggers a response in the amygdala, and the child experiences anxiety and discomfort. To avoid that anxiety, the psyche begins suppressing unacceptable thoughts, ideas, and desires so quickly that the child doesn't even have time to register them consciously. This is the creation of the personal shadow.

Why would we suppress a positive trait that could be a life-enhancing source of deep personal fulfillment? Socialisation is one reason. The socialisation process begins at birth. The definition of the socialisation process is "to acquaint individuals with the norms of a collective." The process serves both the individual and the collective in that it trains the individual to control violent impulses, share resources, and work towards a common goal.

In a world dominated by the Machine, socialisation leans heavily towards reinforcing behaviours and thoughts that fit into the Machine's superstructure and agendas. The Machine requires collective consent. Unruly individuals with minds and wills of their own are a danger to that structure. The DMV is the American Psychiatric Association's 'bible.' In the 1980s, they concocted a new disorder called *oppositional defiant disorder* or ODD. The symptoms include:

- Often argues with adults.
- Often questions rules.
- Temper tantrums.
- Uses mean and hateful talking when upset.

While the FDA has yet to approve medications for the treatment of childhood, oops, I mean 'ODD,' some psychiatrists in the United States are submitting thousands of children to Aripiprazole and Risperidone, two antipsychotic medications to treat this supposed psychiatric disorder.

In his article, "The Systematic Crushing of Young Non-Conformist and Anti-Authoritarians," Dr. Bruce Levine writes:

Heavily tranquillising antipsychotic drugs (e.g., Zyprexa and Risperdal) are now the highest-grossing class of medication in the United States ($18 billion in 2011). A major reason for this, according to the Journal of the American Medical Association in 2010, is that many children receiving antipsychotic drugs have non-psychotic diagnoses such as ODD or some other disruptive disorder; this especially true of Medicaid-covered paediatric patients.

Over the past 75 years, collective norms have been manipulated by social engineering via multi-layered propaganda to a degree never before seen in recorded history. Now mind-altering pharmaceuticals are being used in addition to social conditioning. Socialisation is a form of mind and behaviour control. Some of it emerges from human nature, but much of the most recent socialisation is purely ideological. The most recent set of collectivist norms masquerade as humanism while actually being anti-human. Is it any wonder then that both the individual and collective shadows have densified exponentially?

There is a difference between individuation and individualism. One is a process; the other is an ideology. Society is an essential part of human existence. Without a collective to act as both opposition and support, there could be no flowering of individuality. Individuation is, as Jung said, "Coming to selfhood" as an integrated consciousness that is characterised by wholeness. Wholeness is a state in which the conscious and unconscious work together in harmony. When I had my personally poignant insight on the fourfold structure of the earth symbol (circle with quadrants), I had never studied or read anything from Jung. The fact that I had that sudden insight, independent of any direct external influence, is proof of Jung's statement from *The Self*, Ibidem, par. 59:

> Although "wholeness" seems at first sight to be nothing but an abstract idea (like anima and animus), it is nevertheless empirical in so far as it is anticipated by the psyche in the form of spontaneous or autonomous symbols. These are the quaternity or mandala symbols, which occur not only in the dreams of modern people who have never heard of them but are widely disseminated in the historical records of many peoples and many epochs. Their significance as symbols of unity and totality is amply confirmed by history as well as by empirical psychology.

As he says, modern people who have never even heard of or understand these *quaternity symbols* will dream of them. The unconscious speaks. Jung believed that the spontaneous production of quaternity images, whether consciously or in dreams, is an indication of the ego's capacity to assimilate unconscious content.

Making the most of our capacity to assimilate unconscious content is vital to the merger of the light (what we're conscious of) with the shadow, and into the persona. These symbols represent the beginning of the unification process but don't guarantee it.

Jung points out in *The Psychology of the Transference*:

> These images are naturally only anticipations of a wholeness which is, in principle, always just beyond our reach. Also, they do not invariably indicate a subliminal readiness on the part of the patient to realise that wholeness consciously, at a later stage; often they mean no more than a temporary compensation of chaotic confusion.

Encountering the positive aspects of our shadow side can be surprising, so surprising that we can scarcely imagine that we're capable of such creativity and resourcefulness. This is when having the courage to stand against the tidal wave of tyrannical *normality* and learning to have faith in yourself comes into play.

But what of the "chaotic confusion" that Jung refers to above? It can be any number of things but as concerns the shadow, that chaotic confusion is a common experience when one initially encounters their dark side. When I set out to encounter my shadow, it knocked me silly. I went wobbly in the truest sense of the word. It took almost two years of full-time work and immense determination to begin to merge, and that's despite my years of self-inquiry and inner work. Shadow work is an ass-kicker.

Encountering shadow is extremely difficult to prepare for precisely because you are utterly unaware that the things that are torturing you are part of you. They will seem genuinely separate from the self. It's no small shock to discover that the demons of the world, are in truth, your own.

Embracing the Beautiful, Ugly Beast

This thing of darkness I acknowledge mine. —William Shakespeare

For I do not understand what I am doing, because I do not practice what I want to do but I do what I hate. —Romans 7:15

Creation is bound to destruction. A pristine, blank canvas is a space of infinite potential, but as soon as we cover the canvas with a work of art, we've destroyed that potential by collapsing it. When we speak, we destroy the silence. In your life, you may have known someone who hated your guts. You've also likely known someone who told you that you're one of their favourite people. Which of these people knows the real you? Who is correct in their assessment of you? Neither. You are an infinite potential that is constantly collapsing potentiality in order to create.

Everyone has had a murderous thought, *everyone*. Perhaps someone pissed you off in traffic, and a satisfying image of running them off a cliff entered your mind. Maybe some kid stole your crayons in the first grade, and you wished the wicked witch would gobble him up.

Millions of people play video games so that they can release the destructive energy that modern society requires they contain. People of all races and both genders think bigoted, angry, and accusing thoughts at some point in their life. Anyone of any race, culture, or gender who claims they haven't is either intentionally lying or totally unconscious. Everyone has experienced jealousy and envy. We can be greedy, manipulative, deceptive, and predatory creatures.

To be human means to map a territory that includes the highest peaks of beauty and the lowest ravines of depravity. We humans are consciousness-mapping cartographers.

The challenge we face isn't the nature of the darkness within, but our identification with, and condemnation of the beast. Neville's beast wasn't ugly because his thoughts were evil, but because he judged them as such. Entering life as a human means entering a realm of predation and uncertainty. The predation of the natural world is not of ill-intent, it's built into the system. A wolf who kills a rabbit doesn't kill because he wants to cause harm; he kills because he wants to eat, that's the only way he knows how to survive.

We easily forget that we're also animals, and our primal instincts are to survive by being the fittest, the fastest, and the most cunning. The entirety of human existence is characterised by a battle between our lower and higher natures. We're normally humble enough not to identify as saints or infallible gods, but we find it remarkably easy to identify with the devils of our primal nature because we've been taught to fear them. What we push away with force will always magnetise back to us. Thoughts come and go; they pass by in a constant stream. Thoughts can self-organise and create thought entities with their own agendas. Our psyche is a densely populated universe full of imaginary characters; the saint, the sinner, the virgin, the whore, the hero, the coward, the jester, the wise man, the fool—the list goes on. But we, as beings, are neither sinner nor saint. To be either of those things would mean that the relative self possesses a permanence that can be categorised. It doesn't, and it can't.

We have access to will. We can decide which actions to take, but we can't decide which thoughts pop into awareness. Thinking happens so fast that we have no conscious way to prevent it. We can only observe, decide if it's something we want to examine further or let pass. One of the fastest ways to assimilate the negative contents of your shadow is to stop identifying with a rigid, dualistic endeavour to be a "good" (versus a "bad") person. Labelling everything as good or bad is a gross oversimplification and results in repression, which creates shadow.

We must stop conforming to culture and group-think. Aim to be a conscious, truthful, and an actualised person who is okay with the fact that you'll have dark thoughts and impulses on occasion. Learn to be okay with being chastised and rejected if people can't handle your authentic self, speech, and perspectives. Live as an Awareness of infinite potential. An Awareness that is conscious of, and actively uses, its will to co-create.

Leave the herd behind.

Shadow Physicians

Humour is in our DNA. It's one of the most essential aspects of mental health and resiliency. Humour is a trait of transcendent strength, along with spirituality, hope, awe, and gratitude. Laughter lowers cortisol and blood pressure. It also creates intimacy. You've probably noticed that you feel suddenly closer to someone with whom you've shared a genuine, deep belly laugh. Humour releases tension and momentarily dissolves blocks between people.

Psychologists have been studying positive humour for a while now. By "positive," they mean humour that's not mean or snarky. To limit our understanding of the benefits of humour by focusing on the *nice* and ignoring the value of the *naughty* is to miss the tremendous power that humour has to help us process our collective shadow.

> *It's always funny until someone gets hurt. Then it's just hilarious.*
> —Bill Hicks

Humour has the power to subvert. It's a powerful weapon against collectivisation and propaganda. The Jester's role is to mock the constrictive social mores that we hide behind like masks. He pulls the curtain back and reveals what's hidden in shadow. The Lakota people of the Great Plains call their jester *Heyoka*. The Heyoka is considered sacred. He can do or say anything during his performance. It's they Heyoka's job to ask uncomfortable questions, and say things that no one else will. The primary purpose of the Heyoka is to catalyse emotional healing. They play the role of our mirror-selves, doing things backwards, wearing clothes inside-out, and saying the opposite of what society considers to be true.

> *When two or more people agree on an issue, I form on the other side.*
> —Bill Hicks

I consider all comedians to be sacred, Shadow Physicians.

Ideology, decades of machine-like corporate professionalism with its tightly regulated, impersonal social behaviour, and its robotic exploitation of humans (who are seen as nothing more than cogs in a machine), centuries of religion and spirituality that encourage exclusive identification with the "light side," and the more recent "political correctness," have resulted in an enormous densification of the collective shadow.

Is it any wonder that comedians, our Shadow Physicians, have come under attack? Individuals with especially dense shadows, magnetised to each other, use social media and corporate pressure and to hunt and cannibalise anyone that poses a threat to their systematic shadow repression. They don't stop until they're satisfied that they've destroyed their target's reputation and cut off their means of income. They're predators.

We *need* our comedians, and they need us. They stand before us—a people who have almost always internalised our collective pain. It's no surprise that many comedians have a history of depression. But they've discovered that unadorned truth is healing. Anyone who stands on a stage with the express purpose of making others laugh is brave. They could be booed off the stage. It takes courage. They do it for themselves and for us.Virtually everyone has heard the phrase, "Laughter is the best medicine." Let's not forget that the most potent of this medicine is administered by vulnerable, courageous, insightful, honest Shadow Physicians.

The best kind of comedy to me is when you make people laugh at things they've never laughed at, and also take a light into the darkened corners of people's minds, exposing them to the light. —Bill Hicks

Another way to assimilate our shadow is to work with our energies through dance, art, exercise, martial arts, music, sport, and a healthy sex life. Storytelling and writing are also helpful. The work of author Stephen King is an example of using writing as a medium for the expression of the personal and collective shadow.

I always wondered who I am when I write because once I'm doing it, I'm not really in the room with myself. —Stephen King

Our Spooky-Cool Power and Shadow

During an interview on the show *Thinking Allowed*, author and researcher Michael Talbot discusses experiences in which the contents of his shadow manifested as phenomena around him and in his home for years. It's fascinating. Instead of describing it here, I encourage you to stop reading now, and go watch part 1 and part 2 of the interview called "Michael Talbot: Synchronicity & the Holographic Universe" on the YouTube channel Caharvey2007. Now that you've watched that interview in full, especially part 2, it's probably clear to you that the unconscious is constantly exteriorised and at work in the world.

What lies in shadow has the power to create and destroy. There is nothing evil about destruction, just as there is nothing inherently good about creation. We misunderstand what it is to be *good*. Goodness isn't the absence of evil, it's an understanding of it, which leads to mastery of ourselves. We also misunderstand what it means to be *perfect*. Perfect doesn't mean flawless. To be perfect is to be *real*. Or at least as real as we can be as waves traveling through an ocean of consciousness. Look at the natural world. Mountain tops are man's peaks of awareness, deep caverns are our underworld, fish are facts, so varied and numerous, swimming through the waters of our mind. Forests are the neural networks in our brains. The process of self-knowledge is like mapping a landscape. In the end, we discover that the topography of the relative self is the topography of the world we inhabit, both psychologically and physically.

Catching the Wave

Again, transformation is a wave. An ocean wave is an energy current moving through water. Each wave has its own unique and significant form. As ocean waves impact the global climate, we each have an impact on world consciousness.

Like meditators in an Ashram, dedicated surfers awake before dawn with a singular purpose; to catch the perfect wave. Arriving at the beach, a surfer takes a contemplative stance as she surveys the shore. Every beach is unique; each has its own constellation of underwater forms. There are reefs, rocks, sandbars, and ravines. This unique underwater landscape determines wave patterns. It also determines when (according to the tide) and where a wave will break. Surfers aren't looking to catch the crest of a wave; they go for the pocket that's created under the breaking point. Catching a wave is no easy thing. To reach the wave, a surfer needs to paddle as if their life depended on it. Once there, she must find her centre of gravity in the middle of the board. Once she's caught the wave, she needs to pop up, to get on her feet, and stay there.

Self-inquiry is like surveying the self's shore and learning about the landscape under the surface of the water. Finding the perfect wave is like finding a transformation vector (area of life and being) that we can identify and are willing to work on. Contemplative practice and emotional intelligence help us find our centre of gravity, and sheer will gets us up on our feet. Just like in surfing, there will be stokes of ecstasy and wipeouts that we experience as moments of suffering. But the surfer is never defeated. Each new wave she catches and rides is a rebirth. At the end of our lives, we'll be like surfers who are glad that they chose to spend the day braving the overwhelming power of the ocean, rather than sitting comfortably under a beach umbrella.

As you move forward, remember these words from Carl Rogers, "The good life is a process, not a state of being. It's a direction, not a destination." You are not an insignificant accident in a random universe. You're tremendously significant to the world, not because you're special or talented or gifted or blessed. You matter not as an illusory 'self' but as an individuated expression of infinite potential, the potential to *be and become*. As you awaken, you'll understand that the 'self' is not the wave. The wave is *your transformative life*, i.e., all your choices and creations. Your life affects the world, all the people you encounter, and even those you'll never meet.

You are worth the effort you put into your own becoming.

The more you know yourself, the more clarity there is. Self-knowledge has no end;
you don't come to an achievement, you don't come to a conclusion.
It is an endless river. —Jiddu Krishnamurti

Chapter 16
RECOVERY OF VISION

I never go anywhere without my Blake. Just read Blake for yourself,
don't listen to what scholars write about his work because many of them
don't understand it themselves! —Neville Goddard

Neville and William would have been fast friends. They both witnessed eternity and couldn't help but speak about it. Whenever I listen to Neville's lectures in his own voice, I feel like he's a sort of Kāru. Kāru is Sanskrit for "poetic singer." Kārus have something magical in their voice, just the sound of it lifts you to higher states, and makes you feel like your heart and mind are expanding.

Blake was also a Kāru. We can't hear his actual voice, but a Kāru is also a composer. The poetic songs they compose have a transformative effect on the listener. In Tantric Buddhism, Abhisheka is a form of prayer that serves as a prelude to initiation. Reading Blake's work is a form of Abhisheka; the work itself is a Kāru. Therefore, it's important to read it for yourself instead of relying on others to tell you about it. Blake's complex poetry awakens preexistent, unconscious gnosis within the reader and catalyses transformation.

Blake was a man on a mission. He was at constant war with what he called the "Single Vision of Newton." When he wasn't waging war on Single Vision, he was insisting that we understand the Zoas, especially Urizen, and how they run amok in our world. Blake laments humanity's lost vision. He wrote, "*If the doors of perception were cleansed every thing would appear to man as it is, Infinite.*"

Cleansing the doors of perception leads to a recovery of vision, specifically what Blake calls Fourfold Vision. He wrote:

Now I a fourfold vision see
And a fourfold vision is given to me
Tis fourfold in my supreme delight
And three fold in soft Beulah's night
And twofold Always.
May God us keep From Single vision & Newton's sleep.

Blake despised Single Vision and "Newton's sleep." Newton's sleep is the sleep of those who rely exclusively on five-sense data, live in a dualistic reality, and perceive linearly. It's a limited way of interpreting reality. Single Vision is also the literal-mindedness of rational materialism and religion. For a person with Single Vision, a tree is just a tree. Single Vision isn't vision at all; it's blindness. It sees *with* the eye, instead of *through* it. Blake said that we're deceived when we view the world this way. In *The Everlasting Gospel*, he writes,

It leads you to Believe a Lie, When you see with, not thro' the Eye.

Single vision is also linear; it sees the past as static and unalterable *fact*.

Twofold vision is symbolic association and the very first level of poetic perception that's aware of the interrelatedness of things. This vision shows us that reality is analogue, but Twofold vision is incomplete because it relies exclusively on the mind to interpret reality. Even though those with Twofold vision can conceive of metaphor and symbolism; they cannot yet incorporate feeling and spirit into their perception. They can't see with the heart or perceive with the spirit.

To see a world in a grain of sand
And a heaven in a wild flower,
Hold infinity in the palm of your hand
And eternity in an hour.
—William Blake, "Auguries of Innocence"

Blake equates Threefold Vision with Beulah. In Beulah, you can "hold infinity in the palm of your hand, and eternity in an hour." Beulah is the midpoint between duality and non-duality. It's where contraries are equally true. Understanding that contraries are equally true leads to authentic—or what Blake would call true—intellect. In Beulah, you can see the poles but you are never polarised. A person with Threefold Vision can always see and understand *all sides* of an issue. Threefold vision reconciles rationality and imagination. Once you've attained Threefold Vision, you no longer see the rational and the irrational as opposites. In Beulah, there's a reconciliation of the rational intellect with the spiritual imagination.

Threefold Vision reveals karma. Every cause has an effect because all things are inextricably connected to one another. Still, if we attain Threefold vision and stay there, never attaining the Fourfold, Blake warns that this leads to ignorance because you mistake the part for the whole.

Fourfold Vision is imaginative perception. It's what Blake considers the pure intellect (true intelligence) of Eternals. While traveling through Generation as a human on your return to Eternity, Fourfold Vision means living life like you would a lucid dream. In Tibetan seven-point Mind Training, they're referring to Fourfold Vision when they direct the practitioner to be an illusory person (and to see others as illusions) between meditation sessions.

This is often misunderstood by those who lean towards solipsism. In a lucid dream, you understand that all the characters in your dream are aspects of yourself. In the waking world, when using Fourfold Vision, you see all the characters as aspects of the Absolute Self and treat them as you would want to be treated. But like in a dream, you don't take anything personally; you don't get offended; you don't seek praise or crumble under criticism for two reasons: 1. It's just a dream, and 2. You can change the dream if you want.

With Fourfold Vision, you will see that time is not only *not* linear; it doesn't exist at all. It's an illusion created by movement. Change of form is movement. Trees grow, children grow, and things wax and wane. Planets and stars move in a pattern. When the mind perceives this movement in and of matter, it creates the illusion of time and believes that the future is unknowable, and the past fixed. With Fourfold Vision, you know that present can revise the past, and the future can communicate with the present. Blake did this in his poetry.

Imagine a book in which one verse can alter the preceding verse in what seems to be an impossible and contradictory way. I won't use Blake here, let's make something up:

1 — *Dark was the world until high in the black firmament, appeared one, lonely star. It shone down on a world of perpetual unknowing, the only light within a shadowy dream.*

In this Dream World, a young man named Ambrose, in awe of the sudden appearance of the star, turned his eyes toward the sky and its new light. Walking without regard for his or anyone else's path, he stumbled accidentally upon a maiden who also stood in wonder of the new light. Falling in love with her immediately, he asked, "Fair One, tell me if you know the name of this mysterious radiance."

The maiden Bélen admitted that she knew not its name but swore that if Ambrose could pull the radiance down for her, she would name it in his honour.

Inspired by the new light, the two fell in love.
But their love lasted only 1000 heartbeats.
At the 1001 pulse of the drum, Bélen's heart faltered in fear that the light may leave them.

Her lover took great, personal offence at her wavering inconsistency and fled. In her despair, Bélen ripped out her heart and flung it towards the dark sky.

And where it landed in the heavens, there appeared the first star. The only light in a lonely sky.

2 — *Alone in a dense wood, Ambrose wept over Bélen's rejection. Hearing his cries a small bird asked him, "Why do you weep? A light has come into the world, look skyward and rejoice!" Looking up, he beheld the first star and its light, a radiance that reminded him of his love for Bélen. Cursing his pride, he ran back to her.*

He found his love under the light of the star, looking up at it, smiling without fear, and yet touched by sorrow. When finally she pulled her eyes away, she noticed her returned Love. Throwing her arms around his neck and weeping from joy, she asked him through her tears, "Do you know the name of this light? I've known it before and called it home, but its name escapes me."

With a kiss on her lips, he answered her tenderly, "I do not my love, but if you'll pull it down for me, I'll name it in your honour."

In this story, the second part revises the first. In the first part, there was a star in the sky at which the two were looking. The second part tells you that there was no light and no star in the sky until Bélen tore her heart out and threw it skywards. In this story, the present choice to tear out her heart changes the past. Now there was no light in the sky in the past. Since it wasn't there, how did the two lovers see the star in the sky on the night they met? If Ambrose hadn't left Bélen, would the original star of the first part have remained in the sky?

Blake does this kind of revision constantly, and in even more complex ways. He does this as a means to drastically alter the reader's perception of a pre-existent foundational order and narrative so that the reader understands that the world is not pre-organised in parts. The world and reality itself are like reading a book that you can change as you read. There is no temporal unfolding towards a future end to the story. The story repeats over and over, constantly changing across time and space. Blake is trying to let us know that our lives are exactly like this. We're in a cycle of Eternal Return; all storylines are playing out in multiple realities, and we can revise the past just as much as we can create the future. This is Fourfold Vision.

Fourfold Vision is the moment when all dimensions cease to appear as separate strata and reveal themselves to be different *modes of perception,* that only appear to be different strata of awareness, within One Mind. The One Mind itself is an all-encompassing, all-pervading light that has been misperceived by itself! If you've ever held two mirrors at an angle to each other and looked at yourself, you see your reflection repeated infinitely. Imagine doing that but not recognising yourself. When you gain Fourfold Vision, you regain your ability to see yourself, not as a reflection but face-to-face. This is when you see yourself looking back at you from someone else's eyes, as I had the unexpected and unearned privilege of doing at the age of eighteen.

Neville Goddard addressed dreams within a dream, revision, and the secret of changing karma—all of this only available to those with Fourfold Vision:

> Within the framework of God's grand dream there is another dream—my dream, your dream. And these that have unnumbered experiences—we aren't going to change His dream for us but we can modify and change within the framework of His dream the things that we will encounter. And if I use the Law wisely I will avoid repetition tomorrow when the wheel turns again. I won't break the foot the next time; I won't have the distorted arm the next time; I won't have anything the next time if now I revise it. So I say: if there is one thing I have been brought into this world to tell you, it is the secret of revision: that if something today is unpleasant, you don't like it, don't let it slip by. The Bible speaks of redeeming the time. Every moment, if it is unpleasant, it should be redeemed, because you are going to meet it tomorrow as the wheel turns.

> Learn art of revision. At the end of each day, review your day. If some unlovely thing in the day, don't allow it, rewrite it. Take that same scene and rewrite it, and having rewritten it replay it. In your imagination you imagine the action to be unfolding and you replay everything in the world; as you replay it as you ought to have played it the first time you've changed it. The present moment is never receding into a 'past' as people think, the moment is advancing circularly. And so you will change the pattern, for the wheel is turning and you can't stop it.

Redeeming the Zoas within Ourselves

Sudden down fell they all together into an unknown Space
Deep horrible without End. Separated from Beulah far beneath
The Mans exteriors are become indefinite opend to pain
In a fierce hungring void & none can visit his regions
—The Four Zoas

To understand Blake's Zoas and archetype in general, three statements must be made:

1. Consciousness precedes matter.
2. Mind is nonlocal.
3. There are many strata and individuations of awareness but one only mind.

Blake's *unnamed forms* (archetypes) exist at what we would call higher and lower (in relation to our location on the 'map' of consciousness) levels. The *supra*-conscious can be described as operating above and outside of normal human consciousness. The subconscious is described as operating below. Blake makes it clear that mankind's consciousness has shrunk; the greater part of the fallen Zoas remain outside of man's awareness.

The Zoas, Tharmas, Urizen, Urthona, and Luvah, fell from their transcendent states into division and, as the verse above describes, fell *even below Beulah*. Still, as one studies the Four Zoas and Blake's cosmology, it's clear that the Zoas are both above (supra-conscious) and below (subconscious) normal human consciousness.

In our normal state of awareness, we're unconscious of these strata, just as we're unconscious of the *daimonic* 'sage outside of time' and the *chthonic* 'underworld.' These strata (or realms) contain thought-forms. We must remember that dimensions aren't only stacked vertically, they're also *sideways* and enfolded within each other, like a cosmic onion. Blake uses the imagery of a vertical fall from above, to below but you can fall *sideways* too.

All advanced meditators quickly learn two things:

1. We do not exist in a vacuum.
2. Our normal human consciousness is, quite literally, mind-numbingly limited.

The fall of the Zoas represents the collapse of both human and *divine* vision. Blake makes it clear that the Zoas are *fallen* and yet still *supra*-conscious divisions of Albion, the broken man. Each Zoa is imbedded within our being. Urizen's influence is most ubiquitous; it takes control of our perception by limiting and directing it.

The Zoas are not merely subconscious *projections*. Nor are they mere abstractions. They are <u>poetic representations</u> of a very real, contemporaneous influence, that corrupts human life.

THE MUNDANE EGG

Milton 33

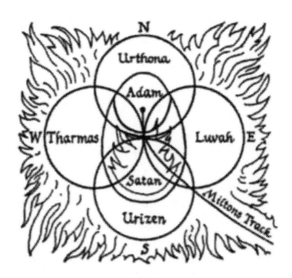

A Broken Man

Albion represents all of humanity. Blake implores us to see ourselves in this broken, Divine Man, Albion. A being in need of self-awareness, he must have the will to change. The only way to restore him is to restore ourselves and become, once more, an Eternal One, a person of timelessness. The re-unification of Albion does more than just restore him to his pre-fallen state; it makes him something far greater than he ever was before. Therefore, Neville Goddard insisted that the fall wasn't accidental at all. It was intentional, regardless of how tragic it appears. The process of fragmentation, incarnation, suffering, and regeneration results in a perfection previously unknown to Albion.

To get a better understanding of how the fallen Zoas impact our lives and the world, let's consider the Zoas in more detail.

Out of all of the Zoas, Blake was most insistent that we understand the massive impact that the Urizenic archetype has on humanity. Sometimes calling him "Nobodaddy," Urizen parodies the God of "Thou Shalt Not..." from the Old Testament. The Book of Urizen reveals just how calamitous the biblical creation story really is. The Book of Urizen opens with an image of horror. A "self-closed" and "all-repelling" demon forms in the abominable void. It's Urizen in his embryonic form, a dark power that is replicating itself through division. This "self-contemplating shadow" comes into existence before the formation of the earth.

Blake writes, *The earth was not, nor globes of attraction.* Urizen speaks and says, "Where nothing was: Natures wide womb." From that, he binds, condenses, and creates a world of solid obstruction. He names himself the One King and One God and declares that there shall be but One Law. The Eternals watch in horror as his pale face emerges from the void in rage and intense indignation. His fires roar but are without light. Reminiscent of the smokeless, dark fire of the Jinn. The Eternals stand by as Urizen's world is formed. It appears to them as a black globe that struggles and beats like a human heart.

The stars stand wide apart from the dark globe. Note that the Zoas did not create the stars. Los, the fallen form of Urthona, sweeps into the picture now and keeps watch over Urizen until the Eternals can confine his dark world and keep it from growing. They do so by creating a tent to separate Urizen's world from their own. As Urizen is rent from Los' side, ripped away from eternity, Los gives a material form to Urizen, who becomes a 'Clod of Clay,' reminiscent of the spiritually dead hylics of Gnosticism. It's Los that gives Clod of Clay the five senses, each sense called "a dismal woe." Urizen is both within and without his abominable, dark creation.

All of the Zoas are referred to as "he," but they are, in fact, androgynous. They have female counterparts, which are independent emanations of their feminine side. It's funny how they give themselves hell by emanating feminine forms. They fuss and fight with their female counterparts, but these females *are* the Zoas.

Urizen's counterpart is Ahania, and she represents his intuition and his longing for true intelligence (which is not reason). Unfortunately, Urizen casts out Ahania because he fears her visions and because he'll tolerate no equal. He seizes her by the hair and throws her to the earth saying,

> *Am I not God said Urizen. Who is Equal to me*
> *Do I not stretch the heavens abroad or fold them up like a garment?*
> *His visage changd to darkness & his strong right hand came forth*
> *To cast Ahania to the Earth. He seizd her by the hair*
> *And threw her from the steps of ice that froze around his throne*
> *Saying Art thou also become like Vala? Thus I cast thee out.*
> *Shall the feminine indolent bliss*
> *Set herself up to give her laws to the active masculine virtue,*
> *Thou little diminutive portion that darst be a counterpart*
> *Thy passivity, thy laws of obedience & insincerity*
> *Are my abhorrence.*
> *And art thou also become like Vala? Thus I cast thee out.*

This guy is a real idiot. I'd like to say that he only hurts himself by exiling his feminine side, but sadly that's not the case. By doing so, he damns humanity to a hellish world of law without wisdom, science without sight, and tyranny without end, unless the other Zoas can successfully challenge him. In Urizen's world, reason dominates at the expense of true intelligence. It's a world of industry, machines, law, and the chains of religion and traditionalism.

Urizen is the mind in self-forged chains.

Urthona is called "Earth Owner." He's dark, but this darkness is not the same as the dark ignorance of Urizen. Urthona is dark because he's the Divine Imagination that, when fallen, is driven into the unconscious. Urthona is the creative darkness and superior intelligence of the unconscious. The anonymous writer of "The Cloud of Unknowing" refers to "the mysterious radiance of the Divine Dark, the inaccessible light wherein the Lord is said to dwell, and to which thought with all its struggles cannot attain." This is Urthona.

Los is Urthona's manifestation in the outer world and the greatest challenge to Urizen's self-proclaimed supremacy. Los is the force that initiatives reunification and can redeem Urizen. He's creative imagination. When he awakens imagination in man, he's the true Master Builder of reality since all things begin in the imagination. Urizen is always trying to take Urthona's place as Master Builder. This is another similarity between Urizen and the Gnostic Demiurge.

Blake associates Los with Christ. Los is indeed a redeemer, but he is also in need of redemption because fallen imagination is constantly required to reconcile contraries. Los is fittingly described as a blacksmith. A blacksmith places metal in fire and hammers it out to his desired form. Remember, the Logos is described as the divine fire. It's through our use of imagination that we place images in this fire and hammer them into form. Los' emanation and feminine counterpart is Enitharmon. She creates space and weaves the living human garment (as opposed to Urizen's lifeless Clod of Clay). This pair have a child called Orc. Orc represents the revolutionary spirit. Blake was unsupportive of revolution because it creates continual conflict without true resolution. Los will eventually subdue, forgive, and even grow to love the redeemed Urizen. **You can't subdue or redeem what you don't know how to love**.

Blake's depiction of Urizen. He looks like he's having a bad day.

How the Four Zoas Manifest in the Outer World

Goddard was insistent that useful parts of the Bible, the parts relevant personal awakening, are relevant to the individual because the narrative they portray is contemporary, not historical. In other words, **it's the story of you, right now, today**. It's also the story of human consciousness as it falls, moves through unnumbered states, and then awakens. The same is true of Blake's work. His narrative stresses the contemporaneity of Eternity, fallen vision, and of Empire.

When Blake prophesied the fall of Empire, it's tempting to assume that he was referring exclusively to the British Empire, but Blake described Empire as being one of "industry and religion." Neither of those things has ended, they've only grown exponentially since the 1700s! Along with Empire, religion has also changed robes. We still have organised religion with membership in the billions but we also have the religion of money, greed, modernism, technology, and rational materialism, and they all have their gods. Blake saw Empire not just as a group of states under the supreme authority of one government, but also as an ethos. Understanding that Empire is an *ethos* is key to comprehending what the *fall of empire* really is, and how you personally play a role in it.

The Four Zoas is a twofold, contemporaneous account of both the individual and humanity. It's the story of you, the reader moving from restricted imagination (the ultimate mind control) to liberated imagination (Fourfold Vision). Blake's narrative is simultaneously individualistic and collective, as it's an account of the history of human consciousness, from Eternity to the sleep of Albion, through many states of progressive awakening, until this consciousness awakens.

This is *your* story. It's *our* story.

An <u>ethos</u> of Empire is the antithesis of human fulfillment. If fulfillment and flourishing is your aim, understanding not only the inner environment of your existence but the outer environment that you move through is key. We need to know what a thing is and how it affects us if we're to master it or perhaps disassemble it.

Urizen—The Ethos of Empire and the Machine

If it's not clear by now, **the Machine is a metaphor**. It is a metaphor for a *mode of consciousness*. We could also call it an *intelligence*. It's power without love, sight without vision, and knowledge without knowing. It's also a complex adaptive system born from that mode of consciousness.

At its worst, it constructs an apparatus of lies: violence posing as protection, exploitation posing as humanism, and control pretending to be care. Our consent greases its camshaft and bearings. Our despondency is its fuel. Our dependence provides it with momentum as it bulldozes over organic, human culture and coils its chains around the mind. It siphons the despondent energy of people who believe in a hateful, judgmental god and channels it through towering church spires and election booths. It liquifies our brains with tele*vision* and pollutes our bodies with spirit killing brews.

Colonialism never ended; it shape-shifted. The colonialism of today is psychological and contractual. It's an insidious, multipolar complex of surveillance, corporatism, non-profit entities serving as fronts for not-so-hidden agendas, weaponised social media, weaponised entertainment and a level psychological manipulation never-before-seen throughout all of recorded human history. And while to some, it may seem like some kind of grand, all-powerful conspiracy; it's not. It's a vicious machine that we helped to build. If we built it, we can sure as hell unbuild it.

It's difficult to extract the system from the consciousness that creates it. While it currently does great harm, it is neither good nor evil, and it's not some sci-fi boogeyman, but it *is* ultimately anti-human. Like a machine, it can only perform certain functions. The only functions this mind can perform are containment, stratification, automation, replication, simulation, transmission, and distribution.

The Machine loves algorithms: for markets, to learn as much it can about your preferences and thoughts, and for systematically churning out soulless music. But it's not strictly associated with technology—it's much older than that. When the machine mind is at work in people, it's calculating. You'll see formulas that people develop for manipulating another person's emotions and choices. Take the systematic methods of conquest as an example: *"Read my book about how to get a man to propose!" "Take my course on how to shag any woman!"*

We created the Machine and believe that it's our servant, but is it?

The Machine appears to have a will that attaches itself to the will of humanity, similar to a parasite. Without us, it lies dormant and inactive, like a virus. When we give it life, it embeds itself in our minds and begins to spread like a virus and grow like a cancer. The Machine is what happens when humans allow the fallen Urizen archetype to possess our minds and control our world. If we don't know that we should or even *could* redeem the Zoas within ourselves, we contribute to the propagation of the Machine. It can't exist without our implicit consent.

The Machine is not a creation of empires, it's the other way around. The Machine is the progenitor of empire, both apparent empire and empire as an ethos. The supra-conscious Machine Mind creates a network with structures, compartments, and layers. All of the respective layers interact with and feed each other. The matrix it forms looks like a multipolar organism with the four primary dendrites: Religion, Government, Finance, and Industry. It uses structures within structures to create containment.

The goal of this stratification and syncretism is to scatter and fragment knowledge instead of clarifying it. Centralisation of power is vital for the Machine to sustain itself. Creating apparent empires with monarchs or emperors was the way of the past. When those apparent empires seem to crumble, it's really just that the Machine is reconfiguring itself and moving power into other structures.

Organised religion is an instrument of empire building. As human consciousness evolves, the Machine must, as well. As we moved past the tyranny of overt, religious domination, control has been maintained by other structures: finance and banking, energy, technology, and political unions that require independent nations to sacrifice their sovereignty to unelected officials and centralised authority. All the above are examples of the shape-shifting nature of the unapparent, but ever-present _ethos_ of empire.

Embedded in this system, you'll find a plethora of sub-structures: philanthropic organisations with their agendas, criminal networks, alphabet agencies, cultural think tanks, etc. At the outermost layer are media, entertainment, and journalism. Whenever you see centralisation, digitalisation, and automation that puts *profit before people*, that's the Machine at work. It reduces human beings to nothing more than cogs in the metal-toothed wheel of an inhuman system. The Machine creates a virtual reality by creating a digital copy of nature, which is, in reality, analogue. It's a copy within a copy. That image might remind you of Urizen's self-replication previously described. While Urizen is the primary *ghost in the machine*, Luvah and Orc play a large role as well.

Criminals conspire, they have to if they want to cover up or get away with their crimes. Conspiracy will exist as long as there are dishonourable people willing conspire to accomplish certain aims. But it's very important to one's mental health, actualisation, and enlightenment to not fall down the conspiracy rabbit hole. Reality is too complex to be organised into conspiratorial boxes. It's not an overarching, comprehensive conspiracy that you're looking at, it's a metaphorical *machine,* **a phenomenon that can replicate itself through billions of minds who sustain it through implicit consent.** Some of our consent is conscious; it's easier to go along with the system than stand apart from it. But the largest part of our consent is unconscious.

The Machine is a manifestation of our collective shadow.

The only way to disassemble the Machine and its structures (effectively putting an end to the *ethos* of empire) is to become conscious of the Zoas, what they represent, how they live in each of us, and then strive to redeem them in ourselves. We do this through lucidity, transformation, transmutation, shadow work, and by making truth our guiding principle.

As we examine the impact that four Zoas have on individual perception and the world at large, it might be helpful to look at one of the most obvious divisions in ourselves and the world: Gender.

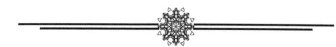

Discussion of femininity and masculinity has become a convoluted mess. No one knows what they're talking about anymore because they don't know what masculinity and femininity actually *are*. They equate the industrialist and the imperial *versions* of masculinity with primeval masculine energy. The same goes for femininity.

Imperial femininity is a creation of the ethos of empire, an ethos that requires the dominance of one pole over the other. The Machine (and its empires) used religion to narrow metaphysical truth into a very strict range of convenient metaphors and then warped that truth even further by creating false historical narratives and preaching them as literal history.

No social science or ideology can tell you what the primeval feminine and masculine are. You must find out for yourself via contemplation and direct experience. Taking a strictly objective approach via examination of the outer world, nature, and human behaviour is helpful. But consider this: if even Beulah, with its *equally true contraries*, leads to distortion by causing us to take the part for the whole, then how much more misleading are our perceptions in Ulro? How can an analysis of phenomena that have been observed and interpreted by a fragmented consciousness, be trusted to produce a holistic understanding?

At the level of matter, what we call *masculine* and *feminine* represents a circumscription of primeval energies that have been configured in a very specific way to make generation within matter possible. Why do people assume that when liberated from matter, these energies will behave in the same way that they do when forced to materialise? Matter is a universal anomaly.

Both far-left progressive feminism, and its apparent antipode, the traditional femininity of the far-right, are mental and behavioural programs used to herd women into ways of being and thinking that ultimately support the Machine. They create machine women for a machine world.

Men don't fare much better. In exchange for the psychological and emotional impotence they feel when the Machine forces them to sublimate the inherent power of the primeval masculine, they're given a weak simulacrum of that power in the form of externalised force. This externalised force belongs to the Machine. Men have been allowed to act as unwitting agents of the Machine by taking up leadership roles in religion, government, and social structures—but they're still slaves.

The demiurgic archetype always goes after women, I hinted to the reason why in chapter 14. Part of Gnosticism will also point to *why*. It first used overt, brutal control. In certain areas of the world, it *still* uses inhumane, physical, and psychological brutality to control the female. In the West, other energies rose to counter the Machine, and so, being a complex adaptive system, it evolved other means suppressing and redirecting the inherent, primitive feminine power: propaganda. It doesn't matter whether it's left or right, liberal or conservative, propaganda is mind control.

Then there's feminism. Feminist ideology is constantly shape-shifting. It's strategically used to keep women confused and fighting amongst themselves over definitions and values. What began as an organic response to a system that designated half of the human race as second-class citizens, was co-opted by Urizenic social structures, and redirected into ideology as a means of controlling the narrative.

Human evolution is a process of refinement. When it comes to ideologies, we evolve when we're able to extract what's *helpful* to our evolution and leave what's *harmful*. Feminism is no different. On its dark side, it represents an attempt to define and collectivise femininity through the Urizenic lenses of law and industry. On its light side, it represents a healthy rebuttal in which Los and Orc challenge conscious and unconscious bias, and unjustifiable hierarchy.

Feminism, as an ideology, will always end up confining, not liberating, thought. *All* ideologies do. The traditionalism of the far-right does the *same thing*: it defines and collectivises femininity through the Urizenic structures of traditionalism, organised religion, and biased science.

Within the current Zeitgeist, a new metaphor has emerged. Recall Tolkien's comment, "The servants of the machine are becoming privileged class." When people first become aware of machine-structures, its tactics, and its servants, they can see the trees but can't see the forest. This leads to two typical responses. 1. They put a lot of energy into investigations of conspiracy, and 2. They look for someone to blame. This finger–pointing means they look everywhere but at their very own selves: their life choices, inner world, behaviour, and shadow.

People still trapped at this level have borrowed a very specific prop that was used in the 1999 film, *The Matrix:* the blue pill and the red pill. Ideologues adapted this metaphor as representative of their ideological, right-leaning, so-called *awakening*. They designate the blue pill for their polar opposite, the far-left leaning liberals. For the truly despondent person, they've also developed the *black pill*. The black pill is for 'woke' people (on both the left and right) who, feeling defeated and hopeless, just want to give up the fight like apathetic Eeyores.

Ideology—The Stupid Pill

By dividing the voter through the political party system, we can get them to expend their energies in fighting for questions of no importance. It is thus, by discrete action, we can secure for ourselves that which has been so well planned and so successfully accomplished. —Montagu Norman, Governor of The Bank of England, addressing the United States Bankers' Association, NYC 1924

The stirring up of conflict is a Luciferian virtue in the true sense of the word. — Carl Jung, Collected Works, 9i, page 179

Ideology is a killer: it kills intellect, contemplation, openness, humility, and empathy. Ideas and beliefs don't automatically make a person ideological. Ideology is defined as "A system of ideas and ideals, especially one which forms the basis of economic or political theory and policy." Ideology is also defined as "a set of normative beliefs and values that lack epistemic justification."

Aristotle described three approaches to knowledge: Sophia, Techné, and Phronesis. Sophia is the type of reasoning that concerns itself with universal truths. Sophia engages with reality through an ongoing, deep contemplation. Phronesis complements Sophia by adding the capability of rational thinking. If Aristotle were here, he'd say that the ideologues of today lack both Sophia *and* Phronesis.

232

Ideology is not about thinking. It creates sub-reality vectors that people live in like bubbles. All of their values and interpretations are derived from their sub-reality. People are drawn to ideologies that best serve their *emotional* and psychological needs, needs that are most often dictated by a person's shadow.

Not all ideologies are created equal, and some ideologies include concepts that point to higher truths. The problem is that any higher truths an ideology may point to will inevitably be distorted and attenuated by the confining structure of ideology.

> *The most thought-provoking thing in our thought-provoking time is that we're still not thinking.* —Martin Heidegger

Ideology is an example of emotionalism posing as intellect. It's Luvah moving into Urizen's spot. Urizen gets in on the action too because it represents an opportunity for Urizen to capitalise on the blind passion of ideologues and their rabid willingness to control others. Ideology is most pernicious when it becomes a person's identity. It effectively divides the world into two groups, those with *right-think* and those with *wrong-think*. Now Orc steps into the picture to stoke the fires of revolution.

The 'Ism' Schism

During the Yellow Vest protest in France, I met a young man who was part of the protest. He told me that he identifies as an "anarcho-communist" and that he had no problem with the destruction of other people's property. I asked him why. His justification was rooted in envy and entitlement.

Looking closely at him, in his eyes and at the way he moved and spoke, four things became immediately obvious. The first was that he was extremely lonely. The second was that he felt unlovable. The third was that no one was really home upstairs. The fourth was his "anarcho-communism"…really?

Apparently, he's a member of the Church of 'Oxymoronism.'

Violent dispositions, emotional instability, envy, self-loathing and isolation create a ticking time bomb. It's remarkably facile to exploit these (and other) qualities in the population. You can predict the direction of social movements based on the emotional and psychological needs of the populace. If you use social engineering (large-scale, psychological manipulation) to either create the *perception* of economic insecurity, *or* manipulate currencies and global markets to effect real, economic instability in certain sectors and nations, while simultaneously convincing the populace that communism is a clear and present danger, you can accurately predict that there will be a massive increase of support for free-market capitalism and classical liberalism. There will be an increase in adoption of construct-challenging ideologies. Construct-challenging ideologies are more problematic for the Machine but not impossible for it. It's highly adaptable and can be configured to suit any agenda.

If, on the other hand, you want to encourage adoption of construct-supporting ideologies, all you need to do is convince the public that the economy creates unfair stratification because it's not regulated enough. If you can convince them that free-market capitalism is the cause of poverty, while simultaneously pushing media (in all of it's forms) to focus on social inequality, unbridled corporate greed, expensive healthcare, systemic racism, and sexism (that you convince the people can only be resolved through social coercion and forced, legal compliance, rather than through personal transformation and growth), you can accurately predict an increase in support for Socialism and Big Government—perfect for the Machine.

Ideologies are like livestock corrals; they're easy to herd people into.

This isn't the way to truth, nor is it a way to a better world. Every ideology will have its counter force with which it has to battle. Ideology creates perpetual war, fortifies ego, and creates a form of mass insanity as a labyrinth for the mind and a most effective means of containment. The ideologically possessed find it very difficult to find true fulfillment or establish a sense of inner quietude and equilibrium.

The battle is within—our reason battles with our hearts. Emotion and reason constantly struggle for dominance when they could learn to work together. Wisdom is, after all, the marriage of unconditional love to reason.

Los and Urizen battle constantly. The seemingly objective, outer world seems so real, so concrete. It's hard to believe that our imagination is powerful. Orc, the spirit of rebellion, and instigator of revolution, is a petulant child. It's the Orc in all of us that would rather rebel than accept responsibility or work to master the system.

Orc never imagines that his personal agency could be put to better use. He's all *re*volve and no *e*volve. Recall Euler's number from the last chapter. Orc eternally revolves around the circle. He lacks the growth and change needed to spiral upwards and off the wheel. More on that wheel in chapter 19…

The passions and hate of a fallen Luvah collide with the indignation of Urizen and create volatile political climates. Seeing the world with Single Vision only, people who are possessed by Luvah and ideology become polarised. Polarisation is the result of Luvah (as hate *pretending to be love*) and Orc (fighting against the *other*) working together. Polarisation short circuits our ability to reason and connect.

We use polarised batteries to fuel our machines. Polarised populations fuel another kind of machine. Polarisation isn't strictly binary. Consider a multipolar neuron. A multipolar neuron possesses a single axon and many dendrites (and dendritic branches) that allow for the integration of a tremendous amount of information from other neurons.

It looks like this[3]:

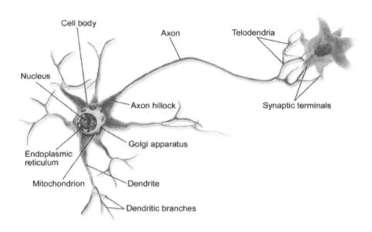

It's creepy looking. One can't help but notice that the endoplasmic reticulum looks similar to the repulsive Eye of Sauron in *Lord of the Rings*.

In 1956, Nelson Rockefeller conceived of the Special Studies Project. The project created panels to look at military strategy, foreign policy, international economics, government reorganisation, and the arms race. In 1961 the project published a book entitled *Prospect for America: The Rockefeller Panel Reports*. The report lays out a detailed plan for creating a multipolar world with one central authority. It calls for "a world divided into smaller units but organised and acting in common effort." On the same page, they add, "It would presumably consist of regional institutions under an international body of growing authority."

Multipolarity *always requires a central axon*. Without a central axon connected to the axon hillock (part of the cell body), it wouldn't be a multipolar organism.

[3]Image created by Bruce Blause and confirmed to be available for free use by anyone for any purpose under the Creative Commons Attribution 3.0 and states that there is no requirement to request permission for use. Link to the license: https://commons.wikimedia.org/wiki/File:Blausen_0657_MultipolarNeuron.png

In 2014, the phrase *multipolar world* began appearing in news articles all over the world. There are many dozens of instances of the phrase "multipolar world" appearing in media since 2014. Every passing year has seen an increase in the use of this phrase and promotion of the idea.

How about a multi-node world instead of multipolar? Multiple, thriving nodes would appear naturally, and without a central authority, if people weren't forcibly dislocated from their social groups by government-regulated markets and government interference in community creation. Markets have existed as long as humanity; they're not in any way inherently inhuman, but humane markets are regulated by *naturally organising social relations*, not governments or financial institutions. Social regulation of a market is maintained largely by non-statutory ties.

Self-regulating markets are not truly *self*-regulating. Governments create the conditions for free markets by dissolving the social regulation of the market and replacing it with government regulations that ignore social preferences. Now the market becomes machine-like, whereas before it was reflective of a kind of deep social ecology of human beings and their relationships.

Humans thrive and flourish, not from money but from stable, lasting social ties. People don't want wealth nearly as much as they want social ties and social recognition. People go into debt to create social status. In a disconnected world, many people can't imagine any other way to be. They're missing the ties that bind because the Machine moves humans around like cogs. When massive structures of State dominate and absorb the smaller, localised structures of naturally magnetised social groups, they homogenise, which is the opposite of diversity. This homogenisation diminishes efficiency and cripples will of the people.

Humans are magnetised to each other **not** by race, gender or sexuality but by a shared vision, which creates resonance. If we refuse to allow ourselves to be divided by the age-old, 'Divide and Conquer' tactics that ruling classes have used for millennia, we can accomplish anything.

I must create a system or be enslaved by another man's. —Blake

The answers we are looking for are not found in capitalism, fascism, communism, socialism, or any *ism*. As soon as we unplug from the Machine and hopefully disassemble it, the answers will seem self-evident. I'm not suggesting yet another ideology. I'm suggesting a new level of individual and collective *contemplation* and *cooperation*.

Humans will always use automation as a means of making work more efficient and to give us more time to create, contemplate, and enjoy life. Could we build new something new, something more humane? New, metaphoric machines that serve us without creating the ethos of empire all over again? If humanity developed Fourfold Vision, what kind of technology could we create? Anything that ameliorates social trust will have an extraordinary impact on a socially regulated market. What improves social trust more than shared vision, personal relationships within community, familial ties, and a shared love of wisdom?

Our collective wisdom is reflected in our choice of leaders. We are, therefore, being led by the least among us. What could we create if we put personal agency, self-determination, and contemplative life at the core of education? Would we still be drawn, by the *billions*, to sophomoric, debased, violent entertainment?

The Machine has tried to mimic authentic social confluence with so-called *social* media. There is nothing 'social' about it. It's been a disaster and only densified shadow. By now, we all know that social media creates narcissism and isolation and has slowly conditioned the public to accept increasing levels of censorship. Politicians add their two cents worth and call for peace. They'll be about as effective at making the internet peaceful as they are at establishing world peace. There is no such thing as peace in, or through, politics. All politics are about control. There can be no peace when every side is constantly trying to prove the other side wrong. When politics dictate economy and human relations, peace and true human flourishing are utterly impossible.

Virtually all of the problems of our world stem from our collapsed vision and fragmented psyche.

It's not all our fault, the Zoas fell first, remember? But we have something that they don't have. We have a spark, a fractal embedded within us.

We redeem them; they don't redeem us.

Redeeming the Zoas *in ourselves* is the first step. As we build up and out, from the individual to the community, the redeemed, unfallen Zoas will be reflected in the markets, systems, and nations that we build. Unique communities, unique markets, unique individuals magnetised according to their *own will*, not the will of a Tyrannical Machine.

There will be no one world order, unified under a *central authority* because, as Jean Markale so aptly observed, "Unity of thought is impoverishment of thought." When the Zoas unify, their unique, individual expressions of the Divine are neither annihilated nor subsumed. They're *enfolded* and *entangled* and yet <u>unique</u>. Blake's Albion is more than the sum of his parts.

No Zoa can claim supremacy or dominance and establish itself as a central authority. Blake writes:

> *Empire is no more! and now the lion & wolf shall cease.*
> *Chorus*
> *Let the Priests of the Raven of dawn, no longer in deadly black, with hoarse note*
> *curse the sons of joy.*
> *Nor his accepted brethren whom, tyrant, he calls free; lay the bound or build the*
> *roof.*
> *Nor pale religious letchery call that virginity, that wishes but acts not!*
> *For every thing that lives is Holy*

As to how the Zoas impact our individual perception and steer our lives, it's probably already clear to you that chapter 12, *The Quest for Love*, was all about Luvah. The chapter on imagination was dedicated to Urthona. Chapter 6, *Here Enters Beauty*, is dedicated to all the feminine emanations of the four Zoas. Chapter 9, *The Purpose of Pain*, is about the furnaces of affliction. Chapter 5, *Forgiveness*, is about Los' forgiveness of Urizen and acceptance of Orc, about Tharmas widening the circumference of *self* and Luvah's recovery of love. Chapter 15, Transformation, was about all of the Zoas, especially Dark Urthona.

The first 15 chapters of this book have been about the restoration of the Zoas within each of us and everything it takes to do that. Self-awareness, humility, forgiveness, phenomenological re-orientation, will, agency, transformation, truth, beauty, love.

This book outlines a recovery arc, the reunification of our fragmented being, and the restoration of Albion. To this aim, there are just a few more things to consider. If you'll recall, I compared us human beings to "consciousness-mapping cartographers." Mapping contraries is our way of adding elevation to the map, but what about the cardinal directions? And will our map remain two-dimensional, or can we create a four-dimensional map to go with our new, Fourfold Vision? Thankfully, Blake's shared knowledge that can help us with that.

The Perfect Geography

Have you ever contemplated what north, east, south, and west *really* are? Ancient traditions compared the universe to an egg-shaped orb, with layers of concentric circles, like an onion. There are eggs within eggs. Imagine the outermost layer of an onion. That's the earth. On a map of the universe, the red, You-are-Here dot would be at the outermost layer.

The centre of the onion is the unmanifested Godhead (Brahman, Paramatma). A few esoteric texts speak of the "orient," but they don't mean the Far East. In this context, *orient* means your orientation within the Universal onion. The Cardinal Directions are figurative of an inner orientation.

Blake's cosmology assigns a direction to each of the Zoas. There are two geographies; that of Ulro and that of Eternity. Ulro is a third- and fourth-dimensional geography because it includes time and space. The other geography is the infinite, five-dimensional geography of the unfallen, unified Zoas in Eternity.

Geography of Ulro

Four Universes round the Mundane Egg remain Chaotic
One to the North, named Urthona: One to the South, named Urizen:
One to the East, named Luvah: One to the West, named Tharmas
They are the Four Zoa's that stood around the Throne Divine!

But when Luvah assum'd the World of Urizen to the South:
And Albion was slain upon his mountains, & in his tent;
All fell towards the Centre in dire ruin, sinking down.
And in the South remains a burning fire; in the East a void.

And the Four Zoa's clouded rage East & West & North & South
They change their situations, in the Universal Man.
Albion groans, he sees the Elements divide before his face.
And England who is Britannia divided into Jerusalem & Vala
And Urizen assumes the East, Luvah assumes the South
In his dark Spectre ravening from his open Sepulchre. —Jerusalem, Plate 59

Within the fallen realm of Ulro, Urthona (imagination and spiritual sensation) is in the North. The South has been taken over by Luvah, but it's not his rightful place. Emotion and passion have taken over reason. This leaves a void in the East, which Urizen moves into, causing his fallen reason to create systems devoid of love. Urizen is reason without love. In the geography of Ulro, Tharmas and Urthona remain in their rightful places. Tharmas is in the West.

The Perfect Geography of Eternity

In Eternity, the geography is turned upside down and inside out. It's not just that Urizen (the linear, rational aspect of our mind) and Luvah (feeling and emotion) return to their rightful places. **Our concept of what and where the directions *are* is undermined completely**. Blake's ideal geography of eternity is a model of the perspective of those who are no longer living in the fallen world of Ulro. Both Ulro and Eternity (within and without) co-exist simultaneously and are connected and work upon each other. Blake describes it as such:

And the Four Points are thus beheld in Great Eternity
West, the Circumference: South, the Zenith: North,
The Nadir: East, the Centre, unapproachable for ever.
These are the four Faces towards the Four Worlds of Humanity
In every Man. Ezekiel saw them by Chebars flood.
And the Eyes are the South, and the Nostrils are the East.
And the Tongue is the West, and the Ear is the North. —Jerusalem, Plate 12

Blake doesn't offer any clarification as to what this means, he forces us to contemplate. Urthona is associated with the ear; hence "Ear is in the North." Tharmas is associated with both taste and touch sensation because he unifies them, hence the "Tongue in the West."* You can guess the other two. Think about pheromones. Who would be the nostrils? And the eyes? Where does light enter? Who represents the "light of reason?"

In the passage above, Blake is describing the four faces (aspects) of humanity *in every person*, as they are beheld in Great Eternity. It's the mode of perception of one who is awakened to eternity. In Eternity, the Four Zoas are not separate qualities that exist independent of each other in differentiated states. In their transcendent form, they're enfolded within each other in the unity of transcendent, eternal Being. This Eternal Being has its own geography, what Blake calls the "Perfect Geography." It is:

West is **circumference**. It's the way that individuated being is maintained with the Divine Body that is comprised of many beings. The circumference denotes individuation within a unified body and a level of energy that establishes one as a life-giving spirit. Without Tharmas providing circumference, there could be no continued sense of individuation.

Tharmas is the parent power because he's the *source* of all power: Will. Electromagnetic energy is an extremely stepped-down version of his power. Tharmas is so powerful that his energy overloads the human mind, causing humanity to filter out spiritual sensations and use only the five senses. In Eternity, with a unified mind, this isn't a problem.

North is the **nadir**. It's divine imagination, and as the nadir, it's the foundation upon which Divine Man stands, i.e., perceives.

242

South is the **zenith,** which is Divine Wisdom. It's Urizen's transcendent form. Compassionate Wisdom is the zenith of the Divine Man and all individuated Eternals.

The East is the "unapproachable centre." It's unapproachable because infinity has no centre. As Empedocles said, "God is a circle whose centre is everywhere, and its circumference nowhere." Eternity has no centre, but an individuated Eternal perceives the East as their centre of gravity (so to speak). The centre is Luvah in his unfallen form, i.e., Divine Love.

The image of east as centre, west as circumference, north as nadir, and south as zenith might seem confusing to the mind that thinks three-dimensionally. Our perception of the four-directions is a psychologically flattened-out, three-dimensional representation of a multi-dimensional reality, just as a two-dimensional drawing of the four-directions is a flattened out diagram. Blake's perfect geography of Eternity is an enfolded, five-dimensional model of a spiritual Being and its awareness.

Ok, what does all of this have to do with us? Is there any way to bring all of this down-to-earth and make it applicable and useful to our lives? Yes!

To unify the Four Zoas within ourselves, we're called not just to unify our fractured beings, but to transcend the fallen states.

This is what that looks like:

Luvah: To make unconditional love our 'centre of gravity.'

Tharmas: By activating our will and working to develop spiritual sensation, the higher form of what we call intuition (recall that Blake considers human intuition as a fallen form of spiritual sensation), while simultaneously striving to complete the process of individuation and actualisation. In doing so, we never lose sight of the truth that while we are individuated beings, we are still One Body of humanity. It's neither wholly individualistic nor collective, like the Druids, one rejects this duality. To know Tharmas in his unfallen state is to cast off false ideas of self and find authentic being and **true power** that flows from an inexhaustible source. Does this remind you of chapter 14 on Will?

Urthona: Imaginative perception becomes our foundation, our *default mode of perception, our True North*. A perception that we then act upon, *fully conscious of our creative power*. Our actions and speech reflect total faith that our vision will become reality. More on that in chapter 17…

Urizen: A zenith is an imaginary point directly above a particular location. Now, instead of being our limiter, Urizen transcends reason and develops true intelligence. Merging with the unfallen Luvah, he becomes compassionate Wisdom. As we re-unify ourselves and transcend fractured perception, that compassionate wisdom becomes our guiding star.

It's only when we have redeemed the fallen Zoas within ourselves, re-oriented ourselves to the perfect geography, and attained Fourfold vision that we find a measure of fulfillment—that is extraordinarily rare and precious in this world.

Chapter Note: I'm going to go out on a limb here and share something for any esotericists, mystics, and dream yoga practitioners who may be reading this. It's highly relevant to esotericists who use lucid dreaming because some of the ancients called the sense of touch (within a dream) "the Western gate," and sight, the "Southern Gate." Anyone who has used either sight or touch in a lucid dream will immediately recognise and understand why they encounter what they do when they travel via dream yoga. If you hear music in a lucid dream, if you focus on it with absolutely all of your attention, you can travel through the sound. You can do the same with sight, by focusing on an object you're looking at within the dream. If you're an evangelical Christian and still reading this book, first of all, thank you! Secondly, if this sounds extremely odd, take a deeper look at the Book of Ezekiel and then come back and compare it to Blake's visions. Take note of "The Four Mighty Ones" of Ezekiel.

PART II
THE ANTARALA

I've divided the book into three parts:

1. The Inner Sanctum
2. The Antarala
3. The Mandapa

Hindu temples are built to represent fractal models of the cosmos. Like these beautiful examples of architecture, the human being is also a temple. I divided the book to reflect these three primary areas of Hindu temples. The first part—chapters one through sixteen, is meant to demonstrate that deep, abiding fulfillment is established in a central core—the Inner Sanctum, and is attained through:

1. An inner orientation—oriented towards *within* not *without* and includes an ongoing, inner dialogue with, and openness to, the Daimon.
2. Self-Inquiry—a deep understanding of the relative self and how it's constructed.
3. Forgiveness
4. Acknowledgment and processing of pain
5. Will
6. Willingness to transform
7. Personal responsibility—self-reliance
8. Imagination
9. Unconditional Love
10. Coherence, which is true beauty.

The second part of the book—chapters seventeen through twenty, is the Antarala. In a temple, the Antarala marks the liminal space between the exterior world and the inner world. Faith, hope, innocence, wonder, and unforced gratitude are all liminal states in which the inner and the outer touch. It's in the Antarala that the inner Being and the exterior world take each other's hands in a dance.

Chapter 17
FAITH

I STOOD among my valleys of the south,
And saw a flame of fire, even as a Wheel
Of fire surrounding all the heavens: it went
From west to east against the current of
Creation, and devour'd all things in its loud
Fury and thundering course round Heaven and Earth
By it the Sun was roll'd into an orb;
By it the Moon faded into a globe,
Travelling thro' the night; for from its dire
And restless fury Man himself shrunk up
Into a little root a fathom long.
And I asked a Watcher and a Holy One
Its name. He answer'd: `It is the Wheel of Religion.'
—William Blake

Organised religion is helpful for many people. If the numbers are any indicator, it's helpful for billions. Exoteric, organised religion provides a structure that can, if used wisely, take a mind from Single Vision to Threefold Vision. Local churches perform a function for communities. They create a safety net and centre for socialising around which social adhesion is created.

My husband and I love to occasionally attend both Catholic and Protestant churches in Paris. Nevertheless, my husband and I don't have to agree with the dogma to care about and enjoy the people at church. We're humans and social animals like everyone else. Some of the best people I've ever met, I met through attending various churches and a few of my biggest heroes were Catholic.

Religion provides a framework for moral and ethical development for those who long for a parent-like authority that makes them feel loved and tells them what is right and what is wrong. They need borders because they don't yet fully trust themselves. They lack self-confidence, which is the truest, most powerful form of faith. As philosopher Ken Wilbur observes, organised religion is for *growing up*. The Mysteries provided a similar structure for the evolution of consciousness, but their target group was those individuals who were *waking up*.

Since the 15th-century, the word *faith* has been braced to the scaffolding of religions that implore their followers to have faith in an externalised, saviour god who will wipe away their *sin* and bring them into a place called Heaven when they die. If not, it's straight to hell for you! Who wouldn't have faith with such a threat hanging over their heads? The Abrahamic religion's manipulation of language is clever because it creates psychological containment: the faith they promote is always in something higher and separate from the transient self. The word faith comes from the proto-indo-European *bheidh,* meaning "a word that implies confidence, trust."

In "Literature and Dogma" (1873), Matthew Arnold writes, "And faith is neither the submission of reason nor is it the acceptance, simply and absolutely upon testimony, of what reason cannot reach. Faith is: the being able to cleave to a power of goodness appealing to our higher and real self, not to our lower and apparent self." I agree and disagree with his statement. We most certainly *do* need to have faith in our lower, apparent self's ability to strive, connect, create, awaken, and succeed. Without that faith, we're easily manipulated and controlled. The subtle suggestion in Arnold's statement is that the lower, apparent self isn't *good.* It's subtle, but it's there, and religion is built around that same subconscious message, *lower self baaad, higher Self gooood.* This is more of the good vs. evil dichotomy that's been hammered into humanity's collective head for thousands of years.

Faith does incorporate the higher form of Urizenic reason, but it then steps above it, to a higher power; *your* higher powers, of creative imagination and will. Dogmas that insist upon the annihilation of the relative self are effectively removing purpose from the Universal Mind. They treat the Universal Mind like a dumb animal that creates out of instinct and then says, "Whoopsie, I accidentally created all of these mirror selves. No problem, they can be annihilated." The deep, esoteric *knowing* of the West is one of refinement and incorporation, not total annihilation.

If you've chosen to believe any of the following:

1. Faith in an externalised saviour god, combined with good works (follow the rules and be nice), is all it takes to get into paradise and leave this messed-up world behind; or

2. Total annihilation of the lower self, along with all of its experiences leads to Nirvana and allows you to escape Maya; or

3. Refuse both of the above, and opt for the Single Vision, rational materialism that many (but not all) Atheists have laid claim to.

You don't have much cause or motivation to make the most of your creative imagination by developing Fourfold Vision and then *consciously participating in reality* by activating your will, and doing the inner work that is necessary to become an embodiment of love, wisdom, and centred being-ness. In other words, you'll never redeem the Zoas within yourself. The kind of self-neutering of creative power that results from any of the three aforementioned paths is very convenient for the powers-that-be, who want to maintain the status quo.

Before transformation, one prays *to* God, after transformation, one prays *through* God, which is our awakened, willful use of imagination. It's through our use of creative imagination and our faith (confidence) in our vision that our self-directed prayers come to fruition. Before transformation, an Atheist doesn't pray, they plan, but without Fourfold Vision, planning is laborious and requires all kinds of systems and models. Eventually, someone suggests visualisation and voila! Here we go…

Faith involves a creative surrender, a surrender of doubt. Surrendering your doubt to absolute faith in **your vision** and **your ability** means that you refuse to be paralysed by the illusory objectiveness of the outer world. Surrender is another thing that's easy to misinterpret. **Surrender is part of creation**; it's not total passivity. There's a time to envision, will and act, and a time to be passive. It's like baking a cake. You grease the pans, mix the ingredients, etc. Then when you put it in the oven, you sit back passively while the heat does its job. Then you act again by taking the cake out before it burns.

Like all things human, we're invited to **master the art of balance**: the balance between the part you play, as a co-creative being, and the part the Universe plays in this cosmic *video game* we're living in; a game with principles and laws; like the law of consciousness and the principles of correspondence, polarity, karma, vibration, etc. Like Blake, Goddard, and Meister Eckhart, I have faith in something higher, but not at the expense of personal agency. You can place your faith, your confidence, wherever you wish. Blake had faith in his countrymen. He supported nations, not oppressive, global empires with their militaristic, legal, or psychological colonisation of other lands because he recognised that a nation is closer to the will of the people who form it.

His support was for organic, bottom-up community building that eventually creates a nation of free, truly self-governing people. His support was for the people, not the State. His wasn't the Neo-nationalism that we see today, and most definitely not coercive, forced national socialism or communism. Blake argues that all religions stem from the same source, the universal, Poetic Genius. Poetic Genius manifests most powerfully among organically occurring groups of people who are magnetised to each other by their shared vision.

Isn't it telling that anything truthful and profound is also always deeply personal and individualistic? When faith is holistic and right-minded, it makes the individual key to all accomplishment. This is why I feel, and perhaps you do too, as William felt when he wrote,

I rest not from my great task!
To open the Eternal Worlds, to open the immortal Eyes Of Man
inwards into the Worlds of Thought, into Eternity
Ever expanding in the Bosom of God, the Human Imagination.

This personal task, to open your immortal eyes inward and into eternity, demands that you have confidence (faith) that you're up to the task.

How Faith Works

In chapter 14, I described imagination as a realm, envisioning as an engine, and faith as a **binding agent**. Faith is the binding agent because it binds your vision to your will. Some have suggested that faith comes in degrees, like "if you have enough faith, you can move mountains." This statement seems to equate faith as a force of movement. When read that way, it leads one to confuse faith with will. Remember, will is the *directing force* that drives the inexhaustible, implosive energy of spirit into, and through, this electro-magnetic realm we call home.

Faith is like an X-marks-the-spot. You're saying, "Hey, Mr. Will, you know all that power that you're directing? Here is where I want you to direct it towards." You point towards your vision, mark it, and continue, "This is my vision, Will, I want you to *bind* my vision to that creative energy that you direct so that the same energy that all fuels creation will manifest my vision into this holo-fractal reality."

So how do we bind will to vision? Through a belief that is so absolute, that we're able to surrender. All our actions will then imply either a preparation for the fulfillment of our vision or that the wish is already fulfilled. If you really want to move, but don't yet have a place, you'll not only envision moving to your ideal location, you'll already have your things packed and your kids registered in their new school. "Faith, without works, is dead."

We have to *feel* that it's already done. This belief isn't a thought; it's a *feeling* in our being, a liminal state binding Eternity to Generation. "Feeling is the secret." That feeling is one of inner peace and *knowing* (that your will, will be done), is the actual binding agent. You just *know*.

Chapter Note: Note in the passage above that Blake capitalises the word 'STOOD' for emphasis. He's standing among his "valleys in the South." Notice that religion is flowing west to east, *against* the current of creation. In the perfect geography of eternity, the current of creation flows from the East to West, from the Unapproachable Centre then Westward, through the Divine Body with it's perfect, spiritual sensation, then continues North, through Divine Imagination and then South, which is the zenith, Divine Wisdom and then back to centre (East). If you imagine a three-dimensional model of the directions and trace this current, with your finger beginning in the centre (east), you'll find yourself tracing a figure 8, the symbol of eternity. By going west to east, against the *current of creation*, the fallen sensation (imperfect intuition) that creates religion (with a little help from Urizen) tries to push its imperfect perception upon the unapproachable, unknowable centre. In other words, religion is an example of Man making God in his own image.

Chapter 18
THE ESSENCE OF GRATITUDE

I don't feel grateful and am sick of people telling me that I ought to force gratitude when what I really want to do is tell someone to pick up their dog's shit off the sidewalk! —Anonymous in Paris

Do you find something refreshing about the display of authentic feeling, even when it's unrefined and a little brutal? I do. It's human, honest, and real.

Gratitude has been a hot subject over the last twenty years. For whatever reason, several organisations have been engaged in the hard sell of gratitude to the masses. They've even gone so far as to develop what they call the *science of gratitude*. It's curious that the organisations that are encouraging thankfulness have yet to identify what gratitude is. What gratitude *really* is, is obvious and yet they can't seem to define it. Why? Maybe because those who are profiting from gratitude (even indirectly) are incapable of fully understanding it because they're Single Vision salesmen.

The Templeton Foundation has provided funding to The Greater Good Centre as part of an initiative to study the science of gratitude. Most answers to the question, "What is gratitude?" are ambiguous. In one paper, the Greater Good Centre quotes Robert Emmons and Michael McCullough, who defined gratitude as a two-step process. The first step is a recognition that one has "obtained a positive outcome." The second step is "recognising that there is an external source for this positive outcome."

According to these two gentlemen, gratitude first requires that something is *obtained* and secondly that it come from an *external* source. Other gratitude studies suggest that gratitude is an emotion, while others suggest that it might be an evolutionary response encoded in our DNA.

Much of this confusion is the result of a collision between religion and rational materialism. One side says you need an external source (a personal, exteriorised God) to give you a reason to be grateful.

The other side goes to the opposite extreme and de-spiritualises of our world completely. For them, gratitude is nothing more than *reciprocal altruism*. What? If altruism depends on reciprocity, it's not altruism. Trying to force gratitude when you don't naturally feel it creates more suppression and shadow. If we can't understand what something is, we'll never know what to do with it, or know if we should do anything at all.

There are two types of gratitude: mental gratitude and what I call essential, or authentic, gratitude. Mental gratitude plays out in the mind as a mental acknowledgment; it's the most basic and superficial form of thanks. The other form is much deeper and is difficult to name. I sometimes call it essential (as in the *essence of* something, not as a necessity) or authentic gratitude, and other times I call it *the touch*—I'll explain why.

In German, you could call it *Wesen der Dankbarkeit*, in Latin perhaps *Essentia Gratitudo*. There's no official name for it, so let's use the term authentic gratitude. Authentic gratitude is not an emotion, nor is it purely psychological or evolutionary.

There is a spiritual sensation that arises in awareness (in the soul) as a response to the four primary attributes of Transcendent Being: Love, Truth, Beauty, and Grace. We filter and interpret this spiritual sensation as *feeling*—this is authentic gratitude. Let me put this way:

Authentic gratitude is a feeling that arises in awareness as a response to the <u>very existence</u> of Love, Truth, Beauty, and Grace.

The fact that those things *exist at all* and can *touch* us in this messed-up world, evokes a response in our being. It doesn't matter what a person believes; they can be a hardcore nihilistic atheist and still be moved by love, beauty, truth, and grace. The soul doesn't care what your mind believes. When the soul is touched by light, it responds. No external, personified deity is required here. This is an internal response to inner truth.

Within humanity, Love, Truth, Beauty, and Grace manifest themselves in myriads of ways: selflessness, the beauty of nature, inner beauty, charity, kindness, generosity, goodwill, opportunity, forgiveness, etc.

Authentic gratitude is mysterious, you never know when it's going to hit. The more attuned you are to the Four Attributes, the more this sensation arises and embeds itself your awareness.

In his article, "Overselling Gratitude," Alfie Kohn suggests that if you don't believe that sunsets were created deliberately for their beauty, it makes no sense to respond with gratitude. The only issue with his statement is that he's assuming that the only gratitude is mental gratitude and that it's a *conscious choice*. It's not. You can't force yourself to feel something that you don't. Authentic gratitude arises from the unconscious as an *automatic response*.

If you feel grateful for the beauty of a sunset, it's a response to the existence of beauty and your ability to perceive it. However, when a sunset moves me, it's not just because beauty exists and I can perceive it, it's also because that beauty *touches, and moves through me*. I merge with it. At that moment, the sunset, with all its beauty, is part of my being. That sensation and recognition is the highest form of gratitude.

Some studies performed by psychologists suggest that gratitude is, in itself, a personality factor. Because they tend to keep everything at the level of the psyche (so that they can measure and analyse), many psychologists miss the deeper, spiritual catalysts that give rise to states of being. Deeply spiritual people operate from states of being that can't be quantified or deconstructed by psychoanalysis. The word gratitude is insufficient to describe how this particular state feels.

Gratitude has been marketed as a conscious choice into which you can hypnotise yourself. I'm not sure why. Surely most of the people doing this are well-intentioned. If you feel unhappy and think that the problem is that you're just not grateful enough, someone or something has misled you. Forcing thankfulness is a bandaid over a wound, not a healing salve.

Now that we know what gratitude is, we can go straight to the source, which is in you. No external source required.

Think of a time when you felt an automatic, profound, genuine sense (again, it's a spiritual sensation) of gratitude that arises from within your being. This sensation feels energetic; you can sense it arise from the heart and, if it's very powerful, flow out and surround you like a field. What was it inspired by? Can you spot love, beauty, truth, or grace in the scenario?

Some part of your being responded to one of those things, no matter how deeply it was buried within the event. If someone gave you a second chance at your job or in a relationship and you experienced a powerful sense of gratitude, that response was to the existence of love, grace and perhaps forgiveness (depending on the circumstances).

Think about it: What is it really that caused such a response in you to make you say, "I am grateful?" This kind of essential gratitude is a state of being that you automatically shift into as you come into contact with the pure essence of either Love, Truth, Beauty, or Grace or any combination of those things. Instead of looking for events and situations to be grateful for, why don't we go straight to the source and start giving other people a reason to experience this state of being? Being touched by the Four Attributes is powerful. Being the vessel through which those things touch others is one hundred times stronger.

People are creating various forms of *gratitude practice*, like journaling, or taking a few moments of each morning to list things for which they're grateful. It's a helpful practice, but if you're looking for something, give it to others, and you'll discover that you had the thing you're searching for all along.

The highest form of gratitude practice is to give others cause to feel the presence of love, truth, beauty, and grace in the world. Be a vessel for the essence of those attributes to flow into the world and touch someone else. You can meditate on gratitude if you want, or you can contemplate the nature of Love, Truth, Beauty, and Grace and how you could bring more of that into your life and the lives of others.

Neither authentic gratitude, nor human fulfillment, can be forced. If it could be, it wouldn't last because everything unreal is transient. Nothing true requires coercion. For that, I'm *mentally* grateful.

Chapter 19
HOPE

I once attended a lecture in Ireland given by writer and self-titled 'Life Teacher.' Let's call him Mr. Stumpf. Sitting in a crowd of about four-hundred people, I watched as he approached the podium, adjusted it and then said, "Hope is for fools." He then launched into a soliloquy on the virtues of "hard, cold truth" and the worthlessness of hope.

His tirade sounded like a personal manifesto, written with ink made from the tears of every person who ever got close to him. Based on his words, Mr. Stumpf was angry at God, women, and Starbucks. He made a very good case, albeit an intellectually dishonest one.

Stumpf's assertion was that hope requires a form of mental gymnastics and naïveté. He argued that hope is constructed around mental projections of the future that keep people disengaged with the present moment. He could have been convincing if he weren't so ornery, depressed, and obviously at odds with the world. This gentleman, who was well past sixty and doubtlessly experienced, could have lectured about *anything*, but he raged against the one thing he had lost…hope.

Mr. Strumpf considered hope as being the antipode of realism, and that was one of the primary fallacies in his argument. He also equated hope with optimism, as if these two things are identical. They most certainly are not. Hope stands apart from all these things as something unique. Let's examine the temporal orientation of hope and its implications.

Hope is not just about the future; it's also very much about the present. The popularisation of the *present moment* has given people the notion that both the past and the future are utterly non-existent because they're mental projections. Technically speaking, the present moment is also a mental projection. There is no time. The past and future *do* exist **because everything is happening all at once.**

If you can *imagine* the present moment (and you are, right now), then you can also imagine other present moments (call them *past* or *future*) that your awareness (at the level it's operating at) isn't currently perceiving, but *can* perceive from another level of awareness. You do this via *imaginative perception*, which is a form of *conception*.

There are two ways to think of this:

1. In the first scenario, you're *being moved*. You're a point that is moving along the circumference of a circle. Draw a circle on a piece of paper. Place your finger at one point on the circle; it doesn't matter where. Now, begin to move forward in either direction, remember the point at which you began. Regardless of which direction you move, that point the you leave behind as you move forward is also a future point that you will arrive at and pass through. What we call the *moment* is the *entire wheel*, not any given point that you perceive (i.e., *imagine*) that you've arrived at. We are always projecting the condition of our inner space onto the screen of outer space. The present moment is just as much an imaginative projection as the past and future.

2. In the second scenario, the circle (a.k.a. the wheel) is moving *through* you. Draw a wheel on a piece of paper, imagine that the wheel is turning. It doesn't matter which direction. Draw a dot at any point on the wheel, that's you, and you're static. You don't move, the wheel does. Any movement by you is an illusion because, in this scenario, you're not a self-moving entity; you're *being moved* or *transformed* by something else that acts upon you. You can change form (grow old, taller, etc.) and change location on the earth, but you never actually move along the wheel; the wheel moves *through you*.

As in the first scenario, the *entire wheel* is still the moment, and what we perceive as present, past, and future are, in reality, *whatever we imagine* as the wheel flows through us. Within the illusion of time, what we imagined (perceived) yesterday, circles around and flows back through us tomorrow because our imaginations create personal imprints on the wheel.

As you can see, in both scenarios, the present moment never recedes into a static past because that past is also your future, which also isn't static; it exists as multiple, super-positioned, quantum potentialities. Using your imagination (what you believe to be true about yourself and the world and how you feel about it), you can, and do, create imprints *anywhere* on the wheel, and those imprints will come back to you as the wheel turns. Whatever imprint is currently flowing through you, you project onto the *screen of space* and experience as your relative reality, within the framework of our consensus reality.

And this is where hope enters the picture.

Hope is both a feeling and a liminal state. It's our way of *sensing* desired potentialities that are super-positioned in the imaginative (quantum) realm. You plant the seeds of hope through imaginative perception. Hope is positive expectation, and faith adds the dimension of confidence that the seeds you plant will sprout. Hope is not passive wishful thinking, as some might suggest. Even the word *wish* isn't as passive as our use of the word would lead us to believe. The word *wish* comes from the PIE root *wen*, which means "to strive for."

There's a proverb that says, "Surely there is a future, and your hope will not be cut off." Another proverb says, "Know that wisdom is such to your soul; if you find it, there will be a future, and your hope will not be cut off." In Hebrew, the word for *hope* means "expectation." If you expect something, that means you're convinced that it's coming, you have faith in the inevitable eventuality of it. We've already examined what faith is, and now you can see why faith and hope are so tied to each other.

There is a saying in Tibetan, 'Tragedy should be utilised as a source of strength.' No matter what sort of difficulties, how painful experience is, if we lose our hope, that's our real disaster. —The Dalai Lama

Hope is crucial to a healthy human existence. Hopelessness kills joy, one of the highest of all states. It's also is one of the strongest indicators of suicide. Why? Because it blocks our connection to our inner source.

When people describe a black cloud of depression, that cloud is hopelessness. It's been proven that hopelessness shortens lifespan even in people that aren't suicidal at all. When the elderly lose hope, their life expectancy decreases markedly. Although it's been almost two decades, I still clearly remember that the first change I noticed as my depression lifted was a re-covery of hope. Hope *grows* and *brightens;* it truly is a spark.

There's a children's film called *The Neverending Story.* In this film, the lack of imagination in *our* world leads to hopelessness and despair and, eventually, the end of *another* world. When all is consumed by a great, black void of Nothingness (which represents hopelessness in the film, but shouldn't be confused with the radiant 'No-thingness' that mystics describe), the only thing that remains is one small spark in the hand of a child: the spark of hope and potential.

Hope is a birthright of every human being. It leads us to strive and not stagnate. Hope <u>evokes</u>, without it, there's no inspiration. It's *in* the spark that Aeon Sophia breathed into mankind, as her own hope…for us.

Hope is the thing with feathers
That perches in the soul
And sings the tune without the words
And never stops at all. —Emily Dickinson

Chapter 20
WONDER & AWE

Beyond our mental maps, there is a place without location, a realm without space, and yet incomprehensibly vast. As my body fell into the suspended animation we call sleep; I remained awake until I felt the shift. It's at that moment that I can slip through one of the folds in my being. I drifted in this no-place quietly, without moving. There was either nowhere to move to, or I was simply incapable of moving myself. I don't know why, but question arose, and I asked no-one in particular, "Where am I from?" A beautiful, female voice responded immediately as if she'd been waiting for the question.

I felt her power take hold my immaterial body as if pushing me from behind and holding me firmly. She moved me across what I knew was a vastness too large for my mind to ever comprehend, and yet we arrived at the other side of this universe in no-time.

In front of me appeared a veil of aether and she pushed me through it. Lights shone everywhere, unnumbered lights, and the female voice said, "You come from the world of the stars. There, there are many lights. You are one of those lights." —My Dream Yoga Journal, 2013

The Mystery Schools ended for a reason. Humanity passes through stages. We take the pearls from each age and incorporate them into the next.

I've always been drawn to mystery, most specifically to mysterious feelings, emotions, sensations, and states like intuition, knowing, gratitude, hope, and awe. I couldn't help but see people, feelings, and emotions as enigmatic caves full of treasures. I tried to enter the caves of feeling and sensation like a spelunker, sure that I would find caverns and tunnels leading to the centre of the earth, and the ground of soul.

Awe is especially enigmatic. In moments of awe, time stops, the mind goes blank, and the self is dwarfed by suggestive sensation. You feel that if you could manage to hold on to this moment just a *little* bit longer, you could step through a hole in the world and disappear.

It works that way in dreams, why not in the waking world?

Awe does something very special. The phenomenological reorientation that we've considered so far in this book is a reorientation towards the inner, supra-conscious world. The wonder that we feel when confronted with the magnitude of the outer world reminds us not only that we're small, but that it's *okay* to be small! Small is not insignificant; it's delicate and precious.

Albert Einstein said, "One cannot help but be in awe when contemplating the mysteries of eternity, of life, of the marvellous structure of reality. It is enough if one tries merely to comprehend a little of the mystery every day. The important thing is not to stop questioning, never lose a holy curiosity."

"Holy curiosity," what a perfect way to put it!

They say that in each hemisphere, on any given night, there are only 4500 visible stars in the sky. One February night, a few years ago, my husband, in-laws, and I exited a manor house that a family member had rented for a wedding reception. I've seen a lot of night skies, but when I looked up on this clear night, I saw a sky unlike any before.

Intellectually, I know and accept that my eyes are incapable of seeing any more than 4500 stars, even on the clearest of nights, but on this night, I swear I beheld *hundreds of thousands,* and they seemed to be *layered.* The sky looked like a supernatural, massive metropolis of celestial lights, some of which were different colours. I wasn't hallucinating because my husband also stopped and said, "Wow!" Neither of us was drugged or drunk. I stopped walking, stopped thinking, and just…beheld.

Oddly, my husband's parents didn't seem to notice it at all. They looked back at us, like, "What's holding you up?" They cast a cursory glance to the sky and kept going as if nothing was out of the ordinary. Later, I asked my husband what he saw, and he said, "The sky was full of stars." I asked him how many he thinks he saw, and he said, "I can't tell." Unlike me, he didn't notice the different colours.

Urizen and Urthona battled in me. Rationally, I know that my eyes didn't see hundreds of thousands of stars, but my Urthona says, "You *did* see them, just not with your eyes." Awe and authentic gratitude are the root emotions of a primeval 'Christianity' that has been here from the very beginning. It didn't just appear two-thousand years ago, it's not a religion, it's not a person, it's a perpetually unfolding *pattern*. Any awe that we're fortunate enough to experience in this life is a mere foreshadowing of the awe one experiences during hypostatic union, as the pattern completes itself in the individual.

There is no amount of money, no pleasure, and no worldly accomplishment that compares to the calm ecstasy and silent reverence of awe. We become what we revere.

The Mystery Schools may have ended, but mystery remains.

Chapter 21
PRACTICAL FULFILLMENT

We've now arrived at the temple Mandapa. The Mandapa is the social area of a temple. It's where people meet to sing, dance, and perform rituals together. Some Hindu temples have more than one Mandapa. If so, each one has a particular function.

The practicalities of fulfillment always involve our interaction with the outer world. It's the area of our life that is influenced by, and influences, other people, places, and organisations like church, work, school, community, etc.

In the Inner Sanctum, all our attention is placed on our core, the innermost self, the well, and the wellspring. We process pain, rediscover the power of our imagination, work on the recovery of our fractured way of being, come into contact with true beauty, and find that at our core, we *are* love. We then learn to activate our will by opening the valve wider as we accept more and more personal responsibility. We begin to transform. Grace enters the stage. What was once a shimmering, potential of grace, has now intensified and radiates.

This transformation reshapes the temple and pillars appear in the Antarala: faith, authentic gratitude, hope, and awe.

Now it's time to bring all of ourselves, as who and what we *really* are, into the Mandapa. If we've genuinely worked on our core, on showing up in the world as our authentic self, this phase isn't difficult, but it does require some calibration as we learn to interact in an entirely new way. It takes time to integrate the insights that we gleaned in the Inner Sanctum.

Insights arrive in a flash; they're often fleeting and forgotten. Integration is capturing those evanescent insights and systematically stabilising them by integrating them into our experience, thereby creating coherence. Coherence connects and harmonises seemingly disparate insights into a more comprehensive understanding of life. It permanently alters one's perception.

When working with my clients, I ask, "What does fulfillment *look* like for you?" So far, the answer has always been some version of the following, "I want to do a job I love, and be with people I love, and I'd like to believe (or trust) in myself more." Some people add other things, but no one has ever excluded those criteria.

Clients often bring up mindset. There are hundreds of books, seminars, and workshops that teach various methodologies for developing a mindset of success, positivity, growth, etc. Changing our mindset and reaping the benefits of that change works best when we address our core in parallel with addressing our thoughts and habits.

If we try to apply mindset methodologies without doing the core work first, we're bypassing, and our results will be inconsistent. This can cause us to falter and lose faith in ourselves. That said, mindset techniques can help you with the core work—if transformation is your goal, combining mindset practices and techniques with counselling, coaching and/or therapy can be incredibly helpful.

Contemplation

Ongoing contemplative practice keeps us centred and encourages continual evolution. It's the most effective means of stabilising insights. Contemplation is a mental posture, a way of perceiving that arises from the harmonisation of the rational and irrational, the left and the right brain, and the inner world with the outer world.

There are many contemplative practices you can choose from and experiment with, like deep listening, beholding, singing, qigong, silence, forest bathing, meditation, poetry, reading transformational texts—the list is long.

If you'd like to learn more, there are various organisations devoted to contemplative practice. You can find them online and in your local community centre. These practices can be individual and social.

Reclaiming Language

Reclaiming language isn't about politics or ideology. Language will never be perfect. I'm certainly not suggesting that the language of previous centuries was ideal, but it was closer to the roots of meaning. We need to remember that language preconditions consciousness and pre-conditioned awareness is, at times (but not always), the *enemy of knowing*.

The Sufis who wrote poetry and perfected the art of calligraphy believed that the shape of the letters and the words they formed had no real existence, for the Sufis, the true power was in the ink!

What really and concretely exists is nothing but the ink. The existence of the letters is in truth no other than the existence of the ink, which is the sole, unique reality that unfolds itself in many forms of self-modification. One has to cultivate, first of all, the eye to see the self-same reality of ink in all letters and then to see the letters as so many intrinsic modifications of the ink. —Toshihiko Izutsu

Recent attempts to redefine words and coerce language are intellectually dishonest. They assume that you're an imbecile with no ability to see what's truly going on. Language is dynamic, it's constantly evolving, but there's a world of difference between the natural evolution of language and intentional social programming via linguistics.

As I wrote this book, the editing software I used repeatedly highlighted my use of the words "man" and "mankind" and informed me of the following, I quote: "*Some readers may find the word mankind to be non-inclusive and outdated. Consider using **humankind**.*" Although the word *human* appears multiple times throughout the texts, the words man and mankind (gender neutral) are also employed. "Man" is derived from the Sanskrit "Manu." Manu was the <u>genderless,</u> divine, primeval Being. Albion before he/she was broken on the rocks.

The word *human* is a Latin variant. *Hum* comes from the Latin *Humus* which means *earth or ground*. It also means *lowly*. The root is found in words like *humicubation*, which means, "The act of lying on the ground in penitence and self-abasement." We also see it in the word *humiliation*. Human literally means *lowly*, gender-neutral man of the earth. It still means *man, but* it's the lowly man of clay, not of spirit.

Throughout Tolkien's Silmarillion and Lord of the Rings sagas, he never used the word *human*. Tolkien was an accomplished linguist that understood the power of language. He was a linguistic genius that learned French, Latin, and German by age twelve and later learned Medieval Welsh, Welsh, Spanish, Italian, Finnish, Gothic, Old English, and Middle English. He understood the grammatical structure of Danish, Dutch, Lombardic, Norwegian, Russian, Serbian, and Swedish.

Tolkien preferred "man" over the Latin-influenced "human" because he was well aware of the root meaning and implications of the word *human*. Tolkien described a world in which each member of mankind was a fractal of *Eru Ilúvatar*, the primary, genderless divinity. Unlike the Elves, Mankind had the ability to transcend time through 'death.'

A *Man* is no lowly thing, and gender has naught to do with it.

The word humanity isn't in any way more inclusive than the word man. It's only inclusive in that it implies that a female is just as low and dirt-like as the male; she's a "clod of clay" with a womb. Nothing particularly progressive there!

Agendas that invert meaning and claim to be one thing when, in truth, they are something else entirely, brings the following Blake passage to mind:

> *TRULY, my Satan, thou art but a dunce,*
> *And dost not know the garment from the man;*
> *Every harlot was a virgin once,*
> *Nor canst thou ever change Kate into Nan.*
> *Tho' thou art worship'd by the names divine*
> *Of Jesus and Jehovah, thou art still*
> *The Son of Morn in weary Night's decline,*
> *The lost traveller's dream under the hill.*

Lucid people can distinguish the garment from the man. The lucid among us are not robots. They can't be programmed.

Presence and Mastery

Mindfulness is an awareness of your inner and outer environment that is discerning and alert. It responds instead of reacting. When we master mindfulness, our observation sensations, thoughts, feelings, intuition, images, and movements become effortless and highly lucid. A lucid dream is a dream in which a person becomes mindful.

Mindfulness during our daily life is the same. We're no longer caught up on the dream of life as unconscious players who are being acted upon. Mindfulness is key to imaginative perception. Presence is a perpetual stabilisation of mindfulness. Our engagement with the outer world becomes masterful, artful, and effective.

Work

Masterfulness changes how we work—being intentional about our personal fulfillment changes the *why* and the *what*. If someone values wealth above everything else, money will remain their why. But for others, the meaning of money is transmuted, money is just another form of energetic exchange. You can have lots of it, it just flows to you, but it's not the reason you do what you do.

"Do what you love," sounds a bit ambiguous. What does that mean? When someone suggests that they're saying to do what brings you joy. You may not even need to change your work, but most people do. When you've transformed from the inside out, your situation will too. When your perception radically shifts from Single Vision, linear time, and rigid subject-object duality, everything in your world will shift.

Throughout the book, we've looked at alignment, specifically how our thoughts, actions, and choices align with our authentic being and create coherence. We are dynamic beings; we're evolving, and expanding over the course of our lives. Considering this, the concept of having only one career over a lifetime is very limiting for some people, but for others, it can be deeply rewarding.

In chapter 15, we looked at values and the topography of the self. Creating a fulfilling career path means aligning our work to our values, strengths, skills, and interests but most of all, to our true joy.

There are a myriad of tools and assessment programs designed to help us find our strengths. Here are a few:

The Gallup CliftonStrengths®
MAPP Career Test®
Meyers-Briggs Type Indicator®
Holland Code (RIASEC) Test®
Riso-Hudson Enneagram Type Indicator®

These kind of assessments can be helpful, but it's important that we use them as an indicator or suggestion, rather than a closed box to live in. Consider such assessments as an opportunity to do some more self-inquiry. Don't take the results of any standardised test as *gospel truth* about yourself.

Many people in their twenties aren't yet sure of what their inherent talents are or what will bring them the most joy. This blindspot isn't a fault or a sign of failure; in fact, it's not a blind spot at all. It's the natural progression of life; they're still developing, still evolving and on the first leg of a journey that lasts anywhere from eighty to one hundred years.

If you're a young person reading this, just know that *you will change*. If you don't change at all, something is wrong. Don't pressure yourself to figure it all out before age twenty-two.

Can you see the immediate reality gap between the natural human and the system? We're asking our young people to choose a path before age eighteen. We send them to institutions of higher learning and expect them to have it all figured out before they graduate. This is changing and has been changing for a while now.

But why wait for the system to change completely before you act? You don't need a piece of paper before you can start building your life and aligning your work with your authentic self. The same goes for people who have been working for decades; you can change!

I've seen so many people go into their jobs, place all of their focus on a narrow scope of activities, and do nothing else. Because they think of themselves as *employees* and because their main objective is to collect a pay check, they never really look around at the organisation they're a part of or the market and movements of markets. Entrepreneurs make personal agency the priority. Even if you prefer to work for an organisation rather than creating your own business, learn to think and behave like an entrepreneur. When you live your life like an entrepreneur, your eyes are always open, and you're always learning.

Finances and current circumstances might dictate that for a while, you need a certain job with a reliable salary until you establish yourself in your new area of work, but you have complete control over your attitude, development and learning. Learn the art of self-teaching; learn to love learning. Consider working with a mentor or a coach to help you discover your joy and reconnect with your innate talents. A mentor or coach can also help you determine your current skill-set and map out a plan to augment it. Create a strategy but don't forget the power of imagination and will, they are the catalysts that launch you into each, successive phase of life and work.

Many people deny their desire to change their work, location and social circle because they fear to lose what they've already built. Someone told me once, "Look at all that you have and all that you have accomplished and how much you can now do because of that process. If you gave it all up tomorrow you could easily create it all over again. In fact, you would create even more."

The material and circumstantial things in our lives have no real substance, they are all transient. **It's the underlying, structural relationship between things that has eternal reality**. It's a bridge. It's a door. That's why the Christ says, "I am a door".

Hold not to the *things* themselves, **hold instead to the musical rhythm, love, and coherence of the underlying relationship**—because that's where

God is. This is true in absolutely every aspect of life. The relationship between two seemingly separate entities (and/or situations) is a clue to the truth: you aren't really separate at all. Your relationship to your work isn't about the title, the tasks, the events or the accomplishments—**It's about your relationship to yourself, as you make yourself manifest in your work.**

Making a big change can be exhilarating and scary. Ironically, it's the people that succeed that often feel the most insecure. I have an uncle that went to university for the first time at the age of forty-eight. He has a wife that is unable to work due to a severe back injury, and at the time he was attending school, he was also taking care of both of his elderly parents and working full-time.

After he finished his undergrad degree, he decided to become a lawyer. He graduated from law school and passed the Bar exam in his fifties. When you ask him about his work now, he glows! But listening to him over the years, I've noticed that he still doesn't give himself the credit that he deserves for what he accomplished. Part of that is humility, but there's another dimension to his words that suggests something deeper.

Photographer and author, Sally Mann, was named 'America's Best Photographer' by Times magazine and was the 2016 winner of the Andrew Carnegie Medal for Excellence in Nonfiction. When asked by a journalist, "Who would you say you are?" Sally replied, "The fundamental thing about my personality is that I think I'm an imposter." Hearing a successful person say they feel like a fraud might seem implausible, and some might interpret such a statement as false modesty; it's not. Imposter syndrome is a real thing and impacts all of us, at some point in our lives.

Imposter syndrome is defined as a psychological pattern in which an individual doubts their accomplishments and has a persistent internalised fear of being exposed as a fraud. When we think of the word "imposter" today, the general implication is that someone is a fraud and a fake, trying to pass themselves off as something they are not.

The root of imposter is *impost*, and we see this root in another word, a word that I think better describes the inner experience of a person suffering from imposter syndrome, that word is *imposition*. In the past, I often felt like I was an imposition to others, like no matter how much I knew, no matter how good my ideas and results were, I didn't merit my success. In my psyche, everyone else belonged, but I was an outsider. I can tell you exactly when that belief first took hold; it was Friday, October 31, 1980. I was seven.

The Watchtower organisation of Jehovah's Witnesses doesn't allow its members to celebrate holidays. They also don't do the pledge of allegiance, or sing the National Anthem. This meant repeated embarrassment for me as, on the first day of every school year, my mother would approach my new teacher, explain our families religious affiliation and instruct the teacher that I was not to partake in any birthday parties, stand for the pledge of allegiance or participate in holiday activities.

That's tough for a child; the isolation, the strange looks from other kids, the humiliation as day-after-day, I was forced to remain seated as the rest of the class pledged together. I longed for a Christmas tree, for a birthday party, for permission to collect copious amounts of toxic candy dressed up as a Jedi. I can't remember Halloween in the first grade, but I will never forget my first foray into forbidden territory as I found a way to join the festivities on Halloween, 1980.

All of the kids came to school wearing their costumes. I showed up dressed as usual. As I entered the classroom by way of the coat drop, I realised that my raincoat was the most beautiful shade of green, it was shiny and had a hood and, if I imagined hard enough, I could imagine that my hood had ears. As I faced a group of classmates, all decked out in their colourful attire, one of them asked me, "Where is *your* costume, why aren't you dressed up?" I promptly replied, "I *am* dressed up. I'm Pete the Magic Dragon!" Pete, who for those of you who don't know, was the most wonderful shade of green, the exact shade of my raincoat.

I share this story because I believe that curing imposter syndrome requires deeper insights into the individual causation and layered complexity of personal experience.

To call something a syndrome implies not just one attribute or symptom but a collection of them; a collection that creates concurrence, which in this case is a set of beliefs and behaviours that are harmful in the least and completely paralysing at the most.

The circumstances and events that fostered my eventual imposter syndrome weren't limited to negative experiences. I was also singled out at an early age because I was considered 'gifted.' My first intelligence test was at the age of six. I was pulled out of the classroom, placed in a room in the library with large, glass windows so that the psychologist could supervise, and given a series of tests.

They didn't have a program for gifted children at our elementary school and weren't sure what to do with me so, between the 1st and 4th grades, I was tutored privately through extra activities, anything they could think up, like learning to type, helping in the principal's office, learning to use the old 1980s computers, and even learning about the stock market through mock trading with a teacher. I loved it. But it also meant that yet again, I felt singled out, isolated and alien.

What many don't realise is that Impostor Syndrome tends to impact those who have overcome odds and worked incredibly hard to earn their success. —Robert Glazer

Why is this? Could this be a natural response to a culture that rewards conformity (diplomas, titles, and the accepted ways of doing things) and sends the constant message that unless you are X, Y or Z, you're not qualified? Layered into this are other contributors like persistent stereotypes and unexamined group-think.

The accumulative result is a whole smorgasbord of 'messed-up'. There are millions of highly adept, talented and intelligent people who don't 'fit the bill' in terms of background, degrees, titles and expected attributes but who could and do, impact the world, business, their neighbours and colleagues in positive and sometimes miraculous ways; all the while feeling that they don't deserve to be where they are.

My imposter syndrome continued throughout my early career, up until I made a big shift in my perception of Self-worth. Knowing that you're not alone and opening up about your insecurities is the first step.

"I thought it was a big fluke. I thought everybody would find out, and then they'd take the Oscar back." —Jodie Foster

There is a slew of web content and books that give advice on how to overcome imposter syndrome with recommendations like: "Dress for success,"—"Just know that others don't know everything" and "Learn to project confidence." I appreciate what the people who shared that advice were trying to do but employing such superficial tactics is like spraying perfume on cow dung and expecting it to magically transform into potpourri.

Here are the first steps that one can take to overcome and change the limiting beliefs underlying Imposter Syndrome and other feelings of insecurity at work.

1. Find the Origin

For some, this is easy; for others, it requires more contemplation. It's sometimes uncomfortable to dredge up old memories, but it's important to re-examine our own lives, not with the aim to blame but with the intent to unfold and review our experiences through new lenses.

2. Instant Replay

As I was examining my life and reactions during those formative years, I found that replaying the experience as if it was happening right now, within the imaginative body of my younger self but with the wisdom of an adult, to be very enlightening. I realised that as much as I hated having to remain seated during the pledge of allegiance, it taught me to never fear a group and never to be afraid to stand out. It was ironic, but much of what fed my imposter syndrome was also the cure!

3. Make Peace with the Imposter

As you re-examine your life, you'll most likely find a collection of experiences that snowballed upon each other. Each successive confirmation of your false belief (that you don't belong, or that your success is unmerited) cemented and became an aspect of your personality that is harmful to you. Know that much of what you think is just you, isn't you at all, it's a construct with many layers. Maybe you are different. Maybe you've overcome obstacles that others didn't have to face or perhaps you've simply taken a route that's unique to you. What if the nasty voice in your head that's telling you that you don't belong and are unworthy, is just trying to protect you, albeit it a very misguided way?

That voice is the true imposter because it's pretending to be you. Separate that voice from your stream of consciousness. Call it out, challenge it. Here's an example: the imposer voice says, "You don't really belong here, your success is pure luck." So challenge that statement. Use Byron Katie's technique from *The Work*: Can you know the statement "my success is pure luck" to be an absolute, universal truth? Yes, or No? If your answer is "no," ask yourself, "What would I be without the thought that my success is based on pure luck?" Sit with that. Understand that the majority (if not all) of our binary and polarising beliefs are untrue. Underneath all of them is a part of our psyche that just wants to protect itself. Examine it, examine the beliefs, acknowledge the intention to protect (however misguided), and make peace with it. Then let it go.

4. Trust Others

It's also about learning to trust the discernment of others while not relying on them to confirm your worthiness. In a funny way, imposter syndrome is a bit of an ego-trip. It indicates a lack of trust in the wisdom of others. It's essentially saying, "The rest of the world isn't smart enough to see me as I am, to see my strengths and weaknesses. In their ignorance, they project good things onto me, but eventually, they might realise they were wrong." Which leads to the next step towards recovery:

5. Share Your Vulnerability

As you go back in time in your imagination to unpack your experiences, you will act as an invisible coach from the future to your younger self. In the present, it's helpful to find someone to coach your adult self. You can work with professional coaches, psychologists, and consulting philosophers, but you can also open up at work with your colleagues, manager, and HR and share your insecurities. Openness is a powerful cure. You'll be surprised to discover that virtually everyone deals with some degree of imposter syndrome. You'll also be surprised by how caring, supportive, and understanding people can be. Ultimately, imposter syndrome is about far more than our career; it's a matter of inherent worth, precisely our awareness of our own value as human beings. Bring joy into the work you do. Whatever it is, find the joy in it. If you do decide to make a big change; you will bring the skilfulness that you developed by means of your inner work and apply it to all reconfigurations of your outer life in the Mandapa.

Friends & Lovers

Inspiring conversations, fulfilling lovemaking, shared interests, deep attraction, laughter, emotional support, fun…these are the things that most people associate with relationships, but as wonderful and enriching as they are, these are transient experiences. **The real relationship between two people is in the silence between them**. Relationships are self-revealing. If you know that, and if you've passed through the furnace of deep self-inquiry and the initial stages of transformation, your relationships will reflect your evolution.

We've been told that, "It takes two to tango" and that if the other person isn't willing to change, there is nothing you can do. Both of those ideas are untrue. It only takes one person to transform any relationship.

Although it may appear that opposites magnetically attract, that level attraction is an attraction between the personality construct of two relative selves. At the deeper level, those contraries are equally true. Let's take an example of a couple: an outgoing man and an introverted woman. The man is broadcasting and embodying a polarity: Extraversion. He's suppressing the other polarity, his need for introversion. The woman in this scenario broadcasts and embodies introversion, but suppresses her need for extraversion.

This reveals a truth. **We always attract what we are deep inside** (but *might* be repressing or unaware of because it's in shadow). The soul desires unifi-

277

cation, resolution, and the reconciliation of opposites within itself. Relationships give us an opportunity to explore those parts of ourselves.

But here's the rub, when we resolve those contraries within ourselves, our motivation for forming an intimate relationship changes drastically. It's not so much about mirroring our relative self in others, but about learning to behold and love another person for what they truly are: the Absolute Self... and infinite. That's the Self that Blake beheld when he wrote, "*I am in you and you in me, mutual in divine love.*"

When we love and live this way, we become like mature trees. As all knowledgable foresters know, trees give more than they take.

Chapter 22
THE POETIC LIVES OF WALKING TREES

His roots were loosening themselves from the earth. "It is right so; it is best," said the tree, "No fetters hold me now. I can fly up to the very highest point in light and glory, and all I love are with me, both small and great. All are here."
—Hans Christian Anderson

They said that we appear to them as men, walking like trees.
—Neville Goddard

We *are* the earth. Nature is a stream that flows through us. She's not the tree, the toad, the stone, or the flower; she's the *spirit* of those things. She's a dryad, a salamander dancing in fire, and the wind spirits that blow away fallen leaves at the end of every autumn. On their own, Nature's spirits have no memory of Eternity; they came into being outside of it and are bound to the Great Wheel.

They learn from us and give back to us what we give to them. If some of the inhabitants of the Otherworld are notoriously capricious, fickle and cruel, it's because that's what we've taught them to be. Los and Enthiharmon may provide the pattern, Tharmas may provide the energy, but *we* are the *urth*-onas[4].

---

[4] Earth Owners

Like Blake, Neville Goddard was a visionary and mystic. Neville used to say that he occasionally met the inhabitants of other realms. Not the Otherworld of the Celts, but some other parallel dimension. These people told him that they shuddered at the very thought of living in our world. He said, "They call our world the 'Woodland' and say that to them, we appear as men, walking like trees."

If you've ever touched a human corpse, you'll know that the body becomes very wooden.

We *are* trees. Our limbs are branches, our spine a trunk, and our brain a dense forest. Our roots are psychological; they bind us to our stories, and our stories enslave us to time. Writing this book was an interesting exercise because, in order to share the process of my personal apocalypse, I needed to think about the past as if it's static, an unalterable book, even though I know it's not. I had to remember the girl (and woman) I used to be, her experiences and interpretations—but *I* am not her. My roots have loosened.

The woman I used to be remains a beloved and cherished part of me; a transmuted cell in the imago[5] of my Being.

> *We who are poets know that the reason for a poem is not discovered until the poem itself exists. The reason for a living act is realised only in the act itself.*
> —Thomas Merton

Unlike the great oak, we can move, or better yet, we are *being moved*—we pitter and patter about upon the surface of the earth. We may not notice it, but there's a pattern and a rhythm to our movements. The function of poetry is to move, transform, transmute, and transport. If trees ever evolve enough to create poetry, they'll begin to walk.

Like stars, poets are made of a quintessence. Wordsworth alludes to this when he writes, "Poetry is the breath and finer spirit of all knowledge; it is the impassioned expression which is in the countenance of all science."

---

[5] Imago is the final stage in the metamorphosis of a butterfly. Webster's Dictionary notes that: "Linnaeus's conception was that the imago was the *true representation* of the creature, the earlier stages of larva (Latin *larva*, taken to mean "ghost") and pupa (Latin *pūpa* "doll") being in a sense illusory." The same could be said of the relative self—it's an illusory and yet necessary part of the process towards the emergence of the actualised Self.

Poetry restores experience, charred and disfigured by the mind, to its original purity. It seizes the soul by the shoulders, rips her roots out of the bedrock of time, and puts her back on her feet again. Poetry is a number, the number *e*. It rescues us from the finite, otherwise inescapable geometry of space. It twists our guts and brains and hearts until we become spiralling tourbillions with wings, capable of escaping the gravity of fallen reason.

Poets are visionary, intuitive mathematicians, nourished on ambrosia while they sleep. A poet is a stellar traveler. She sojourns a while in the earth, running her hands up nature's skirts, resting beneath the fallen leaves of maturity. Gliding into the lake of transcendent, human emotion, she'll dive deep, and discover a secret, primeval current.

A poetic life is the highest expression of human fulfillment. There's a cadence to it. It's ordered, although it may seem at first chaotic. A poetic life is constructed, layer by layer, as the poet gathers the pieces of her broken self and remoulds them into a fractal model of the eternal cosmos, which is her original body—but she or he doesn't stop there. The poet imagines something greater for himself and all of humanity. Like Blake, he'll prophesy a destiny of his own making. A poetic life is an imaginative life, and yet, at its core, is independent of images.

The title and concept of this book had been in my mind for over five years before I began to write. I wrote and completed it within a ten-week period. Although initially unsure for whom I felt so compelled to write (I suspected that it was just for me, as a bookmark in my life), I realised in the process of writing that this book *was*, and *wasn't*, written for myself. There was no dire need to put it on paper; it lives inside of me. Ultimately, I wrote it for you.

As I wrote, I imagined hands, holding this book, as their owner read. There were young, smooth female hands, one with a fine gold bracelet on her left wrist. There were aged male hands with blue veins protruding through the skin. There were rich brown hands with fresh, pink fingernails, pale, peach hands with chipped polish, weathered hands, hands with pinkie rings and wedding rings, hands belonging to young, strong men with fine hairs below the knuckles, hands attached to wrists with oval cufflinks on a blue, pin-striped shirt, and one hand with melted chocolate coating three of its fingertips. Don't worry—books are meant to be stained.

It's my hope that you found something of value in these pages because you helped to write them. As you read, the book took formation. Your act of reading in what is, at this moment, *my future,* helped me to write in what is now, *your past.* We've written this book together, you and me, across time, heart-to-heart, mind-to-mind. We began the day we were born and will finish in timelessness.

Through my writing, and by your reading, we've placed this book on a shelf in a magical library. It doesn't tell one how to cast spells, but how to *break* them: the spells of randomness, apathy, language, glamour, single-vision, linear time, mirroring, projection, and sleep.

There are countless unique and valid ways of being in the world. Fulfillment is singular and unique to each individual. In this book, you've glimpsed just a fraction of someone else's spiral, another person's story of *being* and *becoming.*

What will yours be?

I believed that I wanted to be a poet but deep down I just wanted to be a poem.
—Jaime Gil de Biedma

ACKNOWLEDGMENTS

This is normally the most boring part of any book.

Acknowledgement sections are like Oscar speeches; they're only interesting when the speaker goes off-script and says something real. My whole life has seemed off-script and I'm glad it's been so! There are people who have held me, supported me and given me unconditional love from the very beginning. They are the only reason I could ever write this book.

Firstly, thank you to my editor who understands that my writing, like my life, requires that some rules be bent—and that, in daily conversation, people sometimes end sentences with prepositions.

For my Husband,

When we first met, I was determined to master unconditional love in a romantic relationship but I was so wary of romantic love, that it took me a while to surrender and open up to you. You were patient, insistent, and never wavered. You gave me everything I needed to thrive and blossom.

Thank you for the unconditional love that you have given me since the day we met in Paris. Thank you for *just knowing* before I did, and for holding to that knowing. You've held my hand and had my back and never thought twice about it. After almost ten years of marriage, our bond is stronger than ever. This book would quite literally have never been written if it weren't for you.

Damaris,

When we were children, I was convinced that you came into this world with the express purpose of annoying me and getting me into trouble. This lasted for eighteen years. It took forty years for me to recognise what a wise woman my little sister is. Fortunately for me, you put up with my *big sisterness*. Thank you for being you, and for listening to all of my contemplative thoughts and pondering. Thank you for picking up the phone when I called in the middle of the night (my time, not yours) to share a eureka moment. You used to dislike that your name means *gentle cow* but you know what? Cows are considered holy in India and I can't think of anyone more deserving of a name that describes a gentle, holy creature with large, soulful eyes, than you.

Dear Son,

Your grandmother used to sign all of her letters to me with, "*To my Dana, you and me against the world.*" She wrote this because right after she had me, your grandparents divorced, and although I was her second child, she felt like I was the first one that really belonged to her. She married when I was two-and-a-half years old, so she didn't end up raising me alone.

As you know, from the moment you were born, it was just you and I, alone in the world but not without support from our extended family. It's hard to believe that you'll turn twenty-six soon.

We've come along way since you boarded that plane to Munich with me at the age of six. You and I will never be "against the world," we were meant to learn to welcome it and love it, which we have done. If it weren't for you, I wouldn't be who, or where, I am now. You're the first light in my life and the brightest by far.

For Magdalena and Olga,

For almost twenty years, we have witnessed each other's *becoming.* Through relationships, unwise but sometimes satisfying love affairs, child-rearing, new adventures in foreign countries, endless chats and boundless support…no one could have better friends. Olga, *per aspera ad astra.* Magdalena, "*We are such stuff as dreams are made on, and our little life is rounded with a sleep.*"

I love you all.

RESOURCES AND RECOMMENDED READING

For updates and more resources from material mentioned in the book, visit the book's website: www.theartofbecoming.com

Books

The Holographic Universe: The Revolutionary Theory of Reality—Michael Talbot (available for free at the internet archive)
Complete works of Neville Goddard: including all of his lectures—start at www.realneville.com
Complete work of William Blake
The Complete Lectures of Meister Eckhart - available on sacredtexts.com
The Flowing Light of the Godhead - Mechthild of Magdeburg
The Mirror of Simple Souls - Marguerite Porete
The Lamsa Bible New Testament
The Druids - The Celtic Priest of Nature - Jean Markale
Complete works of W.B. Yeats
Wholeness and the Implicate Order - David Bohm
Science and the Akashic Field - Ervin Laszlo
Thus Spake Zarathustra - Friedrich Nietzsche
Being and Time - Martin Heidegger
The Candle of Vision — AE George William Russell—available on www.sacred-texts.com
The Egyptian Book of the Gates
Selections from Three Works of Francisco Suarez, S. J. (Natural Law Paper)
The Natural Law According to Aquinas and Suárez (Thomist Tradition Series)
The Upanishads
The Nag Hammadi Scriptures: The Revised and Updated Translation of Sacred Gnostic Texts
The Silmarillion - Tolkien
Stolen Legacy - George G.M. James

History: Fiction or Science? - Anatoly Fomenko
DMT: The Spirit Molecule - Rick Strassman
Tao Te Ching
Man and His Symbols - Carl Jung
The Book: On the Taboo Against Knowing Who You Are - Alan Watts
Becoming a Person - Carl Rogers
The Kybalion - Three Initiates
Buddhism without Beliefs: A Contemporary Guide to Awakening - Stephen Batchelor

Audiovisual
Dark City 1999
Aldous Huxley interviewed by Mike Wallace : 1958 (Full)—available on youtube.com
("The price of freedom is eternal vigilance" - Huxley)
The Peace Pilgrim talk at college—view on youtube
Michael Talbott interview with Thinking Allowed - view on youtube

Thought-Provoking Fiction
Dark City - 1999 film
A Delicate Dependency - a novel by Michael Talbot

INTERESTED IN MORE?

Are you interested in ordering copies of this book <u>in bulk</u>? Contact us at: contact@theartofbecoming.com

Public Speaking: Dana Hutton is available to speak at events, enterprises and available for podcast discussions. To learn more, email at the address above.

Consulting: Mrs. Hutton specialises in working with enterprises that are committed to putting people before profit and creating a People-First work culture. She has more than twenty years of experience as a professional trainer and facilitator.

NO ONE TO CHANGE BUT SELF

A Partial Transcript of One of Neville Goddard's Lectures
1948

We become what we contemplate. For it is the nature of love, as it is the nature of hate, to change us into the likeness of that which we contemplate. Last night I simply read a news item to show you that when we think we can destroy our image by breaking the mirror, we are only fooling ourselves.

When, through war or revolution, we destroy titles which to us represent arrogance and greed, we become in time the embodiment of that which we thought we had destroyed. So today the people who thought they destroyed the tyrants are themselves that which they thought they had destroyed.

That I may not be misunderstood, let me again lay the foundation of this principle. Consciousness is the one and only reality. We are incapable of seeing other than the contents of our own consciousness

Therefore, hate betrays us in the hour of victory and condemns us to be that which we condemn. All conquest results in an exchange of characteristics, so that conquerors become like the conquered foe. We hate others for the evil which is in ourselves. Races, nations, and religious groups have lived for centuries in intimate hostility, and it is the nature of hatred, as it is the nature of love, to change us into the likeness of that which we contemplate.

Nations act toward other nations as their own citizens act toward each other. When slavery exists in a state and that nation attacks another it is with intent to enslave. When there is a fierce economic competition between citizen and citizen, then in war with another nation the object of the war is to destroy the trade of the enemy. Wars of domination are brought about by the will of those who within a state are dominant over the fortunes of the rest.

We radiate the world that surrounds us by the intensity of our imagination and feeling. But in this third-dimensional world of ours time beats slowly. And so we do not always observe the relationship of the visible world to our inner nature. Now that is really what I meant. I thought I had said it. That I may not be misunderstood, that is my principle. You and I can contemplate an ideal, and become it by falling in love with it. On the other hand we can contemplate something we heartily dislike and by condemning it we will become it. But because of the slowness of time in this three-dimensional world, when we do become what we contemplated we have forgotten that formerly we set out to worship or destroy it.

As you know, all of the Bible stories are *your* stories; its characters live <u>only in the mind of man</u>. **They have no reference at all to any person, who lived in time and space, or to any event that ever occurred upon earth.**

Because consciousness is the only reality I must assume that I am already that which I desire to be. If I do not believe that I am already what I want to be, then I remain as I am and die in this limitation. Man is always looking for some prop on which to lean. He is always looking for some excuse to justify failure. This revelation gives man no excuse for failure. His concept of himself is the cause of all the circumstances of his life. All changes must first come from within himself; and if he does not change on the outside it is because he has not changed within. But man does not like to feel that he is solely responsible for the conditions of his life.

I may not like what I have just heard, that I must turn to my own consciousness as to the only reality, the only foundation on which all phenomena can be explained. It was easier living when I could blame another. It was much easier living when I could blame society for my ills, or point a finger across the sea and blame another nation. It was easier living when I could blame the weather for the way I feel. But to tell me that I am the cause of all that happens to me that I am forever moulding my world in harmony with my inner nature, that is more than man is willing to accept. If this is true, to whom would I go? If these are the words of eternal life, I must return to them, even though they seem so difficult to digest.

When man fully understands this, he knows that public opinion does not matter, for men only tell him who he is. The behaviour of men constantly tell me who I have conceived myself to be. If I accept this challenge and begin to live by it, I finally reach the point that is called the great prayer of the Bible. It is impossible for anything to be lost. In this divine economy nothing can be lost, it cannot even pass away. The little flower which has bloomed once, blooms forever. It is invisible to you here with your limited focus but it blooms forever in the larger dimension of your being, and to-morrow you will encounter it. All that thou gavest me I have kept in thy name, and none have I lost save the son of perdition. The son of perdition means simply the belief in loss. Son is a concept, an idea. Perdido is loss. I have only truly lost the concept of loss, for nothing can be lost.

I can descend from the sphere where the thing itself now lives, and as I de-scend in consciousness to a lower level within myself it passes from my world. I say, "I have lost my health. I have lost my wealth. I have lost my standing in the community. I have lost faith. I have lost a thousand things." But the things in themselves, having once been real in my world, can never cease to be. They never become unreal with the passage of time.

I, by my descent in consciousness to a lower level, cause these things to disappear from my sight and I say, "They have gone; they are finished as far as my world goes." All I need do is to ascend to the level where they are eternal, and they once more objectify themselves and appear as realities within my world. The crux of the whole 17th chapter of the Gospel of St. John is found in the 19th verse, "And for their sake I sanctify myself, that they also might be sanctified through the truth."

Heretofore I thought I could change others through effort. Now I know **I cannot change another unless I first change myself.** To change another within my world I must first change my concept of that other; and to do it best I change my concept of self. For it was the concept I held of self that made me see others as I did. Had I a noble, dignified concept of myself, I never could have seen the unlovely in others.

Instead of trying to change others through argument and force, let me but ascend in consciousness to a higher level and I will automatically change others by changing self. There is no one to change but self; that self is simply your awareness, your consciousness and the world in which it lives is determined by the concept you hold of self. It is to consciousness that we must turn as to the only reality. For there is no clear conception of the origin of phenomena except that consciousness is all and all is consciousness.

You need no helper to bring you what you seek. Do not for one-second believe that I am advocating escape from reality when I ask you to simply assume you are now the man or the lady that you want to be. If you and I could feel what it would be like were we now that which we want to be, and live in this mental atmosphere as though it were real, then, in a way we do not know, our assumption would harden into fact. This is all we need do in order to ascend to the level where our assumption is already an objective, concrete reality.

You always bear fruit in harmony with what you are. It is the most natural thing in the world for a pear tree to bear pears, an apple tree to bear apples, and for man to mould the circumstances of his life in harmony with his inner nature.

You have no life in my world save that I am conscious of you. You are rooted in me and, like fruit, you bear witness of the vine that I am. There is no reality in the world other than your consciousness. Although you may now seem to be what you do not want to be, all you need do to change it, and to prove the change by circumstances in your world, is to quietly assume that you are that which you now want to be, and in a way you do not know you will become it.

There is no other way to change this world. "I am the way." My I AM-ness, my consciousness is the way by which I change my world. As I change my concept of self, I change my world. When men and women help or hinder us, they only play the part that we, by our concept of self, wrote for them, and they play it automatically. They must play the parts they are playing because we are what we are.

You will change the world only when you become the embodiment of that which you want the world to be. You have but one gift in this world that is truly yours to give and that is yourself. Unless you yourself are that which you want the world to be, you will never see it in this world.

Do you know that no two in this room live in the same world. We are going home to different worlds tonight. We close our doors on entirely different worlds. We rise tomorrow and go to work, where we meet each other and meet others but we live in different mental worlds, different physical worlds.

I can only give what I am, I have no other gift to give. If I want the world to be perfect, and who does not, I have failed only because I did not know that I could never see it perfect until I myself become perfect. If I am not perfect I cannot see perfection but the day that I become it, I beautify my world because I see it through my own eyes. "Unto the pure all things are pure." Titus 1:15

No two here can tell me that you have heard the same message any one night. The one thing that you must do is hear what I say through that which you are. It must be filtered through your prejudices, your superstitions, and your concept of self. Whatever you are, it must come through that, and be coloured by what you are. If you are disturbed and you would like me to be something other than what I appear to be, then you must be that which you want me to be. We must become the thing that we want others to be or we will never see them be it.

Your consciousness, my consciousness, is the only true foundation in the world. This is that which is called Peter in the Bible, not a man, this faithfulness that cannot turn to anyone, that cannot be flattered when you are told by men you are John come again. That is very flattering to be told you are John the Baptist come again, or the great Prophet Elias, or Jeremiah. Then I deafen my ears to this very flattering little bit of news men would give me and I ask myself,

"But honestly who am I?"

If I can deny the limitations of my birth, my environment, and the belief that I am but an extension of my family tree, and feel within myself that I am Christ, and sustain this assumption until it takes a central place and forms the habitual centre of my energy, I will do the works attributed to Jesus. Without thought or effort I will mould a world in harmony with that perfection which I have assumed and feel springing within me.

Our ordinary alterations of consciousness, as we pass from one state to another, are not transformations, because each of them is so rapidly succeeded by another in the reverse direction; but whenever our assumption grows so stable as to definitely expel its rivals, then that central habitual concept defines our character and is a true transformation. Jesus, or enlightened reason, saw nothing unclean in the woman taken in adultery. He said to her, "Hath no man condemned thee?" John 8:10 "She said, No man, Lord. And Jesus said unto her, neither do I condemn thee; go, and sin no more." John 8:11

No matter what is brought before the presence of beauty, it sees only beauty. Jesus was so completely identified with the lovely that He was incapable of seeing the unlovely. When you and I really become conscious of being Christ, we too will straighten the arms of the withered, and resurrect the dead hopes of men. We will do all the things that we could not do when we felt ourselves limited by our family tree. It is a bold step and should not be taken lightly, because to do it is to die. John, the man of three dimensions is beheaded, or loses his three-dimensional focus that Jesus, the fourth-dimensional Self may live.

Any enlargement of our concept of Self involves a somewhat painful parting with strongly rooted hereditary conceptions. The ligaments are strong that hold us in the womb of conventional limitations. All that you formerly believed, you no longer believe. You know now that there is no power outside of your own consciousness. Therefore you cannot turn to anyone outside of self.

You have no ears for the suggestion that something else has power in it. You know the only reality is God, and God is your own consciousness. There is no other God. Therefore on this rock you build the everlasting church and boldly assume you are this Divine Being, self-begotten because you dared to appropriate that which was not given to you in your cradle, a concept of Self not formed in your mother's womb, a concept of self conceived outside of the offices of man. The story is beautifully told us in the Bible using the two sons of Abraham: one the blessed, Isaac, born outside of the offices of man and the other, Ishmael, born in bondage.

Sarah was much too old to beget a child, so her husband Abraham went in unto the bondservant Hagar, the pilgrim, and she conceived of the old man and bore him a son called Ishmael. Ishmael's hand was against every man and every man's hand against him. Every child born of woman is born into bondage, born into all that his environment represents, regardless of whether it be the throne of England, the White House, or any great place in the world. Every child born of woman is personified as this Ishmael, the child of Hagar.

But asleep in every child is the blessed Isaac, who is born outside of the offices of man, and is born through faith alone. This second child has no earthly father. He is Self-begotten. What is the second birth? I find myself man, I cannot go back into my mother's womb, and yet I must be born a second time. "Except a man be born again he cannot enter the kingdom of God." John 3:3

I quietly appropriate that which no man can give me, no woman can give me. I dare to assume that I am God. This must be of faith, this must be of promise. Then I become the blessed, I become Isaac. As I begin to do the things that only this presence could do, I know that I am born out of the limitations of Ishmael, and I have become heir to the kingdom. Ishmael could not inherit anything, although his father was Abraham, or God. Ishmael did not have both parents of the godly; his mother was Hagar the bond-woman, and so he could not partake of his father's estate.

You *are* Abraham and Sarah, and contained within your own consciousness there is one waiting for recognition. In the Old Testament it is called Isaac, and in the New Testament it is called Jesus, and it is born without the aid of man.

No man can tell you that you are Christ Jesus, no man can tell you and convince you that you are God. You must toy with the idea and wonder what it would be like to be God. No clear conception of the origin of phenomena is possible except that consciousness is all and all is consciousness. Nothing can be evolved from man that was not potentially involved in his nature. The ideal we serve and hope to attain could never be evolved from us were it not potentially involved in our nature.

Let me now retell and emphasise an experience of mine printed by me two years ago under the title, THE SEARCH. I think it will help you to understand this law of consciousness, and show you that you have no one to change but self, for you are incapable of seeing other than the contents of your own consciousness.

Once in an idle interval at sea, I meditated on "the perfect state," and wondered what I would be were I of too pure eyes to behold iniquity, if to me all things were pure and were I without condemnation. As I became lost in this fiery brooding, I found myself lifted above the dark environment of the senses. So intense was feeling I felt myself a being of fire dwelling in a body of air. Voices, as from a heavenly chorus, with the exaltation of those who had been conquerors in a conflict with death, were singing, "He is risen, He is risen," and intuitively I knew they meant me.

Then I seemed to be walking in the night. I soon came upon a scene that might have been the ancient Pool of Bethesda for in this place lay a great multitude of impotent folk -- blind, halt, withered—waiting not for the moving of the water as of tradition but waiting for me.

As I came near, without thought or effort on my part, they were one after the other, moulded as by the Magician of the Beautiful. Eyes, hands, feet -- all missing members -- were drawn from some invisible reservoir and moulded in harmony with that perfection which I felt springing within me. When all were made perfect the chorus exulted, "It is finished."

I know this vision was the result of my intense meditation upon the idea of perfection, for my meditations invariably bring about union with the state contemplated. I had been so completely absorbed within the idea that for a while I had become what I contemplated, and the high purpose with which I had for that moment identified myself drew the companionship of high things and fashioned the vision in harmony with my inner nature.

The ideal with which we are united works by association of ideas to awaken a thousand moods to create a drama in keeping with the central idea. My mystical experiences have convinced me that there is no way to bring about the perfection we seek other than by the transformation of ourselves. As soon as we succeed in transforming ourselves, the world will melt magically before our eyes and reshape itself in harmony with that which our transformation affirms.

We fashion the world that surrounds us by the intensity of our imagination and feeling, and we illuminate or darken our lives by the concepts we hold of ourselves. Nothing is more important to us than our conception of ourselves, and especially is true of our concept of the deep, dimensionally greater One within us.

Those that help or hinder us, whether they know it or not, are the servants of that law which shapes outward circumstances in harmony with our inner nature. It is our conception of ourselves which frees or constrains us, though it may use material agencies to achieve its purpose.

Because life moulds the outer world to reflect the inner arrangement of our minds, there is no way of bringing about the outer perfection we seek other than by the transformation of ourselves. No help cometh from without: the hills to which we lift our eyes are those of an inner range.

It is thus to our own consciousness that we must turn as to the only reality, the only foundation on which all phenomena can be explained. We can rely absolutely on the justice of this law to give us only that which is of the nature of ourselves.

To attempt to change the world before we change our concept of ourselves is to struggle against the nature of things. There can be no outer change until there is first an inner change.

As within, so without.

I am not advocating philosophical indifference when I suggest that we should imagine ourselves as already that which we want to be, living in a mental atmosphere of greatness, rather than using physical means and arguments to bring about the desired changes.

Everything we do, unaccompanied by a change of consciousness, is but futile readjustment of surfaces. However we toil or struggle, we can receive no more than our concepts of Self affirm. To protest against anything which happens to us is to protest against the law of our being and our ruler ship over our own destiny.

The circumstances of my life are too closely related to my conception of myself not to have been formed by my own spirit from some dimensionally larger storehouse of my being. If there is pain to me in these happenings, I should look within myself for the cause, for I am moved here and there and made to live in a world in harmony with my concept of myself. If we would become as emotionally aroused over our ideas as we become over our dislikes, we would ascend to the plane of our ideal as easily as we now descend to the level of our hates.

Love and hate have a magical transforming power, and we grow through their exercise into the likeness of what we contemplate. By intensity of hatred we create in ourselves the character we imagine in our enemies. Qualities die for want of attention, so the unlovely states might best be rubbed out by imagining "beauty for ashes and joy for mourning" rather than by direct attacks on the state from which we would be free. "Whatsoever things are lovely and of good report, think on these things," for we become that with which we are en rapport.

There is nothing to change but our concept of self. As soon as we succeed in transforming self, our world will dissolve and reshape itself in harmony with that which our change affirms.

I, by descent in consciousness, have brought about the imperfection that I see. In the divine economy nothing is lost. We cannot lose anything save by descent in consciousness from the sphere where the thing has its natural life. And now, O Father, glorify thou me with thine own self with the glory which I had with thee before the world was." John 17:5

As I ascend in consciousness the power and the glory that was mine return to me and I too will say "I have finished the work thou gavest me to do." The work is to return from my descent in consciousness, from the level wherein I believed that I was a son of man, to the sphere where I know that I am one with my Father and my Father is God.

I know beyond all doubt that there is nothing for man to do but to change his own concept of himself to assume greatness and sustain this assumption. If we walk as though we were already the ideal we serve, we will rise to the level of our assumption, and find a world in harmony with our assumption. We will not have to lift a finger to make it so, for it is already so. It was always so.

You and I have descended in consciousness to the level where we now find ourselves and we see imperfection because we have descended! When we begin to ascend while here in this three-dimensional world, we find that we move in an entirely different environment, we have entirely different circles of friends, and an entirely different world while still living here. We know the great mystery of the statement, "I am in the world but not of it."

Instead of changing things I would suggest to all to identify themselves with the ideal they contemplate. What would the feeling be like were you of too pure eyes to behold iniquity if to you all things were pure and you were without condemnation? Contemplate the ideal state and identify yourself with it and you will ascend to the sphere where you as Christ have your natural life. You are still in that state where you were before the world was. The only thing that has fallen is your concept of self. You see the broken parts which really are not broken. You are seeing them through distorted eyes, as though you were in one of those peculiar amusement gallery's where a man walks before a mirror and he is elongated, yet he is the same man. Or he looks into another mirror and he is all big and fat. These things are seen today because man is what he is.

Toy with the idea of perfection. Ask no man to help you but let the prayer of the 17th chapter of the Gospel of St. John be your prayer. Appropriate the state that was yours before the world was. Know the truth of the statement, "None have I lost save the son of perdition." Nothing is lost in all my holy mountain. The only thing that you lose is the belief in loss or the son of perdition.

"And for their sake I sanctify myself, that they also might be sanctified through the truth." John 17:19

There is no one to change but self. All you need do to make men and women holy in this world is to make yourself holy. You are incapable of seeing anything that is unlovely when you establish within your own mind's eye the fact that you are lovely. It is far better to know this than to know anything else in the world. It takes courage, boundless courage, because many this night, after having heard this truth will still be inclined to blame others for their predicament. Man finds it so difficult to turn to himself, to his own consciousness as to the only reality. Listen to these words:

"No man can come to me, except the Father which hath sent me draw him." John 6:44 "I and my Father are one." John 10:30 "A man can receive nothing, except it be given him from heaven." John 3:27 "Therefore doth my Father love me, because I lay down my life, that I might take it again." "No man taketh it from me but I lay it down of myself." John 10:17,18.

"You did not choose me, I have chosen you." My concept of myself moulds a world in harmony with itself and draws men to tell me constantly by their behaviour who I am. The most important thing in this world to you is your concept of self. When you dislike your environment, the circumstances of life and the behaviour of men, ask yourself, " Who am I?" It is your answer to this question hat is the cause of your dislikes.

If you do not condemn self there will be no man in your world to condemn you. If you are living in the consciousness of your ideal you will see nothing to condemn. "To the pure all things are pure."

Now I would like to spend a little time making as clear as I can what I personally do when I pray, what I do when I want to bring about changes in my world. You will find it interesting, and you will find that it works. No one here can tell me they cannot do it. It is so very simple all can do it. We are what we imagine we are. This technique is not difficult to follow but you must want to do it. You cannot approach it with the attitude of mind "Oh well I'll try it." You must want to do it, because the mainspring of action is desire.

Desire is the mainspring of all action. Now what do I want? I must define my objective. For example, suppose I wanted now to be elsewhere. This very moment I really desire to be elsewhere. I need not go through the door, I need not sit down. I need do nothing but stand just where I am and with my eyes closed, assume that I am actually standing where I desire to be. Then I remain in this state until it has the feeling of reality. Were I now elsewhere I could not see the world as I now see it from here. The world changes in its relationship to me as I change my position in space.

So I stand right here, close my eyes, and imagine I am seeing what I would see were I there. I remain in it long enough to feel it to be real. I cannot touch the walls of this room from here but when you close your eyes and become still you can imagine and feel that you touch it. You can stand where you are and imagine you are putting your hand on that wall. To prove you really are, put it there and slide it up and feel the wood. You can imagine you are doing it without getting off your seat. You can do it and you will actually feel it if you become still enough and intense enough

I stand where I am and I allow the world that I want to see and to enter physically to come before me as though I were there now. In other words, I bring elsewhere here by assuming that I am there. Is that clear? I let it come up, I do not make it come up. I simply imagine I am there and then let it happen. If I want a physical presence, I imagine he is standing here, and I touch him All through the Bible I find these suggestions, "He placed his hands upon them. He touched them."

If you want to comfort someone, what is the automatic feeling? To put your hand on them, you cannot resist it. You meet a friend and the hand goes out automatically, you either shake hands or put your hand on his shoulder.

Suppose you were now to meet a friend that you have not seen for a year and he is a friend of whom you are very fond. What would you do? You would embrace him, wouldn't you? Or you would put your hand upon him. In your imagination bring him close enough to put your hand upon him and feel him to be solidly real. Restrict the action to just that. You will be amazed at what happens. From then on things begin to move. Your dimensionally greater self will inspire, in all, the ideas and actions necessary to bring you into physical contact. It works that way.

Every day I put myself into the drowsy state; it is a very easy thing to do. But habit is a strange thing in man's world. It is not law, but habit acts as though it were the most compelling law in the world. We are creatures of habit.

If you create an interval every day into which you put yourself into the drowsy state, say at 3 o'clock in the afternoon do you know at that moment every day you will feel drowsy. You try it for one week and see if I am not right.

You sit down for the purpose of creating a state akin to sleep, as though you were sleepy but do not push the drowsiness too far, just far enough to relax and leave you in control of the direction of your thoughts. You try it for one week, and every day at that hour, no matter what you are doing, you will hardly be able to keep your eyes open. If you know the hour when you will be free you can create it. I would not suggest that you do it lightly, because you will feel very, very sleepy and you may not want to.

I have another way of praying. In this case I always sit down and I find the most comfortable arm chair imaginable, or I lie flat on my back and relax completely. Make yourself comfortable. You must not be in any position where the body is distressed. Always put yourself into a position where you have the greatest ease. That is the first stage.

To know what you want is the start of prayer. Secondly you construct in your mind's eye one single little event which implies that you have realised your desire. I always let my mind roam on many things that could follow the answered prayer and I single out one that is most likely to follow the fulfillment of my desire. One simple little thing like the shaking of a hand, embracing a person, the receiving of a letter, the writing of a check, or whatever would imply the fulfillment of your desire. After you have de-cided on the action which implies that your desire has been realised, then sit in your nice comfortable chair or lie flat on your back, close your eyes for the simple reason it helps to induce this state that borders on sleep.

The minute you feel this lovely drowsy state, or the feeling of gathered to-getherness, wherein you feel that I could move if I wanted to but I do not want to, I could open my eyes if I wanted to but I do not want to. When you get that feeling you can be quite sure that you are in the perfect state to pray successfully.

In this feeling it is easy to touch anything in this world. You take the simple little restricted action which implies fulfillment of your prayer and you feel it or you enact it. Whatever it is, you enter into the action as though you were an actor in the part. You do not sit back and visualise yourself doing it. You do it.

With the body immobilised you imagine that the greater you inside the physical body is coming out of it and that you are actually performing the proposed action. If you are going to walk, you imagine that you are walking. Do not see yourself walk, FEEL that you are walking.

If you are going to climb stairs, FEEL that you are climbing the stairs. Do not visualise yourself doing it, feel yourself doing it. If you are going to shake a man's hand, do not visualise yourself shaking his hand, imagine your friend is standing before you and shake his hand. But leave your physical hands immobilised and imagine that your greater hand, which is your imaginary hand, is actually shaking his hand.

All you need do is to imagine that you are doing it. You are stretched out in time, and what you are doing, which seems to be a controlled day dream, is an actual act in the greater dimension of your being. You are actually encountering an event fourth-dimensionally before you encounter it here in the three-dimensions of space, and you do not have to raise a finger to bring that state to pass.

My third way of praying is simply to feel thankful. If I want something, either for myself or another, I immobilise the physical body, then I produce the state akin to sleep and in that state just feel happy, feel thankful, which thankfulness implies realisation of what I want. I assume the feeling of the wish fulfilled and with my mind dominated by this single sensation I go to sleep. I need do nothing to make it so, because it is so. My feeling of the wish fulfilled implies it is done.

All these techniques you can use and change them to fit your temperament. But I must emphasise the necessity of inducing the drowsy state where you can become attentive without effort.

A single sensation dominates the mind, if you pray successfully.

What would I feel like, now, were I what I want to be? When I know what the feeling would be like I then close my eyes and lose myself in that single sensation and my dimensionally greater Self then builds a bridge of incident to lead me from this present moment to the fulfillment of my mood. That is all you need do. But people have a habit of slighting the importance of simple things.

We are creatures of habit and we are slowly learning to relinquish our previous concepts but the things we formerly lived by still in some way influence our behaviour. Here is a story from the Bible that illustrates my point. It is recorded that Jesus told his disciples to go to the crossroads and there they would find a colt, a young colt not yet ridden by a man. To bring the colt to him and if any man ask, "Why do you take this colt?" say, "The Lord has need of it."

They went to the crossroads and found the colt and did exactly as they were told. They brought the unbridled ass to Jesus and He rode it triumphantly into Jerusalem. The story has nothing to do with a man riding on a little colt. You are Jesus of the story. The colt is the mood you are going to assume. That is the living animal not yet ridden by you. What would the feeling be like were you to realise your desire? A new feeling, like a young Colt, is a very difficult thing to ride unless you ride him with a disciplined mind. If I do not remain faithful to the mood the young colt throws me off. Every time you become conscious that you are not faithful to this mood, you have been thrown from the colt.

Discipline your mind that you may remain faithful to a high mood and ride it triumphantly into Jerusalem, which is fulfillment, or the city of peace. This story precedes the feast of the Passover. If we would pass from our present state into that of our ideal, we must assume that we are already that which we desire to be and remain faithful to our assumption, for we must keep a high mood if we would walk with the highest.

A fixed attitude of mind, a feeling that it is done will make it so. If I walk as though it were but every once in a while I look to see if it really is, then I fall off my mood or colt. If I would suspend judgment like Peter I could walk on the water. Peter starts walking on the water, and then he begins to look unto his own understanding and he begins to go down. The voice said, "Look up, Peter." Peter looks up and he rises again and continues walking on the water. Instead of looking down to see if this thing is really going to harden into fact, you simply know that it is already so, sustain that mood and you will ride the unbridled colt into the city of Jerusalem All of us must learn to ride the animal straight in to Jerusalem unassisted by a man. You do not need another to help you.

The strange thing is that as we keep the high mood and do not fall, others cushion the blows. They spread the palm leaves before me to cushion my journey. I do not have to be concerned. The shocks will be softened as I move into the fulfillment of my desire. My high mood awakens in others the ideas and actions which tend towards the embodiment of my mood. If you walk faithful to a high mood there will be no opposition and no competition.

The test of a teacher, or a teaching, is to be found in the faithfulness of the taught. I am leaving here on Sunday night. Do remain faithful to this instruction. If you look for causes outside the consciousness of man, then I have not convinced you of the reality of consciousness.

If you look for excuses for failure you will always find them, for you find what you seek. If you seek an excuse for failure, you will find it in the stars, in the numbers, in the tea cup, or most any place. The excuse will not be there but you will find it to justify your failure. Successful business and professional men and women know that this law works. You will not find it in gossip groups but you will find it in courageous hearts.

Man's eternal journey is for one purpose: to reveal the Father. He comes to make visible his Father. And his Father is made visible in all the lovely things of this world. All the things that are lovely, that are of good report, ride these things, and have no time for the unlovely in this world, regardless of what it is.

Remain faithful to the knowledge that your consciousness, your *I AM-ness*, your awareness of being aware of the only reality. It is the rock on which all phenomena can be explained. There is no explanation outside of that. I know of no clear conception of the origin of phenomena save that consciousness is all and all is consciousness.

That which you seek is already housed within you. Were it not now within you eternity could not evolve it. No time stretch would be long enough to evolve what is not potentially involved in you. You simply let it into being by assuming that it is already visible in your world, and remaining faithful to your assumption, it will harden into fact. Your Father has unnumbered ways of revealing your assumption. Fix this in your mind and always remember, "

An assumption, though false, if sustained will harden into fact."

You and your Father *are one being* and your Father is everything that was, is and will be. Therefore that which you seek you already are, it can never be so far off as even to be near, for nearness implies separation.

The great Pascal said, "You never would have sought me had you not already found me. "What you now desire you already have and you seek it only because you have already found it. You found it in the form of desire. It is just as real in the form of desire as it is going to be to your bodily organs. You are already that which you seek and you have no one to change but Self in order to express it.

Made in the USA
Columbia, SC
20 January 2020

86932198R00190